A THOUSAND WORDS

Grammar and Writing in Context

Andrew J. Hoffman
San Diego Mesa College

Catherine A. Hoffman
San Diego State University

HEINLE & HEINLE
™
THOMSON LEARNING

Australia • Canada • Mexico • Singapore • Spain
United Kingdom • United States

HEINLE & HEINLE

™

THOMSON LEARNING

English Editor: Stephen Dalphin
Development Editor: Jill Johnson
Marketing Manager: Katrina Byrd
Project Manager, Editorial Production: Angela Williams Urquhart
Print/Media Buyer: Elaine Curda
Production Service: Techbooks
Copy Editor: Mary Jo Gregory
Cover Image: PhotoDisc
Cover Printer: Von Hoffman Graphics
Compositor: Techbooks
Printer: Von Hoffman Graphics

Printed in the United States of America
1 2 3 4 5 6 7 05 04 03 02 01

For more information about our products, contact us at:
Thomson Learning Academic Resource Center
1-800-423-0563

For permission to use material from this text, contact us by:
Phone: 1-800-730-2214
Fax: 1-800-730-2215
Web: http://www.thomsonrights.com

ISBN: 0-15-505976-9
Library of Congress Control Number: 2001095542

Asia
Thomson Learning
60 Albert Street, #15-01
Albert Complex
Singapore 189969

Australia
Nelson Thomson Learning
102 Dodds Street
South Melbourne, Victoria 3205
Australia

Canada
Nelson Thomson Learning
1120 Birchmount Road
Toronto, Ontario M1K 5G4
Canada

Europe/Middle East/Africa
Thomson Learning
Berkshire House
168–173 High Holborn
London WC1 V7AA
United Kingdom

Latin America
Thomson Learning
Seneca, 53
Colonia Polanco
11560 Mexico D.F.
Mexico

Spain
Paraninfo Thomson Learning
Calle/Magallanes, 25
28015 Madrid, Spain

CONTENTS

PREFACE

A Thousand Words: Grammar and Writing in Context was written to meet the needs of writing instructors who are frustrated by fill-in-the-blank or multiple choice "workbooks" that fail to deliver on the promise of better student writing. Instructors who teach low-level developmental writing courses face multiple challenges. Often, students are expected to learn the rules of English grammar without any connection to real writing tasks. Instead, students are taken through grammar drills, fill-in-the-blank exercises, or multiple choice quizzes without any direct application to a writing assignment. The result is that at the end of the term—in spite of successfully completing homework assignments and quizzes—many students' writing skills have not improved much. These students then experience difficulties in high-level developmental writing courses that require paragraph and essay writing.

An additional challenge is that these students need work in grammar—the instructor cannot ignore the often frequent errors students in these courses make and merely focus on composition. Compounding the problem is that students in low-level developmental writing courses sometimes have poor study skills, are easily discouraged, and lack confidence in their ability to improve their technical mastery of English.

With *A Thousand Words*, students learn the technical skills they so badly need, and they apply those skills to writing effectively. What makes this textbook distinctive is that in each chapter, lessons in grammar are combined with sentence and writing lessons. All instruction is geared toward producing a written work by the end of the chapter. The instructions are presented in a clear manner, with frequent writing models. The pacing allows students to improve their language skills and integrate them into writing tasks. There is no "disconnect" between the grammar instruction and the writing assignments.

ORGANIZATION

Our title is borrowed from the well-known phrase, "A picture is worth a thousand words." With this title we are drawing attention to a central pedagogical aspect of our text: student writing in response to other works—both pictorial and written. The text is arranged thematically. Each chapter begins with a photograph illustrating its theme and follows with a reading related to the theme. At the conclusion of the chapter, a second photograph provides another source for writing ideas. Thus, instructors will have both the photographs and the reading to stimulate discussion and inspire student writing.

A Thousand Words is a highly teachable text. Instructors can set up their course to grade student writing by portfolio assessment. Portfolio assessment enables instructors to collect and grade assignments less often, but more meaningfully, because a portfolio check reveals each student's writing process. Objective chapter tests can be helpful for reinforcing the grammar and sentence lessons, and although such tests should not be the sole criteria for assessing students' writing abilities, they can serve as an excellent way to determine what students have and have not yet learned. The consistent structure of each chapter helps instructors organize the course so that students know what is expected. The relevance of the photographs and readings to students' lives helps to generate discussion. These discussions help students establish a foundation both of ideas and of concrete details to include in their writing. The variety of materials in each chapter helps keep each class session interesting and the students involved, which always helps the instructor.

A Thousand Words comprises eight chapters. Instructors have many choices for homework assignments within each chapter, including grammar and sentence exercises, writing assignments, and lesson reviews. The textbook requires that students ultimately use all four language skills: reading, writing, talking, and listening.

FEATURES

Each chapter contains the following features:

Chapter Goals: Students first encounter a discussion of the important objectives of each chapter. This enables students to understand the importance of different lessons within the chapter and how these lessons help students write well.

Photograph: Each chapter begins with a photograph illustrating its theme. The photographs are accompanied by questions, which can serve as writing topics or in-class discussion topics.

Reading: The readings are nonfiction articles and essays on topics of relevance to students today. The readings are related to the chapter's theme, such as Education or Family, and are challenging for students in that the readings are complete — not simply a single paragraph excerpt from longer works. The readings are chosen to stretch the students rather than to insult them by being overly simplistic. Every reading is preceded by a vocabulary list with definitions of difficult terms. The readings reflect a variety of cultural perspectives and provide suitable materials for both class discussions and writing assignments.

Writing Assignment: The writing assignment requires students to apply what they have learned in the chapter to develop a work of their own. The writing assignments themselves are flexible; there are questions that correspond to the photograph and the reading and allow students to think critically about other, related questions.

Writing Instruction: The writing lesson introduces the students to the concerns of forming a complete piece of writing. Each Writing Instruction section covers one prewriting strategy and a writing lesson. Over the course of the textbook, besides learning eight prewriting strategies, students are presented with matters such as the structure of the paragraph, the importance of transitions, the use of subject-specific language, and how to write for special purposes (such as a letter or résumé). The Writing Instruction gives only the most basic strategies, in keeping with the needs of low-level developmental writing students.

Writing Models: An important feature of the Writing Instruction is that students are provided with writing models. In fact, the use of models continues throughout the chapter as students develop their own written work. Thus, after being given a writing assignment, students are given a lesson in writing and then apply the lesson to their own writing assignment. The models allow students to see what they need to achieve at each step. Writing models appear at significant points in the chapter: with the writing lesson, with the sentence lesson, and with the grammar lesson. The writing models show the different stages of drafting and revising a work written in response to the writing assignment.

Grammar Lesson and Exercises: These lessons cover matters such as recognizing parts of speech in a sentence, maintaining agreement (subject-verb and pronoun-antecedent), and using punctuation marks correctly. There are some objective exercises but also "blank line" exercises that require students to demonstrate a real understanding of the material. There is also a passage through which students see how the grammar lesson applies to a writing sample created in response to the writing assignment. Then, students apply the lesson to their own writing assignment.

Sentence Lesson and Exercises: These lessons cover subjects such as recognizing basic sentence structure, fixing fragmentary or fused sentences, and avoiding wordiness through combining sentences. There are some objective exercises, but also "blank line" exercises that require students to demonstrate a significant understanding of the material. There is also a passage in which students see how the sentence lesson applies to a writing sample created in response to the writing assignment. Then, students apply the lesson to their own writing assignment.

Lesson Reviews: Each chapter has objective lesson reviews that cover the grammar and sentence lessons. These can serve as effective pretest exercises for instructors who give objective chapter tests.

Zoom-In Practice: This boxed feature appears periodically in each chapter. The practices help students understand key elements of a lesson by giving the students additional opportunities to test their knowledge. The practices are very short, designed to be completed in five minutes or less. The practices provide an excellent tool for instructors to gauge just how well students have understood the material before moving on to new material.

Don't Lose Focus: This is another boxed feature that appears at different points in each chapter. This feature reinforces lessons that may be particularly difficult or confusing to students. By providing students with additional explanations or advice on how to handle a featured problem, the students can feel more confident about their technical skills.

Final Draft Due: At the end of each chapter, students are asked to submit their final draft of the writing assignment. Because the textbook has guided the students throughout the writing process, each student will have at least one prewriting assignment and two rough drafts in addition to the final draft. This makes the textbook suitable for use in portfolio-based classes. Each chapter includes a Portfolio Checklist at the end of the chapter to help students organize their portfolios.

Parting Shot: This is another photo, with questions, that connects to the theme of the chapter. The photo provides additional opportunity for discussion and exploration of a theme.

Goals in Review: This is a bulleted list of the completed chapter objectives. This helps students understand the importance of the different lessons and provides an easy reference guide for review.

ANCILLARIES

An Instructor's Manual includes objective chapter tests, with answers to the tests, the lesson reviews, and all exercises. The IM also provides additional advice for instructors, including sample syllabi, discussion topics for each chapter, more writing assignments, and lists of sources (e.g., movies, novels, magazine titles) that may provide additional support for the teaching of each chapter theme.

ACKNOWLEDGMENTS

We acknowledge the support of many people in the making of *A Thousand Words*. First, Stephen Dalphin, our sponsoring editor at Thomson, visited us on a rare rainy day in San Diego to talk about our new project. For his support and encouragement, we cannot thank him enough. Jill Johnson, our developmental editor, has been a true asset in the process of putting this textbook together. Our trust in her judgment is complete. Amy McGaughey, editorial assistant, pushed through paperwork with cheer and speed. Thanks also to our project manager, Angela Urquhart.

We also thank the instructors in colleges and universities who kindly reviewed several different versions of this textbook: Sharon Cleland, Florida Community College at Jacksonville; Stanley Coberly, West Virginia University at Parkersburg; Judy Covington, Trident Technical College; Mary Eastland, Hill College; Timothy Jones, Oklahoma City Community College; Caren Kessler, Blue Ridge Community College; Robin Ramsey, Albuquerque T-VI A Community College; Joseph Thweatt, State Technical Institute at Memphis, and Fran Turner, Shelton State Community College. We also thank Robert E. Yarber, veteran textbook writer, professor emeritus, and personal friend, whose unflinching critique of an early draft of this textbook helped turn our rough ideas into firm reality.

We would be remiss if we failed also to mention our students. Like most instructors, we learn a lot from our students. Their needs, their struggles, and their successes have guided us in shaping this text. In particular, four different classes used draft versions of this textbook. We are especially grateful to the students in those courses. Their experiences helped us improve the text so that others could benefit in the future.

Finally, we thank our children, to whom this book is dedicated. Sean and Alex are truly our best collaborative effort.

A.J.H

C.A.H.

A THOUSAND WORDS

1

Education

CHAPTER GOALS

In this chapter, you will learn about

- a prewriting strategy called "The Circle of Life,"
- the basic form of the paragraph,
- the parts of speech, and
- the simple sentence.

Learning how to write well can be difficult. So much seems involved—good grammar, correct spelling, and proper punctuation—yet there is much more to writing well than technical competence. You need good ideas, and you have to express those good ideas in a form your reader can follow. A good piece of writing is the result of a combination of factors: using writing strategies that develop your ideas clearly and coherently, applying rules of grammar, and being able to form effective sentences. Meeting these concerns is the writer's task. *A Thousand Words: Grammar and Writing in Contexts* will help you navigate the writing process by presenting instruction on three levels: writing, grammar, and sentence construction.

Education is the theme of Chapter One. Education is an important part of almost everyone's life, and experiences in school and other educational environments help mold us into who we are and who we may yet become. For some students, success

OPENING SHOT

In school seems to come easily. But for many others, school can be disappointing and frustrating, a place of difficulties. With support, however, students can find their way through to meet their goals.

QUESTIONS ABOUT THE PICTURE

1. What obstacles do older students confront when returning to school? What advantages do they have?

2. How can younger students benefit from the presence of older students in a class?

3. What is the make up of students at your college? Are the majority of students under 22, or is there a substantial number of older students as well?

4. Is there a particular age at which learning stops?

READING

Questions to Consider

1. Why do you think it's important to go to college?
2. Is it better to go directly to college after high school, or should you work for a while first?
3. Do you go to college because you're interested in learning or because you want a job in the future that pays well?

Words to Watch

ebbed   diminished or declined

irrelevant   unrelated to the matter at hand

lethargic   characterized by sluggishness or inactivity

cynical   expressing or exhibiting scorn or mockery

fascist   a reactionary or dictatorial person

infanticide the murder of an infant

classics   works generally considered to be of the highest rank of excellence

myth   a story regarded as embodying an aspect of a culture

It's Never Too Late to Get That College Degree
Diane Spear

1   After struggling through a bad breakup and serious fit of depression, then receiving disappointing grades in several music classes, I dropped out of college in 1978. Following five aimless years, my confidence and motivation had ebbed, and I felt neither talented nor disciplined enough to reach my goal—to become a concert pianist. Broke, and without another career in mind, I decided to look for work. A degree seemed irrelevant.

2   During the years that followed, I bounced around in a variety of go-nowhere jobs: restaurant hostess, piano teacher, showroom model, secretary in an investment firm, and finally, editorial assistant at a publishing house. I got by but always felt bored or frustrated with long hours for little pay and hardly any chance for advancement at jobs I didn't care about anyway.

3   As I approached my thirty-fifth birthday, I began to examine the lethargic pattern of my days and question whether I was comfortable continuing to drift instead of acting to make my life more meaningful. With the help of some sensible advice from a friend, and much mental wrestling on my part, I decided to redirect my energies and go back and finish college at night. It was the wisest decision I've ever made.

4   If you're at a similar restless stage, don't be afraid to take the same step. You'll learn so much besides what's taught in class. For instance,

1. Age is just a state of mind.

5   Novelist Walker Percy published his first book at forty-five, and Grandma Moses was no child prodigy, but when I first went back to school, I was intimidated by the prospect of competing against energetic eighteen-year-old whizzes who wore cool clothes and listened to rap music.

6   So I got up two hours early every day to write papers before going to my publishing job. I ate lunch at my desk while reading the assigned material. And I soon found out the kids in my courses were no threat—they complained about homework and skipped classes just as I had at their age. A few seemed as complacent and cynical as residents in a retirement home. My real competition was Mary, a sixty-year-old grandmother who turned in two papers for each assignment! But she was my inspiration as well. When I asked what made her return to school at her age, she said, "I realized that in four years I'll be sixty-four no matter what. And I can be sixty-four with a degree or sixty-four without one."

2. Expressing your ideas and opinions is fun.

7   When I took a class in mythology, I was overwhelmed by the sheer number of gods and goddesses and the complications of their bizarre antics. A few weeks into the course, I found I had absorbed more than I thought. At a party, I was introduced to a woman named Hera. When she left, I joked, "I guess she has to hurry home to Zeus"—and everyone

laughed. Six months earlier, I hadn't known that Hera was a mythological character married to Zeus or that Zeus was king of the gods.

8   Later that semester, I gathered my courage to speak up in class after reading Plato's *Republic:* "He seems like such a fascist to me, with his ideas about censorship and infanticide. But I keep telling myself that he's a great philosopher and I'm a college dropout." The professor laughed and assured me Plato's politics had been criticized on those grounds for centuries and I should trust my instincts.

3. Speaking up is not so scary.

9   Many courses require oral presentations, and I really sweated those at the beginning. I began by painstakingly writing out what I had to say and reading it word for word, never even looking up from the page. After a couple of weeks, though, I had gotten enough encouragement from teachers and classmates that I became much more relaxed, even during formal talks.

10   This new skill carried over into my job at the publishing company. I spoke much more often at office meetings, and I knew I had made a great leap forward when my boss asked me to help with her speech at an important book conference—an event that led to promotions for both of us.

4. "Great books" are actually exciting to read.

11   I can assure you that I wouldn't have opened William Faulkner's *Light in August,* Henry David Thoreau's *Walden,* or Virginia Woolf's *A Room of One's Own* if they hadn't been assigned in class. But I'm glad they were, because I had been too insecure to tackle the classics on my own.

12   Before I returned to school, when someone mentioned a book I hadn't read, I'd feel ashamed to admit I didn't know it. I'd smile and nod, hoping no one noticed my silence. Now when I hear about a book I "should" have read, I don't feel embarrassed or puzzled. I write down the title, look for it in the library, and decide for myself whether it's something I want to read.

5. You can't be intimidated without your consent.

13   After I got over worrying about what my fellow students would think of me, I fretted about my instructors. One teacher, a Hemingway lookalike, intimidated me with his encyclopedic knowledge. I spaced out midsentence during lectures and wound up with notes that resembled a Lily Tomlin monologue with their illogic. When I got up the courage to consult with the professor and confess that my anxiety was getting the better of me, he was surprisingly friendly. He advised me to just try to relax and suggested that I tape the lectures rather than take notes. He also told me about a former student who had similar fears when she returned to school to complete her bachelor's degree. She went on her earn her Ph.D.

6. Career options expand dramatically.

14   College is a great place to find yourself and your direction. I used to think there was something wrong with me because I didn't know exactly

what I wanted to do with my life. After immersing myself in several kinds of classes and group projects, I found that I enjoyed—and had a gift for—working with people. I realized that I could use my "people talent" more fully—and would have a better chance of supporting myself—in social work rather than in music or English, my two previous areas of interest. In school, I discovered that I could make a career out of doing what most pleased me.

15   Other students made career changes too: from reception to teaching program, from Wall Street to a writing job, from bartending to computer graphic design. "From front ends to Freud" is how one classmate describes his move from an auto-parts business to psychology.

7. Your life experience is valuable.

16   Taking freshman composition at thirty-five taught me the value of my past. For our first assignment, we had to write about a cultural myth. At first I was really stymied, having grown up in a culture brimming with more falsehoods than myths. Finally I decided I could write about that. While other students brought in essays with such titles as "Brooklyn Stickball Heroes" and "All Italians Cook Great," I stirred up discussion with "The Lies of the South," about my childhood in one of the towns that put racism on the map.

8. Higher education is worth money.

17   Some large corporations consider schooling an investment in the company's success and will partially or fully reimburse employees for tuition. The personnel or human-resources department where you work can tell you what the policy is. When I decided to return to school, my very encouraging boss allowed me to switch from part-time to full-time, a move that made me eligible for tuition reimbursement. That financial aid enabled me to have a social life instead of living in student poverty.

18   Other companies give bonuses or raises to employees who earn degrees. And many upper-level positions have a degree requirement, so by finishing yours, you become eligible to move from an entry-level job to one with a career track.

9. Finishing what you start is a joy.

19   Because I worked at a full-time job all the way through, my bachelor's degree took another three years to complete—eight altogether—but I felt the time spent was well worth it. At the end of the coursework, in order to graduate, I had to pass a two-hour oral exam on twenty-four books from a variety of disciplines. "Hemingway" was on my orals committee. As I talked easily and comfortably with him and two other professors about anthropology, philosophy, poetry, fiction, psychology, and religion, I realized how much I'd learned, how much confidence I'd gained, how I'd grown. The experience made me feel I could do anything I put my mind to. So I took the next step.

Now I'll be forty when I get my master's degree—on scholarship!

PREPARING TO WRITE

Circle of Life

One common misconception you might have about writing is that it is an innate ability that some people simply do not have. This might lead to the thought that your ability to write has already been determined. However, this is not so. Writing is a skill that can be learned, much like learning how to drive a car or mold a bowl from clay.

A good piece of writing is the result of a process, a series of steps that the writer has followed. You might already be familiar with some elements of the process of writing, such as making rough drafts or proofreading your final work before handing it in.

One important stage of the writing process that is frequently slighted is prewriting. **Prewriting** is the stage at which a writer develops the *ideas* that will underpin the work. Because ideas are not always available to us at a snap of the fingers, prewriting exercises are often necessary. After all, our brains are not really like computers in the sense that we cannot simply find an idea in a part of our memory labeled "Writing ideas." Instead, the good writing ideas that we all have within us have to be pulled out through various means. Some of these means are tightly structured, and some are loosely structured, but all will help you explore the ideas you do have so you can then choose the best ones for your writing situation.

The Circle of Life

Your first prewriting activity is to construct what is called a "Circle of Life." Draw a large circle, and then draw sections (pie-shapes) for each year of schooling you have attended. Label each section, starting with kindergarten, and then all of the other sections. Don't forget to add this year! Then, in the segment for each year, write down some of the important events that occurred or persons you met who had a big influence on you. When you have finished, each slice of the pie will represent a different year in your school life.

Preparing Yourself to Write

To properly construct your Circle of Life, you need to prepare yourself. Talk to friends or family members to discuss your past; try to recapture what and who some of the main events and people from each year of your life were. Look through old photographs and yearbooks. Read through old diaries or letters that you might have kept. Once you have refreshed your memory, you are ready to write your Circle of Life. Here is what a pie chart, done by Karla, a university student, looks like:

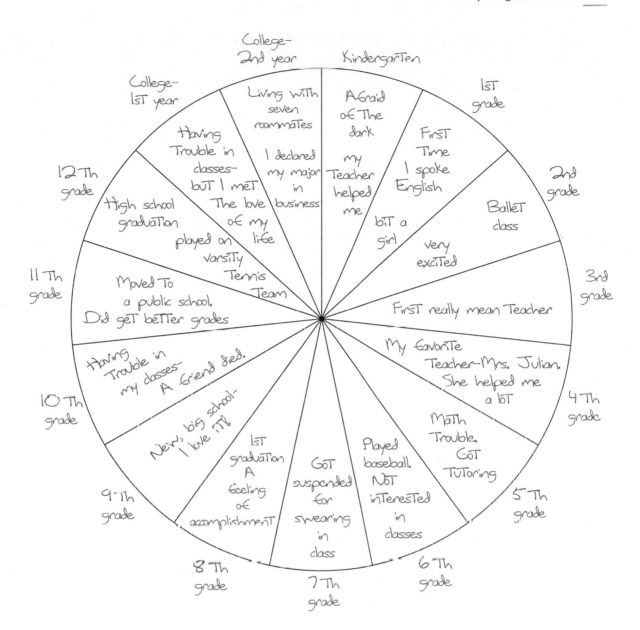

FIGURE 1.1   Karla's Circle of Life

Prewriting

After your preparation is complete, create your own Circle of Life using Figure 1.2. Be sure to include each year of your schooling.

FIGURE 1.2   Circle of Life

Now that you have your Circle of Life, you can see how key events and people have played a part in each year of your school history. If you wish, you can focus on any single year (or slice of your pie chart) and develop ideas from it.

CHAPTER WRITING ASSIGNMENT

Write a 100- to 200-word paragraph in response to one of the following writing assignments. Instructions in the chapter will guide you through the writing process. At different points in the chapter, you will be asked to produce more work on this assignment. By the end of the chapter, you will have completed your final draft.

1. Choose one year of your school life and explain why it was important in shaping your attitude toward school.
2. How has going to college been different from going to high school? Explain by using specific examples.
3. Who has helped you the most in your learning, and how?
4. In Diane Spear's article, "It's Never Too Late to Get That College Degree," she mentions some of her fears about reentering college at the age of 35. Write about any fears, anxieties, and difficulties you have had to overcome in order to attend college.

WRITING LESSON

The Paragraph

While working on the Chapter Writing Assignment, you will find it necessary to decide on a **form** for your writing. That is, your ideas must be presented in some organized fashion. Otherwise, the results will be haphazard—sometimes coherent, but often unreadable. You are probably already familiar with a basic form: the **paragraph.** What you might not know is that paragraphs themselves have organization. Paragraphs contain three basic parts, corresponding to the idea of having a beginning, a middle, and an end: the **topic sentence,** the **support,** and the **wrap-up sentence.**

Topic Sentences

Your paragraph should *begin* with a topic sentence. Simply put, the topic sentence shows your reader what your paragraph is about. Since you are writing a paragraph in response to a specific question—one of the Chapter Writing Assignment questions—your topic sentence will be a specific, direct answer to the question you have chosen. For instance, if you are writing a paragraph in response to a question that asked you to discuss your biggest fears about going to college, you might write the following topic sentence:

> "My biggest fear in going to college is that I'm not as smart as the other students."

This sentence would serve as the topic sentence. It would start your paragraph. The sentence is clear, direct, and specific. Very importantly, it answers the question asked.

When you are creating a topic sentence for your paragraph, you must keep several factors in mind:

- The topic sentence must be a direct statement. In other words, it cannot be a question. Questions might lead readers to a certain answer—or the reader might reach a different answer that the writer did not intend.

  Original:

  What is the worst thing about going away to college?

  Revised:

  Not having my old friends around is the worst thing about going away to college.

- The topic sentence cannot be too broad. Don't suggest more in your topic sentence than can be reasonably covered in one paragraph.

  Original:

  The educational system in the United States needs to be reformed completely.

  Revised:

  My history class would be better if the instructor used more variety in her teaching methods.

- The topic sentence should not try to deal with more than one topic. A second topic needs a different paragraph.

  Original:

  Prices at my college bookstore are too high, and the food in the cafeteria is so unhealthy.

  Revised:

  Prices at my college bookstore are too high.

Support

Of course, one sentence does not usually make a complete paragraph. You must follow that sentence with specific support. That support can be facts, statistics, examples, experiences, or observations that help to back up the topic sentence. In other words, the middle part of a paragraph presents you with the opportunity to *convince* the reader that what you have to say is true, relevant, and important. To support the sample topic sentence, you might write about how past experiences in school have led you to be uncertain of your abilities, that you have heard how competitive college can be, and that you have a good friend who dropped out after a particularly tough semester. These thoughts and experiences will support the ideas presented in the topic sentence.

Wrap-Up Sentences

Paragraphs—just like longer works such as essays, books, or novels—also need to have a sense of completion. One way to present this sense is with a wrap-up sentence, which is a way to tie-off the thoughts, to let your reader know that you have come to the logical end of the paragraph. The wrap-up sentence should not just repeat the ideas in the topic sentence; it should also help the reader experience a sense of having moved forward or of having learned something.

Examine the following paragraph. The topic sentence is underlined, and the wrap-up sentence is italicized. The sentences in between form the support.

My biggest fear about going to college is that I'm not as smart as the other students. After all, I have always had some trouble in school. When I was in elementary school, I loved recess and special projects. However, I was terrible at turning in my homework. As I got older, I started to have trouble in the hard-core subjects, especially math and English. In high school, I even had a teacher tell me never to take her again—that's how bad I was! Because of my trouble, I got turned off to school too, and I know that only made matters worse. I started not caring about my grades and not doing the homework. I barely graduated high school. To make matters worse, my friend Teri, who had always been pretty good in school, dropped out after just one semester of college. She said she couldn't handle the pressure. That scared me too, so I figured that I was done with my education. However, I have since discovered that a high school diploma wouldn't take me very far in the workplace. That's why I made the decision to come back to school. *Now that I'm here, I'm very determined to stay, no matter how hard I have to struggle to make it in the classroom.*

Writing the First Draft

Karla, whose Circle of Life you have already seen, wrote the following paragraph for her first draft in response to Question #1 of the Chapter Writing Assignment. Her topic sentence is underlined.

My fourth grade was a really important year for me because of my teacher, Mrs. Julian. Well, Mrs. Julian was important because she was very nice, and she helped me get excited about school. One thing she did was teach us how to use puppets. Everyone in class made their own puppets, and we even did little plays for the rest of the class. My puppet was a bright orange rooster, and I used some old buttons my Mom used to keep in a jar for the eyes. Of course, we did regular school work too, and what I remember from that was how patient Mrs. Julian was. I had trouble with English because Spanish is my first language, but she seemed to never get tired of helping me with my work. That was important because my parents, who really wanted me to do well in school, couldn't help me a whole lot with my English. Since I'm the oldest child, I didn't have any brothers or sisters who could help me either. The most important thing Mrs. Julian did though was she made me want to come to school because I really wanted to learn. That helped me get through a lot of tough times, even in later years.

Now that you have completed your Circle of Life, and you have learned about the structure of the paragraph, you are ready to write your first draft in response to one of the questions in the Chapter Writing Assignment. Once you have completed your first draft, underline the topic sentence of your paragraph. Then begin the Grammar Lesson.

GRAMMAR LESSON

Parts of Speech

The basic building blocks of writing are words. When you were first learning to speak, you did not start by using whole sentences or even phrases. You used words: one at a time at first, then forming short phrases and eventually sentences. But you began with words.

Words perform different functions in a sentence. To describe these different functions, we use the term "Parts of Speech." There are eight parts of speech in the English language: nouns, pronouns, verbs, adjectives, adverbs, prepositions, conjunctions, and interjections.

Nouns

A **noun** names a person, place, thing, idea, or activity. Nouns answer the questions of Who? or What? is involved in the sentence. Look at the following sentences. The nouns are underlined.

> The plane landed at the airport with 233 passengers onboard.
> Horses require routine care, feeding, and exercise.

Nouns sometimes are used to show possession, usually with an 's.

> Despite their misgivings, Lou's parents finally accepted his decision. ("Lou's" describes whose parents are accepting the decision.)

Note: For a longer discussion of the use of apostrophes with possessives, see the section on "Apostrophes" in Chapter 7.

There are different types of nouns. **Common nouns** refer to general or non-specific people, places, and things. **Proper nouns** refer to specific people, places, or things. **Collective nouns** refer to people and things that consist of more than one person or item, but which are considered one unit.

> Quan was hired by a firm based in Finland. ("firm" is a common noun)
> The students went to the dean, Dr. Quintana, with their complaints. ("Dr. Quintana" is a proper noun)
> The board of education decided not to act at this time. ("board" is a collective noun)

Pronouns

A **pronoun** substitutes for a noun. **Personal pronouns** substitute for the names of people or things. When a pronoun describes the "who" or "what" of the verb, the pronoun is said to be subjective in form. The subjective forms include *I, you, he, she, it, we,* and *they.*

> Even though she had won the lottery, Pamela still lived modestly.
> The brothers were certain that they would be stars in the music world.
> He told his parents not to worry.

Personal pronouns also have a form called the objective, which includes *me, you, him, her, it, us,* and *them.*

> The security guard prevented me from entering the bank without my shoes on.
> Dr. MacMillan left her in the examination room.

Leave <u>us</u> alone!

Personal pronouns can take a form called the <u>possessive</u>. The possessive form includes *my, mine, your, yours, his, hers, its, our, ours, their,* and *theirs.* These pronouns can function as either adjectives or pronouns.

Anne brought <u>her</u> daughter to work last Tuesday.
The bear left <u>its</u> tracks in the mud.
I think that leftover meatloaf is <u>ours</u>.
The final decision was <u>theirs</u>.

Another common type of pronoun is the **relative pronoun.** These pronouns include words such as *who, whom, which,* and *that.*

The woman <u>who</u> bought the coat on Friday returned it on Tuesday.
Find the key <u>which</u> opens this door!
We tried to find the car <u>that</u> dented our fender.

There are several other types of pronouns that are less common but which are still useful to know. They include the following:
Intensive pronouns add emphasis. They include the words *myself, yourself, himself, herself, ourselves,* and *themselves.*

I cooked this dinner <u>myself</u>.
The football players <u>themselves</u> spoke to the assembled fans.
The queen <u>herself</u> helped care for the injured people.

Reflexive pronouns are used to indicate that the doer of the action is also the receiver of the action. The reflexive pronouns are the same as the intensive pronouns.

Martin cut <u>himself</u> shaving.
The company's executives rewarded <u>themselves</u> with large bonuses.
We told <u>ourselves</u> everything would be just fine.

Demonstrative pronouns are used to point out or indicate a person or thing. They include the words *that, these, this,* and *those.*

<u>That</u> is the man Nora saw robbing the bank.
I was afraid <u>this</u> would happen.
<u>Those</u> are the roses that Mrs. Greenfield planted last January.

Interrogative pronouns are used to ask questions. They include the words *who, whom, whose, which,* and *what.*

<u>Who</u> is responsible for this mess?

To <u>whom</u> was the package sent?

<u>What</u> is the name of your bank?

Finally, there is a large group of pronouns known as **indefinite pronouns** because they do not refer to any specific individual. Indefinite pronouns include such words as *all, another, any, anybody, anyone, anything, both, each, either, everybody, everyone, everything, few, many, more, most, much, neither, nobody, no one, nothing, none, one, other, several, some, somebody, someone, something,* and *such.*

<u>Few</u> who have seen the photographs have been left unaffected.

<u>No one</u> in the audience realized that the two characters were being played by the same actor.

<u>Someone</u> needs to shut down the power to the nuclear generator!

Pronouns are discussed further in the section on Case in Chapter 6.

EXERCISE 1.1

Underline the nouns and double underline the pronouns in the following sentences.

<u>*Herman*</u> *was disappointed because* <u><u>*he*</u></u> *had not scored higher on* <u><u>*his*</u></u> *exam*.

1. Tom and Mary took their son to his first class at the new school.

2. When he looked at his grades, Robert realized he had to quit the rugby team, or he might flunk out of school.

3. The instructor who taught class was a graduate student, not a professor.

4. While Clarence enjoyed the atmosphere at the small, private college, he did not think he would be able to attend due to the high cost of tuition.

5. In Russia, teachers place greater emphasis on memorizing information.

6. Jane's math class had so many students in it that some were even sitting on the floor.

7. In spite of her parents' advice, Mimi declared Classics as her major.

8. The valedictorian checked her notes nervously while the dean read his introduction to the audience.

9. Everyone left the library excited about the new computers.

10. Someone called the Student Health Center to ask about free flu shots.

Verbs

A **verb** is a word that shows action or describes a state of being. **Action verbs** indicate that something is being done. Don't let the word "action" throw you off: action verbs do not always show movement. Nevertheless, something is happening in the sentence.

The painter <u>leaned</u> the ladder against the wall.

Her smile <u>washed</u> all of the uncertainty from his mind.

The apprentice <u>rejected</u> the magician's warning.

Every day, Gaston <u>thought</u> about escaping from prison.

Linking verbs show a state of being or existence. They often are forms of the verb *be,* such as *am, is, are, was,* and *were.* Other linking verbs include *appear, become,* and *seem.*

The doctor <u>was</u> skeptical about the new procedure.

My brother <u>is</u> a computer genius.

The test results <u>appear</u> normal.

All of the paperwork <u>seems</u> to be completed.

Linking verbs also reveal the state of being of the subject through the physical senses, such as *see, look, smell, taste, feel, hear,* and *sound,* when these verbs are used to describe something's qualities or characteristics.

The spaghetti sauce <u>smelled</u> great.

The canned mushroom soup <u>tasted</u> terrible compared to Aunt Pat's home-cooked version.

The accident <u>looked</u> worse than it really was.

Many sentences use both types of verbs, action and linking.

Sheena <u>told</u> Amber that her dress <u>looked</u> fabulous. (In this sentence, "told" is an action verb, and "looked" is a linking verb.)

Glenn <u>felt</u> along the base of the wall for any stray nails; he <u>felt</u> certain he had lost at least one. (The first "felt" is an action verb because it shows what Glenn was doing; the second "felt" is a linking verb because it shows Glenn's state of being.)

Verb phrases. Sometimes verbs consist of more than one word. This occurs when two or more verbs work together.

Davene <u>has promised</u> her mother a trip to Santa Fe for her birthday.

The verb "has promised" has two parts: a helping verb ("has") and a main verb ("promised"). Helping verbs are often forms of the verbs *be, have,* and *do*. The main verb is given in the past or present participle form. (The past participle is the *-ed* form in regular verbs, and the present participle is the *-ing* form. For example, in the sample sentence, the main verb "promised" is the past participle of the verb *promise*.)

Other helping verbs include the following words:

can/could	may	might	must	ought to
shall/should	will/would			

When one of these words is used with a main verb, the main verb maintains its normal form:

Jose <u>can see</u> the mountain peaks from far away.

The prisoners <u>must return</u> to their cells in the evening.

The coach <u>ought to encourage</u> her players to play better, not criticize them.

EXERCISE 1.2

Underline the verbs in the following sentences. Above each verb, mark whether the verb is an action verb (AV) or a linking verb (LV). Some sentences have more than one verb.

       LV   *AV*
Susan <u>was</u> certain she <u>would graduate</u> with honors.

1. The critic said the student production of *Othello* was fabulous.

2. Brad never studied, so he failed his chemistry class.

3. The professor forgot that the class had moved to another room.

4. Beth walked through Campus Park on her way to the physics lab.

5. The test sounded hard to Dominic, so he immediately called his tutor.

6. The chairs in Mrs. Sims' second grade class creaked under the weight of the parents who came to the PTA meeting.

7. The school board shelved the issue until the next meeting.

8. The students thought the biology lab smelled awful, but Professor Fremland actually enjoyed it.

9. The adult education program teaches basic computer skills.

10. After failing her first test, Rhonda decided to join a study group.

Adjectives

An **adjective** modifies or describes a noun or pronoun.

Marianne accidentally discovered that her <u>loving</u> husband was actually a <u>cold-blooded</u> assassin.

Wendy used the <u>red</u> wagon to haul <u>heavy</u> bags of fertilizer.

The <u>wooden</u> table split in the <u>dry</u> heat of the desert.

Sometimes possessive forms of nouns and pronouns function as adjectives because they modify a noun or pronoun.

The <u>historian's</u> book collection was worth thousands of dollars. ("historian's" describes whose book collection it was)

<u>Kevin's</u> watch was stolen from the locker room. ("Kevin's" describes whose watch it was)

The nurse carefully put the baby in <u>its</u> bassinet. ("its" describes whose bassinet it was)

Note: While possessive nouns and possessive pronouns can function as adjectives, most instructors classify them as nouns and pronouns, respectively.

Adverbs

An **adverb** modifies or describes a verb, an adjective, or another adverb. Many adjectives become adverbs when an -ly ending is added to them, such as with the following:

Adjective	Adverb
angry	angrily
bad	badly
crisp	crisply
dull	dully
gentle	gently
happy	happily
heavy	heavily
horrible	horribly
light	lightly
peaceful	peacefully
poor	poorly
quick	quickly
rough	roughly
sad	sadly
sharp	sharply
slow	slowly
soft	softly
swift	swiftly
terrible	terribly
true	truly

The heavily promoted boxing match ended up being terribly disappointing.

Dr. Voorhis gradually realized that her patient was not being truthful.

Paula was dressed rather smartly for the evening's festivities.

Note: A word is not an adverb only because it ends in "-ly." For instance, "friendly" is an adjective, not an adverb. You must examine the function of the word to know what part of speech it is.

Other common adverbs include words such as *really, very,* and *too.*

That tie is really ugly.

The traffic accident was very close to being fatal for Mr. Wright.

The suitcase was <u>too</u> heavy for the steward.

Adjectives and Adverbs are discussed more extensively in Chapter 5.

Underline all the adjectives and circle all of the adverbs in the following sentences.

Janelle (quickly) realized that her <u>new</u> instructor was <u>rigorous</u> yet <u>fair</u>.

1. The patient was too heavy to be transported in a regular gurney.

2. The thoroughbred horse raced swiftly around the oval track in record time.

3. The old peanuts were sealed in an air-tight container.

4. Mr. Deitz spoke eloquently about the horrible treatment of prisoners during the war.

5. Sandra wanted badly to be accepted to State University.

6. Heeding the strong call of instinct, the wolf mercilessly slaughtered the wounded sheep.

7. Exhausted and scared, Crystal entered the house quietly.

8. Sam worked late into the night on his desperate plan.

9. The old wharf suffered from decaying timber, rotting rope, and uncertain joints.

10. The pink and white roses smelled sweet to Betty Lou.

Prepositions

A **preposition** is a word that shows the relationship between an object and something else in the sentence. This relationship is usually one of time or space. Here are some of the most common prepositions:

about	according to	after
above	across	against

ahead of	during	out
along	except	out of
along with	except for	outside
apart from	for	outside of
among	from	over
around	in	owing to
as	in back of	since
as for	in case of	through
at	in front of	to
because of	in spite of	toward
before	into	under
behind	like	until
below	near	up
between	of	upon
by	off	with
by means of	on	with regard to
concerning	on account of	with respect to
contrary to	onto	within
despite	on top of	without
due to		

Mason left the wrench <u>under</u> the car <u>in</u> a big pool <u>of</u> motor oil.
The monster crashed <u>through</u> the door.
Maile laughed <u>at</u> the clown.

Note: Some of these prepositions are made up of more than one word. They function, however, to present a single idea.

The airplane stopped <u>in front of</u> the terminal.

Prepositions always are connected to an **object,** a noun or pronoun. In the following sentences, the object of the preposition is double-underlined.

Mason left the wrench <u>under</u> the <u>car</u> <u>in</u> a big <u>pool</u> <u>of</u> motor <u>oil</u>.
The monster crashed <u>through</u> the <u>door</u>.
Maile laughed <u>at</u> the <u>clown</u>.
The airplane stopped <u>in front of</u> the <u>terminal</u>.

The preposition, the object of the preposition, and all of the associated modifiers form a **prepositional phrase.** In each of the following sentences, the prepositional phrases are in brackets.

Mason left the wrench [<u>under</u> the <u>car</u>] [<u>in</u> a big <u>pool</u>] [<u>of</u> motor <u>oil</u>].

The monster crashed [through the door].

Maile laughed [at the clown].

The airplane stopped [in front of the terminal].

EXERCISE 1.4

Put brackets around the prepositional phrases in each of the following sentences.

The group [of students] [in the cafeteria] discussed the current state [of affairs] [at their college].

1. All of the water must be emptied into the trough.

2. The basics of motorcycle riding are easy to learn.

3. Without a doubt, that was the worst film of the decade.

4. The detective found the missing diamond in three days.

5. The letter was sent from Africa to New York without sufficient postage.

6. After her acceptance speech, the actress left the stage with her Oscar trophy in her hand.

7. Take your feet off the table!

8. The examination of the corpse began with a visual inspection.

9. The keys were given to Myra by Tony.

10. The sparrows flew to their nests beneath the eaves of the cathedral.

ZOOM-IN PRACTICE

Without going back to look at the list of prepositions, spend five minutes writing down as many prepositions as you can think of from memory. Over sixty are on the list; space is provided below for thirty. If you cannot come up with at least twenty, you will want to review the list to become more familiar with prepositions.

_____   _____

_____   _____

_____   _____

_____   _____

_____   _____

_____   _____

_____   _____

_____   _____

_____   _____

_____   _____

_____   _____

_____   _____

_____   _____

_____   _____

_____   _____

Conjunctions

Conjunctions are words that join words, phrases, or clauses. The most common conjunctions are **coordinating conjunctions** and **subordinating conjunctions.** Coordinating conjunctions join equal elements of a sentence, such as joining two words, phrases, or clauses. There are only seven in the English language: *and, but, or, so, for, yet, nor.*

Jack <u>and</u> Jill went up the hill.

My grandfather had to choose whether to take early retirement <u>or</u> risk losing his benefits.

The school president spoke about cooperating with the faculty, <u>but</u> then she threatened to fire teachers she didn't like.

Subordinating conjunctions join unequal elements of a sentence—that is, when one idea is joined with a less important idea. The word "subordinate" means that something is of less importance or rank than another. There are many subordinating conjunctions, including the following:

after	even if	provided that	unless	wherever
although	even though	since	until	whereas
as	how	so that	when	whether
as if	if	than	whenever	while
because	in order that	that	where	why
before	once	though		

Little Sophie was featured in all the advertisements <u>because</u> her father owned the company.

<u>Although</u> the bill was passed by a large majority in Congress, the president decided to veto it.

<u>Once</u> we win the lottery, we'll never worry about money again.

Some subordinating conjunctions consist of more than one word.

The athletes played hard <u>even though</u> the outcome of the game had already been determined.

I want that promise in writing <u>even if</u> we shake hands.

Everything will turn out well <u>provided that</u> Ronaldo remembers to bring the Tabasco sauce to the party.

Interjections

An **interjection** is a word or expression that is not a part of the grammar of a sentence. They are often used to show expressions of emotion or strong feeling. When an interjection is used at the start of a sentence, it should be followed by a comma. If it stands alone, the interjection is usually followed by an exclamation mark.

<u>Well</u>, the police officer didn't believe my story.

<u>Hey</u>! Don't touch my French fries!

<u>Ouch</u>! Who left this toy on the stairs?

EXERCISE 1.5

Underline each conjunction and circle each interjection in the following sentences.

(Whoa!) *That exam was hard, <u>but</u> at least now it's over.*

1. My, that young lad sure can sing!

2. Jack and Jill went up the hill, but only Jill came down in a good state of health.

3. Ooops! I broke another cup.

4. Although summer has been terribly hot and last winter was awfully cold, I still find the overall climate here quite nice.

5. Since the team hired the new manager, the players have been trying harder on the field, but I'm not sure they're good enough to win yet.

6. Well, I'm not sure what to say about that, but I'm sure someone else around here knows.

7. Brrr! It sure is cold outside!

8. The breaks have gone against us so far, yet I'm confident about our future.

9. Terry and Madison have left, but Norman and Jack still are hanging around.

10. Golly! That sure is a big pumpkin for Halloween.

ZOOM-PRACTICE

Without looking at the list, write down all seven coordinating conjunctions. If you cannot name them all, go back and review the list until you have memorized them.

_____

_____

_____

_____

_____

_____

_____

DON'T LOSE FOCUS!

Often you cannot tell which part of speech a word is only by looking at the word itself. You have to see the word's <u>function</u> in a particular sentence. Many words, in fact, can function as more than one part of speech. Look at the following sentences:

In the movie *The Ten Commandments,* Moses <u>parts</u> the Red Sea. ("parts" is a verb)

Ken will cast the <u>parts</u> for the opera after auditions next week. ("parts" is a noun)

The <u>well</u> on Grandpa's farm has finally run dry. ("well" is a noun)

Sheila's pet hamster feels <u>well</u> now that it has been given some medicine. ("well" is an adjective, describing the hamster's state of good health)

Because Samantha performed <u>well</u> on her chemistry midterm, she has been named a team leader for the next laboratory experiment. ("well" is an adverb, describing how Samantha performed)

GRAMMAR REVIEW

Underline all of the nouns in the following sentences. Double underline the pronouns.

1. Lawrence looked out the window at his shiny new Corvette as the rain came down.

2. She wondered if she should buy him a train for Christmas, but she decided that a football was a better idea.

3. Someone whispered, "Who is at the door?", but no one answered.

4. Marcus scored 12 points during the second half of the game against Grossmont.

5. Carmen believes jogging is the best exercise, so she runs six times a week.

6. Sun Lee works in the library, but she studies in the cafeteria.

7. Lenny wants to know who will grade his competency test.

8. The two deans, working together, solved the funding problem.

9. The bookstore is having a sale on slide rulers.

10. Most of the schools rely heavily on donations from wealthy alumni.

Underline the verbs in the following sentences and indicate whether they are action (AV) or linking (LV) verbs.

1. The astronomers were awestruck by the satellite's images.

2. The fans waited outside the auditorium to see their favorite rock star.

3. The stage crew impressed the actors with the new sets.

4. Shavon felt a little sick, but she came to class anyway.

5. The celebration marked the university's one hundred years of existence.

6. Sweating profusely, the speaker did not project a good image on television.

7. The home economics class tasted Joanne's latest creation.

8. Professor Yarber's class always seems half-asleep.

9. The new student found the large campus intimidating.

10. The senior faculty hated the library's new computer system.

Applying the Grammar Lesson

In order to demonstrate your understanding of parts of speech, identify one word from your paragraph that functions as a noun, one that functions as a verb, and so on for all eight parts of speech. Use the following code:

Noun	circle	⬭
Pronoun	box	▭
Verb	double-underline	═══
Adjective	parentheses	( )
Adverb	brackets	{ }
Preposition	squared brackets	[ ]
Conjunction	angle brackets	< >
Interjection	back slashes	//

Examine how Karla marked her first draft to identify the Parts of Speech. (Her topic sentence was already underlined.)

My fourth (grade) was a really important year for [me] because of my teacher, Mrs. Julian. /Well,/ Mrs. Julian was important because she was {very} nice, and she helped me get excited [about] school. One thing she did was teach us how to use puppets. Everyone in class made their own puppets, and we even did (little) plays for the rest of the class. My puppet was a bright orange rooster, and I used some old buttons my Mom used to keep in a jar for the eyes. Of course, we did regular school work too, <and> what I remember from that was how patient Mrs. Julian was. I had trouble with English because Spanish is my first language, but she seemed to never get tired of helping me with my work. That was important because my parents, who really wanted me to do well in school, couldn't help me a whole lot with my English. Since I'm the oldest child, I didn't have any brothers or sisters who could help me either. The most important thing Mrs. Julian did though was she made me want to come to school because I really wanted to learn. That helped me get through a lot of tough times, even in later years.

Writing the Second Draft

Once you have identified the parts of speech in your first draft, write the second draft of your Chapter Writing Assignment before beginning the Sentence Lesson. Respond to the revision questions as you work on your rewrite.

Revision questions
- Does your topic sentence directly respond to the question you have chosen?
- Is your topic sentence a question or a statement? If it is a question, rewrite it as a statement. Is your topic sentence too broad for a single paragraph? Is your topic sentence on just one topic?
- Have you used any words that can be cut? If you can cut a word out and keep your intended meaning, cut it out!

After identifying eight parts of speech in her first draft, Karla rewrote her paragraph. In her second draft, Karla checked her topic sentence first. She found that it did answer the question directly, and that it was, indeed, a statement that was not too broad, nor did it attempt to cover more than one topic. Then, Karla reviewed her paragraph with an eye to removing unnecessary words. She cut some of her sentences into shorter ones, so they would be less difficult to follow. Karla also added information, such as the name of her puppet and why her parents could not help her with her English lessons.

Here is Karla's second draft:

My fourth grade was an important year for me because of my teacher, Mrs. Julian. Mrs. Julian was very nice, and she helped me get excited about school. One thing that she did was teach us how to use puppets. Everyone in class made their own puppets, and we even did little plays for the rest of the class. My puppet was a bright orange rooster, and I called him King Orange. I used some old buttons my Mom used to keep in a jar for the eyes. We also did regular school work. I remember how patient Mrs. Julian was. I had trouble with English because Spanish is my first language, but she seemed to never get tired of helping me with my work. That was important because my parents, who really wanted me to do well in school, couldn't help me a whole lot with my English because their English wasn't as good as mine. I didn't have any older brothers or sisters who could help me either. I would have been on my own if it hadn't been for Mrs. Julian. The most important thing Mrs. Julian did was make me want to come to school. I really wanted to learn because of her. That helped me get through a lot of tough times, even in later years when I had teachers who weren't as nice.

SENTENCE LESSON

The Simple Sentence

We usually do not communicate with each other using single words. We string words together to form sentences. A sentence is a combination of words that forms a complete thought. To be a sentence, it must have two important components: a subject and a verb.

You have already seen that verbs are words that show action or express a state of being. Therefore, to understand the fundamental meaning of a sentence, you need to be able to identify the verb of a sentence. In each of the following sentences, the verb is underlined:

Joyce <u>refused</u> to enter the arcade.
Dr. Stein <u>found</u> the tumor at the base of the patient's spine.
The secretary <u>discovered</u> the error in the computer manual.

Remember: Sometimes the verb might consist of more than one word.

You <u>must help</u> the passengers store their belongings.
("must" is the helping verb and "help" is the main verb)

The judge <u>did</u> not <u>find</u> the defense attorney's antics amusing.
("did" is the helping verb and "find" is the main verb)

Some sentences have more than one verb.

Marilyn <u>played</u> soccer, <u>ran</u> track, and <u>swam</u> at the club during the summer.

The **subject** of the sentence tells who or what is doing the action of the verb or whose state of existence is being described. A group of words with a subject and a verb is called a **clause.**

Keisha scanned the employment listings for a good summer job.
("Keisha" is the subject and "scanned" is the verb. The entire sentence forms one clause.)

Aaron feels ill this morning.
("Aaron" is the subject and "feels" is the verb. The entire sentence forms one clause.)

The single word that states the who or what of the sentence is referred to as the **simple subject.** Often, there are words modifying the simple subject. The modifying words and the simple subject form the **complete subject.**

The very old man with the umbrella sat down on the bench.
("Man" is the simple subject; "The very old man with the umbrella" is the complete subject.)

Sometimes a sentence has more than one subject joined by "and." The result is a **compound subject.**

Democrats and Republicans alike oppose the creation of a strong third national party. ("Democrats" and "Republicans" form the compound subject.)

Another aspect of a complete sentence is that it must form a complete thought. This means the logic of the wording is complete; nothing is left unsaid. Look at the following clause:

Although Al Capone had members of the Chicago police force on his payroll.

Because the sentence begins with the word "Although," the reader is left hanging, wanting more information. The word "Although" creates the *expectation* that more is to come. In this sentence, "Although" is a subordinating conjunction. If a clause has a subordinating conjunction, the reader usually expects more information. A clause that has a subject, a verb, and a subordinate conjunction is a **subordinate** or

dependent clause because it cannot stand on its own as a complete sentence. (Dependent clauses and subordinate conjunctions are discussed further in Chapter 3.)

> **Revised:** Al Capone had members of the Chicago police force on his payroll.

The revised sentence is no longer a dependent clause because the subordinating conjunction has been removed. This new clause is an **independent clause** because it has a subject, a verb, and expresses a complete thought. There is no need for anything more to complete the logic of the clause. For this reason, an independent clause can stand on its own as a complete sentence. A sentence that has only one independent clause and no dependent clauses is called a **simple sentence.**

Do not confuse the word "simple" with simplistic or short. Many long sentences are simple sentences. Often what makes a sentence long is the presence of modifiers. **Modifiers** are words or phrases that help to describe the nouns, pronouns, and verbs in a sentence. Modifiers can be adjectives and adverbs. Look at the following:

> The young woman carefully set her brown canvas bag down.
> *adj. adj.*   *adv.*   *adj. adj. adj.*   *adv.*

Phrases

Groups of words, called **phrases,** can also serve as modifiers. Common phrases include *prepositional phrases, participial phrases,* and *infinitive phrases.* These names reflect the type of word that initiates the phrase. A **prepositional phrase,** for example, begins with a preposition and ends with its object. In the sentences below, the prepositional phrases are underlined.

> The long, gray line of graduates of the United States Military Academy has contributed many generals, presidents, and other national leaders to our great country.
>
> Without a doubt, yesterday's lecture was the most important of the semester.
>
> The applicants to the program waited for a response from the director.

The **participial phrase** is introduced by a participle, including the present participle (the *-ing* form) and the past participle. The past participle form of many verbs ends in -ed or -d, but some verbs, called **irregular verbs,** have different forms which follow no predictable pattern.

> Walking into the cafeteria for the first time, Tonya noticed the new orange and brown paint job.
>
> Minh found the lost package, wrapped in holiday paper, underneath the desk.

Told to wait, Max found a seat in the hallway.

The **infinitive phrase** starts with an infinitive, created when a verb begins with "to." The infinitive functions as a noun, adjective, or adverb.

Mac decided to do the work himself. (infinitive phrase as noun)

Exams give students the opportunity to show their knowledge. (infinitive phrase as adjective)

The dog barked to wake up its owner. (infinitive phrase as adverb)

Being able to recognize modifiers, whether they are single words or phrases, can help you know whether or not a sentence is complete.

DON'T LOSE FOCUS!

By recognizing phrases, you can identify the subjects and verbs in sentences. For instance, the subject and the verb of a sentence will not be found in a prepositional phrase. If you can recognize a prepositional phrase, you can eliminate those words from your consideration.

Most of the survivors were found in lifeboats.

If you examine this sentence, you might be tempted to say that "survivors" is the subject of the verb "were found." However, you would be wrong. By striking out all prepositional phrases in the sentence, you will find the subject and verb within the words that remain.

Most ~~of the survivors~~ were found ~~in lifeboats~~.

Now, it is easy to see that the pronoun "Most" is the subject of this sentence.

EXERCISE 1.6

Identify the simple subject(s) and underline the verb in each of the following sentences.

S
The tutoring services are quite helpful on this campus.

1. Until the start of the semester, Terry will live with her mother in West Lafayette.

2. To help her get around at school, Mom and Dad gave Felicia their old Ford station wagon.

3. Many famous and wealthy Americans, such as Thomas Edison, John D. Rockefeller, and Bill Gates, never graduated from college.

4. The work on the Physical Education facility has almost been completed.

5. My friend Susie has a trust fund from her grandmother for college.

6. Three members of the Agriculture Department retired last month.

7. The park in the center of campus is beautiful.

8. Student protesters marched outside of the administration building.

9. The new instructor, Professor Pianta, had trouble finding the library.

10. Henry left the study group during the last week before finals.

EXERCISE 1.7

Underline the phrases in the following sentences. Indicate whether they are prepositional phrases (p.p.), participial phrases (part. p.), or infinitive phrases (i.p.).

> *i.p.*   *part.p.*
> *To better his test scores*, Hank tried *memorizing important information*.

1. After the exam, Adrian met his friends in the cafeteria.

2. At night, Stephanie walked through the parking lot with a friend.

3. Looking for fresh ideas, Howard decided to attend the conference in Dallas.

4. The chancellor of the entire system spoke at the ceremony for all of the guests.

5. Scholarships, along with financial aid, enabled Eileen to attend the college of her choice.

6. The professor misplaced his computer diskettes by leaving them in his laboratory.

7. Sensing trouble, the counselor advised the student to look for other career options.

8. The newest report on SAT scores shows that students throughout the country are improving academically.

9. Lost in thought, Yolanda forgot to take notes during the lecture.

10. Wearing the school colors, the student cheerleaders tried to generate enthusiasm for their team.

EXERCISE 1.8

In the space provided, add words to construct simple sentences.

Studying in the library <u>has many distinct advantages.</u>

1. Jenny liked _____

   _____.

2. The school principal _____

   _____.

3. _____

   _____ into the evening rush hour traffic.

4. Without speaking, the magician _____

_____ his audience.

5. The work on the farm _____

_____.

6. _____

_____ geometry class.

7. Professor Conrad will _____

about _____.

8. _____ invented

_____.

9. Inside the laboratory, the scientist _____

_____.

10. _____

_____.

_____

Sentence Review

In the following sentences underline the verb(s) and write an "S" above the simple subject(s). Remember: some verbs are more than one word long.

1. Dr. Zumwalt, a long-time member of the faculty at Yale, retired in 1973.

2. I just can't remember the words to that song.

3. Without a computer, Steven could not process the information on the diskette.

4. That last experiment appears to be a failure.

5. The MacMillan family has been driving all night long, trying to reach Reno.

6. The two candidates, Mr. Democrat and Ms. Republican, offer different views of the future.

7. The construction workers have finished the new stadium.

8. Judging from the lecture on the first day, my freshman biology class will be quite interesting.

9. Everyone can join the ROTC program on campus.

10. The new computers, while initially impressive, have been more trouble than help.

In the following sentences, underline and mark the prepositional phrases (p.p.), infinitive phrases (i.p.), and participial phrases (part. p.)

1. Trying very hard, Justin studied late into the evening.

2. The party at the fraternity house had unexpectedly tragic results for a new member.

3. Martha had to find George because Ben wanted to dance a waltz with her daughter.

4. Some people like to eat Spam, but Ron uses it to feed his cats.

5. Watching from the window, Nancy saw the boys chasing the geese along the riverbank.

6. Without hope, there is no reason to go on.

7. The new manager of the restaurant refused to take a much needed break.

8. To impress her professor, Gretchen worked hard on her term paper.

9. Faced with certain defeat, Allen knocked over the chess board in a fit of rage.

10. The doctor, led by three orderlies, found the patient lying on the floor next to the bed.

Applying the Sentence Lesson

To see how frequently you use simple sentences, identify all of the simple sentences in your second draft by double-underlining them. Then, consider whether or not you have enough variety—you don't want all of your sentences to be simple sentences, yet if none of them are, you will probably need to break down some longer, more complicated sentences into simple sentences to help provide clarity. Good writing is usually varied in sentence forms.

Look at Karla's second draft, with the simple sentences double-underlined:

My fourth grade was an important year for me because of my teacher, Mrs. Julian. Mrs. Julian was very nice, and she helped me get excited about school. One thing that she did was teach us how to use puppets. Everyone in class made their own puppets, and we even did little plays for the rest of the class. My puppet was a bright orange rooster, and I called him King Orange. I used some old buttons my Mom used to keep in a jar for the eyes. We also did regular school work. I remember how patient Mrs. Julian was. I had trouble with English because Spanish is my first language, but she seemed to never get tired of helping me with my work. That was important because my parents, who really wanted me to do well in school, couldn't help me a whole lot with my English because their English skills weren't as good as mine. I didn't have any older brothers or sisters who could help me either. I would have been on my own if it hadn't been for Mrs. Julian. The most important thing Mrs. Julian did was make me want to come to school. I really wanted to learn because of her. That helped me get through a lot of tough times, even in later years when I had teachers who weren't as nice.

Writing the Final Draft

Once you have identified the simple sentences in your second draft, rewrite it to create the final draft of the Chapter Writing Assignment. Respond to the revision questions as you work on your rewrite.

Revision questions

- Does your paragraph overall have a topic sentence, support, and a wrap-up sentence? These will give your paragraph a sense of beginning, middle, and end.
- Does the support in your paragraph include at least three specific, different details? With any fewer details, your paragraph will lack the support needed to make its points.
- Does your paragraph have at least four simple sentences? If not, make sure that the final draft does.

The rewrite of your second draft will be your final draft. Hand in the final draft, with the Circle of Life, first draft, second draft, and any other materials you created in the process of writing this paragraph.

Karla noticed that she only had three simple sentences in her paragraph. She thought she could improve the paragraph by breaking more of the longer sentences into simple sentences. She also looked for more words that she could remove without changing the meaning of what she said, and she added more details about her teacher. Here is her final draft:

My fourth grade was an important year for me because my teacher, Mrs. Julian, helped me get excited about school for the very first time. One thing I loved that she did was teach us how to use puppets. Everyone in class made their own puppets. We even did little plays. My puppet was a bright orange rooster I called King Orange. I used some old buttons my Mom kept in a jar for the eyes. We did regular school work, too. Mrs. Julian was very patient with me. I had trouble with English because Spanish is my first language, but she never got tired of helping me improve. Her help was important. Even though my parents wanted me to do well in school, they mostly spoke Spanish so they couldn't help me with my homework. I didn't have any older brothers or sisters to help either. I would have probably gotten discouraged and failed if it hadn't been for Mrs. Julian. Because she had such a great attitude and was always ready to help, I really wanted to learn. In later years, when school seemed hard and teachers didn't seem to care, I always remembered Mrs. Julian and what she did for me, and that helped keep me going.

PORTFOLIO CHECKLIST

In your portfolio, you should now have the following:

1. a Circle of Life prewriting exercise
2. a First Draft. The first draft should have the topic sentence underlined. It should also have each of the Parts of Speech marked.
3. a Second Draft. The second draft should have your simple sentences double-underlined.
4. a Final Draft. Make sure you have at least four simple sentences.

PARTING SHOT

1. How important is technology in the learning process?
2. Which is more effective: learning on one's own or by interacting with others?
3. How important is it to have support from family and friends in your education?

GOALS IN REVIEW

In this chapter, you have learned about

- a prewriting strategy called The Circle of Life
- the basic form of the paragraph
- the parts of speech
- the simple sentence

PRACTICE CHAPTER TEST

Part I

In the following sentences, underline the nouns, double-underline the pronouns, and circle the verbs. Remember that some verbs are more than one word long.

1. Your payment is expected by next Tuesday in our office or you will be sent to jail!

2. The park near the station has been converted into a parking garage.

3. The weakness in her proposal was its reliance on voluntary agreements.

4. Most of the chickens were killed by gassing them with poison.

5. Everyone shook hands with his or her partner.

6. The stolen automobiles were found near the border in an abandoned warehouse.

7. Nobody understands teenagers except other teenagers, or so they themselves think.

8. The newspaper ran an advertisement appealing to bald men who still want hair.

9. The English professor traveled to Romania to teach at a well-known university.

10. Who is the woman in the bright, red dress?

11. She did not understand how to operate the new computer.

12. Walking along the beach, Marianne discovered a shell with a beautiful purple interior that she had never seen before.

13. The carne asada smelled wonderful to Andrew as he entered the restaurant.

14. The steering on the used car felt too soft to Beulah, so she decided not to buy it.

15. My cousin Michael is a genius, or so my mother tells me.

Part II

Mark the simple subject with an "S" and underline the verb in each of the following sentences. Be aware that some sentences have more than one subject and/or more than one verb.

1. People who swear in public demonstrate their poor upbringing and lack of manners.

2. Some American writers, such as Ernest Hemingway and James Baldwin, moved to France to do some of their best writing.

3. Honestly, I, along with Penique, cannot say if we will attend the opening performance of the opera season.

4. Many of the travelers were lost in the spacious airport.

5. Doug is sending messages into outer space for aliens to hear.

6. Skiing is an exciting Olympic sport.

7. Kristin has been living in an apartment without heat all winter.

8. The trout tastes excellent with a little lemon.

9. Without saying anything to his friends, Jeremy left San Diego and flew to Seattle.

10. Hoping for a different decision, the lawyer filed an appeal for his client.

CHAPTER 2

Family

CHAPTER GOALS

In this chapter, you will learn about

- branching as a prewriting exercise,
- the importance of transitions in a paragraph,
- word order in sentences, and
- the compound sentence.

The theme of this chapter is Family. Many of us consider our family members the most important people in our lives. Parents or guardians have a tremendous influence on how we think of ourselves. Of course, you might already be a parent, and the relationship you have with your child or children is likely to be a central aspect of your life. No matter what your particular situation, your family can often be a rich source of writing ideas.

OPENING SHOT

QUESTIONS ABOUT THE PICTURE

1. How would you describe this family?

2. What is traditional about this family? What is not?

3. How is this family like your own? How is it different?

READING

Questions to Consider

1. How important is it for parents to give their children privacy? At what age are certain areas of a child's life off-limits to a parent? How does this change as a child grows older?

2. What are a parent's responsibilities concerning a child's safety? How does that change as a child grows older?

Words to Watch

autonomy	independence; self-government
incorrigible	incapable of being corrected or reformed
inquisitiveness	undue curiosity; inclination to investigate
micromanage	to manage with excessive control or attention to details
ramification	a consequence growing out of a problem or situation
snoop	someone who pries into the private affairs of others
vigilance	alert watchfulness

Should Parents Spy on Their Kids?
Andrea Warren

1   Elaine Richmond*, a forty-year-old accountant from Teaneck, New Jersey, is a self-confessed snoop. She wants to know *everything* that goes on in her thirteen-year-old daughter's life—and will go to just about any length to find out.

2   "I've gone through her backpack," Elaine freely admits. "I've read her diary and her computer files. If she wants to go to the movies, *I* drive her there. I want to know who she's with and what she's doing at all times."

---

* Names have been changed.

3   Elaine, who feels that it's her parental responsibility to monitor her child this way, makes no apologies. "I have absolutely no guilt," she says emphatically. "If I find something incriminating in my daughter's things, I'll confront her. We might have a fight about it, but I never say I'm sorry. Most parents are in denial about what their kids do these days. I intend to nip any problems in the bud."

4   Linda Burrows* of Portland, Oregon, is a forty-three-year-old single mother with a very different view on the issue: She places almost no restrictions on her eleven-year-old daughter and her fifteen-year-old son and rarely enters their rooms uninvited. "I trust my kids," she says. "Besides, once they reach the preteens, they do what they want, so why go through all the hassles and fights involved in trying to know what they're thinking and doing every minute? They'd just end up hating me."

5   Of course, Elaine's and Linda's positions represent extreme ways of dealing with an issue all parents confront. Other mothers and fathers find themselves closer to the middle: While they would never resort to spying on their children, they know they have to keep a watchful eye on them. The problem is, the line between too much and too little vigilance can be fuzzy at times. How much freedom from intrusion should a child be allowed? At what point does careful monitoring border on invasion of privacy? And how should a family determine its own standards and set its own rules?

6   The dilemma is a serious one, and how a parent solves it can have long-lasting consequences. "If you don't supervise your children carefully, they could get into trouble, because the world is a dangerous place and kids naturally experiment," says Laurence Steinberg, Ph.D., professor of psychology, Temple University, in Philadelphia, and the author of *You and Your Adolescent* (HarperReference, 1997). "On the other hand, if you spy, your display of distrust can have ramifications just as severe."

7   Complicating the issue is the fact that children can be hypersensitive to even the *appearance* of prying. "When my nine- and eleven-year-old boys come home from school, my husband, Jeff, and I know better than to ask too many questions, even though we really want to hear about their day," says Debi Fast, thirty-eight, of Kearney, Nebraska. "We're *interested,* but the kids think we're just *nosy.* They can get so upset that they won't even tell us the littlest things."

8   Experts agree that children need some freedom from adult interference—and adult inquisitiveness—so that they can develop a sense of individuality and learn to make decisions on their own. Yes, this means parents must sometimes back off. But parents who try to give their children autonomy by *never* asking questions will find that tactic doesn't work—children may interpret it as lack of caring.

9   According to David Elkind, Ph.D., a professor of child study at Tufts University, in Medford, Massachusetts, and the author of *Parenting Your Teenager* (Ballantine Books, 1994), the issue of a child's need to withhold

information versus a parent's need to know should be handled on a case-by-case basis.

10   Clearly, parents who suspect that their child is engaging in forbidden or risky behavior—being sexually active, using drugs—need to act on their worry. Sometimes the warning signs are obvious (your child leaves drug or birth control devices around); sometimes they're subtle (your child suddenly seems uninterested in old friends or starts doing poorly in school). But whenever your observations give you serious cause for concern, your child's right to privacy must give way to your right to be informed.

11   "Freedom from intrusion is a privilege, and children need to know that they can enjoy this freedom in their private lives only as long as they abide by the responsibilities that accompany it," Elkind advises.

12   Carla Wilson*, a forty-five-year-old teacher from Dallas, reached this conclusion when her fifteen-year-old son ran away from home last year. "We were frantic," she recalls. "When we checked with the school, we found out he had been repeatedly truant. They had never notified us of this, even though it could have been a tip-off that something was wrong. We had to search our son's room for clues and uncovered disturbing evidence that he was using drugs—a complete surprise to us. When the police found him two weeks later, we immediately put him into drug rehab. After he returned to us, he was very angry for searching his room. We told him he'd given us no choice."

13   According to Lauren Ayers, Ph.D., a psychologist in Albany, New York, and the author of *Teenage Girls: A Parent's Survival Manual* (The Crossroad Publishing Co., 1994), parents don't need to apologize when concern leads them to invade their children's privacy.

14   "Tell your child why you were concerned, what you found, and what you're going to do about it," Ayers says. "Children may become distrustful if they think their parents are spying on them without cause, but there's a critical difference between reasonable monitoring, such as demanding to know why the liquor cabinet is unlocked, and outright snooping, like reading your child's letters from friends. Older children can understand that difference and eventually learn to appreciate the parent who looks after their interests."

15   Of course, very young children don't understand issues of privacy, which is why they're so guileless about getting into other people's possessions. However, "By the age of five or six, children can reason well enough to understand the concept," says Carlyn Saunders, Ph.D., the director of the Communication Skills Center, in Kansas City, Missouri. From then until age ten or eleven is the perfect time for parents to encourage the kind of interaction that will keep communication lines open.

16   "To help this happen, I tell parents to be quietly available when kids want to talk," says Saunders. "Don't grill and drill them with questions about their day or what they did at a birthday party. Instead, talk about your day and your feelings, so it's safe for them to do the same."

This kind of openness, established when a child is young, will serve parents well when, developmentally, the need for privacy surfaces in preadolescents.

17   "If parents suddenly begin arguing with a twelve-year-old about closed bedroom doors and furtive telephone conversations, they may be setting themselves up for years of conflict," Saunders continues. "Such parents often end up with secretive, rebellious teens, or with teens who are overly dependent and lack self-esteem."

18   Eva Horn of Nashville, Tennessee, is in the midst of negotiating the bedroom privacy issue with fourteen-year-old Marie. "Marie turned moody and secretive seemingly overnight." Last week I noticed a book on her nightstand and asked how she liked it. She demanded to know how I knew what she was reading. Yet she knows I go into her room to put away laundry. I'm just not supposed to see anything while I'm there!"

19   As long as parents know their child isn't breaking a house rule, like entertaining a boyfriend behind a closed bedroom door, they need to beware of reading too much into certain behaviors, says Jerry Wyckoff, Ph.D., a psychologist in Overland Park, Kansas, and co-author of *20 Teachable Virtues* (Perigee, 1995).

20   "If a child wants his bedroom door closed, that doesn't mean something bad is going on. Starting at the age of ten, kids want and need a world that's separate from their parents. Kids who are given space, who have time to be reflective, often make a better transition to adulthood. Parents who are concerned about that closed door should ask themselves, "Why does this bother me?"

21   Elaine Richmond, the mother who needs to know *everything* her thirteen-year-old is doing, may run the risk of alienating her daughter if she continues to spy on her. Even after more than two decades, Angela Hatfield* still seethes with resentment. "My mother was an incorrigible snoop," the forty-year-old Seattle resident remembers. "She would open my mail and go through my drawers. Once, when my older sister was home from college, my mother went through her things and found birth control pills. She yelled at my sister and told her how awful she was. There was no discussion about why my sister had birth control, or why our mother had searched her belongings. It made me very angry, and to this day, our relationship could, at best, be called distant."

22   Like Elaine, Angela's mother may have felt her actions were justified out of concern. But their good intentions are misguided. "Parents should not try to micromanage their children's lives," says Kris Sheridan, an adolescent counselor in Lawrence, Kansas. "Unless a parent thinks her child is in danger, trust—combined with realistic monitoring—is the only thing that works. Children understand the concept of trust and will honor it, provided their parents do. They also understand that they break this trust when they do something wrong. Then they know that their parents have a right—and a responsibility—to do whatever they have to in order to make sure they're okay."

PREPARING TO WRITE

Branching

Prewriting activities help writers develop good ideas before they begin writing. Many prewriting activities work by having the writer generate ideas. These ideas are connected to each other according to the writer's internal logic ("free association" is the term typically used). **Branching** is one type of prewriting activity that moves from one idea to another in a logical fashion, but with the option of having *more than one idea connected to another.* It begins with a single subject at the start, and then moves off in several different directions. Branching involves more than just getting words down on paper; it involves making connections. Therefore, the physical format of the result of a branching activity is highly visual. It looks somewhat like a tree. See Figure 2.1 of a branching exercise developed in response to this chapter theme by a community college student named Sabrina.

The purpose of branching is to see how one idea can lead not to just one new idea, but to several new ideas, and those ideas lead in other directions. Branching can serve two important purposes: to help you see the wide range of topics within a given subject, and to show

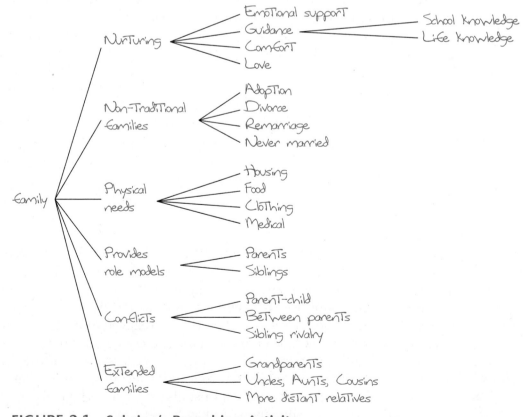

FIGURE 2.1   Sabrina's Branching Activity

the relationships among those topics. By finding topics within a subject, you are able to be more specific and detailed about what you want to say. Instead of speaking about your subject broadly, you are able to narrow the focus of your writing. This helps to define clearly what you have to say.

Branching serves as a way to organize ideas on parallel levels as well, meaning that all items at each level of the branch are of equal type and importance. This means that you can convey to your reader a sense of *hierarchy* or order of importance among the ideas you are presenting.

Preparing Yourself to Write

To prepare for the branching activity, refresh your memory about your family by talking to your parents, grandparents, siblings, or other family members. Look at photo albums, home videos, family Bibles, and other books or documents that record the names, birth dates, and death dates of family members.

Prewriting

Use the general subject of Family or choose one of the questions from the Chapter Writing Assignment and do a branching exercise on the following page. Once you have completed your branching activity, examine the results to see what sort of connections you have discovered. Were any of these unusual or unexpected? What part of your results do you find most interesting? If you wish, you can focus on any single limb or section of the branching activity to form the basis of your Chapter Writing Assignment.

Branching Activity

CHAPTER WRITING ASSIGNMENT

Write a 100- to 200-word paragraph in response to one of the following writing assignments. Instructions in the chapter will guide you through the writing process. At different points in the chapter, you will be asked to produce more work on this assignment. By the end of the chapter, you will complete your final draft.

1. How would you describe your own family? Consider such issues as whether it is traditional or non-traditional, fragmented or united, supportive or not, affectionate or withdrawn. Cite specific details in your support.

2. Write about the importance of a family member in your life. Explain how he or she helped you develop into the person you are today.

3. Can families without either a father or a mother (such as in single-parent families) be as successful in raising children as the traditional two-parent family? Explain.

4. In the article "Should Parents Spy on Their Kids?", Andrea Warren states that most parents try not to be too intrusive in their children's lives or too absent from them. Based on your own experience and observations, what is the best approach parents should take toward learning about their children's activities as they approach their teenage years?

WRITING LESSON

Transitions

Writing a successful paragraph requires that your reader be able to follow what you have to say. A problem writers often face is that they understand what they *mean* to say, but the reader *misunderstands*. It is an essential goal of the writer to avoid misunderstandings.

One frequent source of confusion can be found when writers fail to provide helpful **transitions.** A transition occurs whenever a writer moves from one idea to another. Transitions can occur between paragraphs, but you must also be aware that transitions occur within paragraphs as well. Examine the following paragraph written about a family crisis. Words that show transitions within the paragraph have been underlined.

One of the worst crises in my family occurred <u>when</u> my grandmother was diagnosed with Alzheimer's. <u>After</u> my grandfather passed away from a long illness about eight years ago, we knew my grandmother was not only grieving, <u>but</u> she was exhausted from taking care of my grandfather.

Therefore, when she became forgetful or stopped talking in conversations, no one said much. However, these symptoms did not improve. My mother grew terribly worried, especially since we don't live in the same city as my grandmother. As a result, she was constantly on the phone with her brothers and sisters talking about what to do. My eldest aunt moved my grandmother in with her and her husband, my Uncle Edward. At first that worked, but my grandmother only worsened. For example, not only did she stop remembering names, she stopped knowing who people were, even her own children. Also, she had serious physical problems. Finally, the family had to put my grandmother into a home for Alzheimer's patients. Everyone was upset because now she's living with strangers. On the other hand, this may be harder on us than on her because, to my grandmother, we are strangers, too.

The underlined transitions guide the reader from one thought to the next within the paragraph. Sometimes transitions are a single word, and sometimes they are phrases. The following is a list of transitional words and phrases:

Sequences

and	last, last of all
additionally	in addition
next	furthermore
first, second, third …	moreover
finally	subsequently

Contrasts

however	nevertheless
on the other hand	although
instead	even though

Causal Relations

because	consequently
since	as a result of
for	so

hence	thus
therefore	

Spatial Relations

above	under
below	underneath
in	inside of, outside of
on	nearby
on the left, on the right	in the distance

Exemplification

for example	specifically
for instance	in this case
namely	

ZOOM-IN PRACTICE

Spend five minutes writing about an embarrassing moment in your life. Underline your use of transitional words and phrases that help you show the sequence of events.

Writing the First Draft

When Sabrina did her branching activity on the topic of the family, she was not sure what she would eventually write about. After looking over her branching activity, she realized that while she had come up with both positive and negative ideas about families, when she thought of her own, she mostly thought of good things. She decided to write her paragraph in response to Question #1. She underlined the transitions in her paragraph:

Some people might think my family is not very traditional, but I think it is. On the one hand, my parents are divorced, and both have since remarried. I grew up with my mother. I only saw my Dad a few times each year because he moved away to a different state. However, my family is very traditional in some important ways. First, everyone loves each other. My step-dad has been great. He and my mother have been married for twelve years, <u>so</u> he's been like a second father to me <u>since</u> I was a little kid. I've called him "Dad" for years. <u>Also</u>, my mother and father worked things out so that my sister and I could always visit my father during the summer and for important events, <u>like when</u> he remarried five years ago. What makes my family most traditional, <u>though</u>, are the every-day things, like the smiles, the hugs and kisses, the talking. Even the fights. We love each other so much we know we can disagree with each other and still be a family. <u>Of course</u>, as I've grown older, I've relied less on my family and more on my friends, <u>but</u> my family is still the best, most important thing in my life.

Now that you have completed your branching activity and learned to use transitional words and phrases, you are ready to write your first draft in response to the question you selected in the Chapter Writing Assignment. Once you have completed your first draft, underline all the transitional words and phrases in it. Then begin the Grammar Lesson.

GRAMMAR LESSON

Word Order

If English is your native language, you may not even be aware of how **word order** affects meaning—it is such a well-understood part of how you talk and write. However, one of the characteristics of English is that the meaning of sentences is partly determined by word order.

Take a typical sentence: "Dad eats the pizza." "Dad" is the doer of the action of eating. The "pizza" is what Dad ate. If you reverse the order of the sentence, "The pizza eats Dad," you completely change the meaning of the sentence.

Word order is crucial in proper English. As a result, certain regular sentence patterns have evolved. Here are five patterns:

1. Subject-Verb (only)
2. Subject-Verb-Direct Object
3. Subject-Verb-Indirect Object-Direct Object
4. Subject-Linking Verb-Subject Complement
5. Subject-Verb-Direct Object-Object Complement

Subject-Verb (only)

Examine the following sentences. The subject in each is italicized, and the verb is in bold.

> The *cat* **meowed.**
>
> My *brother,* a heavy sleeper, **snored** all night long.
>
> The *manager* **sat** in the dugout long after the defeat.

This sentence pattern requires only the presence of two words: a verb and a subject that performs the action of the verb. The verbs in this sentence pattern are known as **intransitive verbs** because they do not take objects. In other words, nothing is done *to* anything: The cat meows, the brother snores, and the manager sits.

Remember: As you saw in Chapter 1, the subject and the verb of a sentence can not be found in a prepositional phrase. In longer sentences, you might have trouble locating the subject and the verb. However, if you strike out the prepositional phrases, finding the subject and verb can be a lot easier.

> **Original:** The robber walked into the lobby of the bank without his mask.
>
> **Prepositional phrases struck out:** The robber walked ~~into the lobby of the bank without his mask~~.

Now, it is simple to see that "walked" is the verb and "robber" is the subject.

DON'T LOSE FOCUS!

Don't forget that all sentences have a subject and a verb. The subject-verb only format is marked by the absence of other elements in a sentence, such as a direct object. Remember, the verb in a subject-verb only sentence will *always* be an action verb. If a sentence has a linking verb, the subject will require a complement on the other side of the verb.

EXERCISE 2.1

Examine the following sentences. Put a check in front of the sentences written in the subject-verb only format. Leave blank the ones that are not.

√ The cousins ***ran*** *around the table.*

1. This summer, the family will fly to Hawaii.

2. My grandfather ran an old-fashioned malt shop.

3. Little children grow so quickly.

4. JoBeth got her driver's license with a lot of help from her mother.

5. Standing beside her cousin Jared, Eileen looks tiny.

6. Feeling hungry, the baby cried loudly.

7. My cousin Marty swims each day at the community pool.

8. The family met at the restaurant for breakfast.

9. My son Jim lifts weights to stay healthy.

10. Mothers seldom rest from their busy schedules.

Subject-Verb-Direct Object

Subject-Verb-Direct Object is the second sentence pattern. Look at the following sentences to see examples of this pattern. In each sentence, the subject is italicized, the verb is in bold, and the direct object is underlined.

The *jockey* **rode** the horse to the starting gate.

Gaylee **wrote** a letter to the editor.

Oscar **hired** an attorney.

This sentence pattern contains a subject, a verb, and a **direct object,** which is usually a noun or pronoun. The direct object is the word that answers the question, "To what or to whom is the action of the verb done?" The verbs in this sentence pattern are **transitive verbs** because they require an object. In other words, the doer of the action does the action to something or someone.

EXERCISE 2.2

Examine the following sentences. Put a check in front of each sentence that is written in the subject-verb-direct object format. Leave blank the ones that are not.

√ Caitlin ***bought*** *the silver* <u>*necklace*</u> *on sale.*

1. Gretchen brought the mail into the house.

2. Andrew and Kay made the punch with flour instead of sugar.

3. Feeling tired, Father yawned on the couch.

4. Mother-daughter relationships can be difficult.

5. No one liked Grandmother's new hairstyle.

6. Bobby is like his father.

7. Dinner at the Puppo home was always fantastic.

8. This spring, Justin and his mother, Aunt Cynthia, will travel to Arizona for two weeks.

9. At the dinner table, Sybil passed the mashed potatoes to Eugene.

10. My cousin Alexis bought a new dog, Sparky.

Subject-Verb-Indirect Object-Direct Object

The third sentence pattern is Subject-Verb-Indirect Object-Direct Object. Examine the following sentences. The subject in each is italicized, the verb is in bold, the direct object is underlined, and the indirect object is double-underlined.

> Despite her reservations about his character, *Anita* **sent** Mr. Daley a wedding invitation.
> *Professor Steilen* **wired** his friend bail money.
> The *audience* **gave** the actress a standing ovation.

This sentence pattern explains for whom or to whom the action was taken. That noun or pronoun is the **indirect object.** The indirect object comes before the direct object in the sentence. One way to detect the indirect object in a sentence is that the sentence can usually be rewritten by moving the indirect object into a prepositional phrase.

> Despite her reservations about his character, *Anita* **sent** a wedding invitation to Mr. Daley.
> *Professor Steilen* **wired** bail money to his friend.
> The *audience* **gave** a standing ovation to the actress.

EXERCISE 2.3

Examine the following sentences. Put a check in front of each sentence that is written in the subject-verb-indirect object-direct object format. Leave blank the ones that are not.

√   *The nervous* father ***tossed*** *his teen-aged <u>son</u> the car <u>keys</u>.*

1. Guillermo gave his wife a new dress.

2. Aunt Mary drove her convertible into the garage.

3. The three boys offered Uncle Jack a glass of lemonade.

4. Without question, Sheila's parents will hate her boyfriend.

5. Glenn mailed his relatives Hanukkah cards.

6. Harry flew home first class with stops in Dallas and Chicago.

7. Mark and his brothers went duck hunting in Idaho.

8. Slowly, Marion threw his little sister the football.

9. Carrie wrote her mother a letter from college every week.

10. Having Thanksgiving without any family around is seldom enjoyable.

Subject-Linking Verb-Subject Complement

Another pattern is Subject-Linking Verb-Subject Complement. Examine the following sentences. In each sentence, the subject is italicized, the verb is in bold, and the subject complement is italicized.

Tai **was** *unhappy* about her test results.
Dr. Jerome Jackson **is** a *pediatrician*.
The pitcher's *arm* **feels** *tired*.

The verbs in this sentence pattern are linking verbs because, unlike action verbs, they do not describe actions. A **linking verb** describes a state of being or existence. Linking verbs are often forms of the verb "to be" (such as *am, are, is, was, were,* and *will be*). These verbs are termed "linking" because they link the subject of the sentence with either a noun, pronoun, or adjective that follows the verb. In a sense, the linking verb functions in the same manner as an equals sign in mathematics:

Dr. Jerome Jackson is a pediatrician.
Dr. Jerome Jackson = a pediatrician.

Some linking verbs can be used to describe the physical senses or matters of health. In the sentences below, the verbs are in bold.

The pitcher's arm **feels** tired. (This describes the state of the pitcher's arm, not the action of feeling or touching.)
The spaghetti sauce **smells** spicy. (This describes the state of the sauce, not the action of smelling.)
Grandpa's old sofa **looks** perfect in our new playroom. (This describes the state of the sofa, not the action of looking or seeing.)

Don't be confused. Sometimes these verbs can be used as action words.

Sean **feels** under the bed for his toy.
Aunt Susan **smelled** the roses in her garden.
The sailor **looks** for land from the crow's nest atop the ship's mast.

The **subject complement** is the word or words that rename or describe the subject. A subject complement is usually a noun, pronoun, or adjective. In the sentences below, the subject complements are in italics.

Tai was *unhappy* about her test results. ("unhappy" is an adjective)
Dr. Jerome Jackson is a *pediatrician*. ("pediatrician" is a noun)
The pitcher's arm feels *tired*. ("tired" is an adjective)

EXERCISE 2.4

Examine the following sentences. Put a check in front of each sentence that is written in the subject-linking verb-subject complement format. Leave blank the ones that are not.

√ *The waiting* groom **appeared** nervous.

1. Dick looked out the window to find Rusty.

2. The crisis between the twins appears quite serious.

3. My great-grandfather was a tailor for mobsters in Chicago.

4. The poor dog smelled my father's dirty socks.

5. My sister Gloria's home-made enchiladas smell terrific.

6. Jasmine was excited about her birthday party.

7. On his thirteenth birthday, David's parents gave him a huge bar mitzvah celebration.

8. Sean and Alex play games in their bedroom upstairs.

9. My cousin Ariel sings country music in Nashville.

10. Anna's stomach felt queasy after eating her brother's homemade soup.

Subject-Verb-Direct Object-Object Complement

The final sentence pattern is Subject-Verb-Direct Object-Object Complement. Examine the following sentences. The subject in each is italicized, the verb is in bold, the object is underlined and the object complement is double-underlined:

President Clinton **named** Madeleine Albright the first woman Secretary of State.
Jocelyn **found** Las Vegas boring.
The *bully* **called** Tyler a sissy.

In this sentence pattern, the object receives the action of the verb, but the sentence is not complete without the object complement. An **object complement** follows the direct object of the sentence and re-names or describes it. Object complements can be nouns, pronouns, or adjectives. Object complements often appear in sentences that have verbs such as the following: *appoint, call, choose, consider, declare, elect, find, make, paint, select, show.*

EXERCISE 2.5

Examine the following sentences. Put a check in front of each sentence that is written in the subject-verb-direct object-object complement format. Leave blank the ones that are not.

√ *The little* boy **considered** himself the king of baseball.

1. My father called my mother "Honey."

2. Winston considered his coworkers incompetent.

3. Rose announced her pregnancy to her husband at dinner time.

4. Timothy and Quentin painted the family van deep purple.

5. Justine worked at the laundromat until 11 at night.

6. Eve stole the job from her own sister.

7. The elderly matriarch declared her old will void.

8. My nephews find Uncle Ed's war stories exciting.

9. Sophie named her father the trustee of her money.

10. Teenagers sometimes build walls between themselves and their parents.

GRAMMAR REVIEW

Identify the sentence pattern of each sentence by writing the pattern number in front of the sentence. Use the following number code:

1. *Subject-Verb (only)*
2. *Subject-Verb-Direct Object*
3. *Subject-Verb-Indirect Object-Direct Object*
4. *Subject-Linking Verb-Subject Complement*
5. *Subject-Verb-Direct Object-Object Complement*

_____ **1.** Uncle Richard's motorcycles are muddy from his latest adventure.

_____ **2.** The business executive sent Mister Callahan a large check for his services.

_____ **3.** His grandmother sent him home-made cookies for Christmas.

_____ **4.** Jeffrey called Harold a monster.

_____ **5.** Tired, the cat yawned.

_____ **6.** Nina's newest pet is actually a small computer.

_____ **7.** April rains usually bring floods to the valley.

_____ **8.** Simon drove to Florida all night.

_____ **9.** Melissa discovered the old piano in the attic.

_____ **10.** Cindy declared Elaine the winner.

Applying the Grammar Lesson

In order to demonstrate your understanding of word order, identify different word orders in your first draft using the same number code as in the Grammar Review. Mark just the simple sentences since they have only one clause. (Sentences that have more than one clause have more than one word order format).

Here is how Sabrina, who had already underlined the transitions in her first draft, applied the grammar lesson:

Some people might think my family is not very traditional, <u>but</u> I think it is. <u>On the one hand</u>, my parents are divorced, <u>and</u> both have since remarried. I grew up with my mother (1). I only saw my Dad a few times each year because he moved away to a different state. <u>However</u>, my family is very traditional in some important ways (4). <u>First</u>, everyone loves each other (2). My step-dad has been great (4). He and my mother have been married for twelve years, <u>so</u> he's been like a second father to me <u>since</u> I was a little kid. I've called him "Dad" for years (5). <u>Also</u>, my mother and father worked things out so that my sister and I could always visit my father during the summer and for important events, <u>like when</u> he remarried five years ago. What makes my family most traditional, <u>though</u>, are the every-day things, like the smiles, the hugs and kisses, the talking. Even the fights. We love each other so much we know we can disagree with each other and still be a family. <u>Of course</u>, as I've grown older, I've relied less on my family and more on my friends, <u>but</u> my family is still the best, most important thing in my life.

Writing the Second Draft

Once you have identified word order formats in your first draft, you are ready to write the second draft of your Chapter Writing Assignment. Complete this draft before beginning the Sentence Lesson. Respond to the revision questions as you work on your rewrite.

Revision questions

- Does your topic sentence respond directly to the question you have chosen?
- Have you used enough transitional words and phrases in your paragraph? If not, be sure to add them appropriately.
- Have you varied your word order formats so that you are not repeatedly using the same formats? Try to use some variety.
- Have you made sure that every word counts? Eliminate any unnecessary words.

After identifying the word order formats in her first draft, Sabrina rewrote her paragraph. She worked on shaping her sentences in different ways to provide some variety. She also removed unnecessary words and made sure that all of her transitions went smoothly. She added more specific details about her family.

Some people might think my family is not very traditional, but in the most important ways, we're very traditional. On the one hand, my parents are divorced, and both have since remarried. I grew up with my mother. I only saw my Dad a few times each year because he moved away to take a new job in Arizona. However, my step-dad has been great. He and my mother have been married for twelve years, so he's been like a second father to me. I've called him "Dad" for years. That's how I truly feel about him. Also, despite their divorce, my mother and father made sure my sister and I could visit my father during the summer and for important events, like when he remarried five years ago. What makes my family most traditional, though, are the everyday things, like the smiles each morning when we get up, the hugs and kisses we always seem to be exchanging, and the talking we do late into the night. Even when my sister and I fight, we love each other so much we know that we can disagree with each other and still be a family. Of course, as I've grown older, I've relied less on my parents and more on my friends, but my family is still the best, most important thing in my life.

SENTENCE LESSON

Compound Sentences

In Chapter One, you learned that a simple sentence is made up of a single independent clause. An independent clause contains a subject and a verb, and it makes complete sense. Of course, not all sentences have just one independent clause. Another type of sentence is a **compound sentence,** which has two or more independent clauses. The compound sentence is used to combine ideas that are of equal importance and to show the relationship between those ideas. The independent clauses in a compound sentence can be joined with a comma and a coordinating conjunction, or they can be connected with a semicolon.

Two simple sentences:

Vanessa was an expert at using computers.

She was able to get a good job as a programmer.

With a coordinating conjunction:

Vanessa was an expert at using computers, **so** she was able to get a good job as a programmer.

With a semicolon:

Vanessa was an expert at using computers; she was able to get a good job as programmer.

Using a Coordinating Conjunction to Create a Compound Sentence

There are seven **coordinating conjunctions** in the English language: *and, but, or, so, for, yet, nor.* The different coordinating conjunctions have different meanings. A common error among writers is to overuse the conjunction *and* at the expense of other, more accurate conjunctions.

Original: Claudia earned a B in the course, and she went home happy.

Revised: Claudia earned a B in the course, so she went home happy.

By using *so* instead of *and,* the writer is better able to show the relationship between the two ideas. In the original sentence, the word *and* indicates a sequence of events. In the revised sentence, the word *so* indicates a cause and effect relationship. In other words, Claudia went home happy <u>because</u> of her B.

Here are the seven coordinating conjunctions and their uses:

and   a sequence of events; continuity

but   contrast, contradiction, or exception

or   options

so   a result or effect

for   a reason or cause

yet   a contrast, contradiction, or exception

nor   a lack of options

EXERCISE 2.6

Each of the following sentences contains one independent clause followed by a comma. Create a compound sentence by adding a second independent clause with a related idea and joining the two with a coordinating conjunction. Try to use each coordinating conjunction at least once.

Our family reunion is usually held in Chicago, but this year it will be held in Houston.

1. Aunt Jan loves to prepare for important family gatherings by cooking a ton of food, _____

_____

2. Most of Terry's brothers and sisters have stayed in his hometown, _____

_____

3. The newest member of the family may have her room downstairs, _____

_____

4. Mark, my brother, works in Los Angeles, _____

_____

5. Clara was going to marry Joseph, _____

_____

6. Sean will not listen to his mother, _____

_____

7. During the holidays, Damien seldom forgets to bring gifts for the children, _____

_____

8. Marvin's mother does not want him to play football, ____

_____

9. At 55, my father suddenly changed careers, _____

_____

10. Francesca talked to her sister on her cell phone for over

two hours, _____

_____

Using a Semicolon to Create a Compound Sentence

A second way to create a compound sentence is to join two independent clauses with a semicolon. A semicolon draws the two clauses together, indicating a relationship between them. While any two independent clauses can be joined with a semicolon, you will only want to use a semicolon when the clauses are closely related. For instance, look at the following sentence:

Samuel went to the store; he bought some new socks.

There is no special reason to use a semicolon. The two clauses indicate a sequence of events (one event is followed by another). The clauses work perfectly well as separate sentences:

Samuel went to the store. He bought some new socks.

In other situations, however, using a semicolon can suggest a close connection between the two clauses:

Vicki worked at a clothing store during the day; at night she studied business law.

Sometimes you will want to make the connection or relationship between the two independent clauses more explicit. To do this, you can use a **conjunctive adverb,** which is placed immediately after the semicolon and followed by a comma:

Robyn stopped eating sweets; however, she failed to lose weight.

By using the word "however," the writer is able to show the relationship between the two clauses, which in this case is one of contrast (i.e., she stopped eating sweets, but contrary to expectations, she still has not lost weight).

The following is a list of commonly used conjunctive adverbs:

accordingly	also	besides	finally	hence	indeed
afterward	anyhow	consequently	furthermore	however	instead

meanwhile	next	still	therefore
moreover	nonetheless	subsequently	thus
nevertheless	otherwise	then	

In addition to conjunctive adverbs, you can also use phrases after a semicolon to show the relationship between two clauses. The following is a list of phrases commonly used with semicolons to join two independent clauses:

after all	by the way	for example	in addition	in other words
as a result	even so	for instance	in fact	on the other hand

As when using a conjunctive adverb with a semicolon, do not forget to put a comma after the initial phrase of the second independent clause.

Albert wants to visit his parents during this break; after all, he has not seen them for over four months.

ZOOM-IN PRACTICE

Without consulting the list of conjunctive adverbs, write down as many of them as you can remember in two minutes. You should be able to think of at least ten.

_____   _____   _____

_____   _____   _____

_____   _____   _____

_____   _____   _____

_____   _____   _____

_____   _____   _____

_____   _____   _____

_____   _____   _____

EXERCISE 2.7

Each of the following sentences contains one independent clause. Create a compound sentence by adding a second independent clause containing a related idea and joining the two with a semicolon. Try to use different conjunctive adverbs and phrases for each sentence. Do not forget to use a comma after the conjunctive adverb or phrase that follows the semicolon.

The genealogy expert noted that Eugene's family name had a long, proud, and historic background; however, Eugene only wanted to find out if he was related to anyone rich.

1. Aunt Rose and Uncle Joe moved to Phoenix from Illinois

   _____

2. This spring my parents celebrated their 50th wedding anniversary _____

   _____

3. Forrest wanted to investigate his family tree _____

   _____

4. Annette and Will are going to have their first child in September _____

   _____

5. As children, the two brothers competed with each other constantly _____

   _____

6. Parents have a tough time knowing how strict or lenient to be with their children _____

   _____

7. Julie's first memories are of her mother singing to her ____

   _____

8. Being a good father was tough work for Nathan _____

   _____

9. The survivors gathered to hear the reading of Mr. Samson's will _____

   _____

10. Despite her misgivings, Clara cared for Monique's newborn child _____

    _____

Sentence Review

Examine the following sentences. Put a check in front of each sentence that is a compound sentence. Leave blank the ones that are not.

1. The student was having trouble in class, so she went to a tutor.

2. The baker wanted to expand his business by adding a coffee stand.

3. Without the money, Maureen could not buy the car; she felt deeply disappointed.

4. Looking into her crystal ball, the fortune teller saw a faint image of a man in a top hat and tails standing next to a Model A Ford.

5. Davene quit her job, for she could no longer put up with her boss.

6. The climb up the side of the mountain had been an enormous physical strain on Wayne, so he decided to take a nap.

7. The supervisor removed Nick from the graveyard shift and hired Jerome instead.

8. Abigail loves to watch soap operas, she tapes three each day.

9. Mrs. MacGregor can not operate a computer, but she owns three of them!

10. The contract dispute over, Ellis flew back to Portland to see his family.

Examine each of the following sentences. Insert a comma and a relevant coordinating conjunction into the sentence at the point where two independent clauses meet. Try to use each of the seven coordinating conjunctions at least once.

1. The misery of the poor is easy to see in the photographs they inspire me to want to help others.

2. The army officer tried to get more artillery support for his men there was none to be had.

3. The cattle ranchers had trouble with the government they hired a big-city law firm to represent them.

4. Overtime is not worth the extra effort I can't seem to turn down the opportunity to work overtime.

5. The factory was closing down hundreds of workers were going to lose their jobs.

6. I could move to Seattle I could stay put here in Southern California.

7. The three brothers worked well together on the project they'll probably be asked to do another one soon.

8. Victoria did not work at her last job for long before being fired she will not last long at this new job either.

9. The foreman, Mr. Trent, wanted a new machinist on the floor to do precision drilling Max was the only qualified person.

10. With good marketing the new product will be a success without it, the product will fail.

Applying the Sentence Lesson

In order to see how frequently you use compound sentences, identify all of the compound sentences in your second draft by double-underlining them. (If you have a sentence that has *three* clauses, and at least two of them are independent clauses, double-underline that sentence, too.) Then consider whether or not you have enough variety—you want to make sure you have some compound sentences, but also there should be a number of simple sentences and other sentences which are not simple or compound.

Examine Sabrina's second draft, with the compound sentences double-underlined. Note that her last sentence has three clauses, two of which are independent clauses.

Some people might think my family is not very traditional, but in the most important ways, we're very traditional. On the one hand, my parents are divorced, and both have since remarried. I grew up with my mother. I only saw my Dad a few times each year because he moved away to take a new job in Arizona. However, my step-dad has been great. He and my mother have been married for twelve years, so he's been like a

<u>second father to me</u>. I've called him "Dad" for years. That's how I truly feel about him. Also, despite their divorce, my mother and father made sure my sister and I could visit my father during the summer and for important events, like when he remarried five years ago. What makes my family most traditional, though, are the everyday things, like the smiles each morning when we get up, the hugs and kisses we always seem to be exchanging, and the talking we do late into the night. Even when my sister and I fight, we love each other so much we know that we can disagree with each other and still be a family. <u>Of course, as I've grown older, I've relied less on my parents and more on my friends, but my family is still the best, most important thing in my life.</u>

Writing the Final Draft

Once you have identified the compound sentences in your second draft, rewrite it to create the final draft of the Chapter Writing Assignment. Respond to the revision questions as you work on your rewrite.

Revision questions

- Do you have a clear and direct topic sentence?
- Do you provide effective transitions where needed?
- Have you varied your sentence formats? Doing so will help keep your writing more interesting.
- Have you eliminated all unnecessary words?
- Does your paragraph contain at least two compound sentences? If not, make sure that the final draft does.

The rewrite of your second draft will be your final draft. Hand in the final draft, with the Branching, first draft, second draft, and any other materials you created in the process of writing this paragraph.

When Sabrina did her final rewrite, she felt that she had too many long sentences. She wanted to create more variety in her sentences. She also wanted to say more about her mother and her sister in her family. She also removed more unnecessary words. Here is her final draft:

To some people, my family may not appear traditional since my parents are divorced, but in the most important ways, the family I grew up in is very traditional. I grew up with my mother and step-father. I only saw my Dad a few times each year because he moved away to take a new job in Arizona. However, my step-dad has been great. He and my mother have been married for twelve years, so he's been like a second father to me. In fact, I've called him "Dad" for years because that's how I truly feel about him. Also, despite their divorce, my mother and father made sure my sister and I could visit my father during the summer and for important events, like when he remarried five years ago. What makes my family most traditional, though, are the everyday things. For one, my mother always has smiles for us in the morning when we get up. Next, we're an affectionate family, with lots of hugs and kisses. Also, my mother, my sister and I often sit around talking late into the night. Even when my sister and I fight, we know that we can disagree with each other and still be a family because we love each other and always have. As I've grown older, I've spent less time with my family and more with my friends, but my step-dad, mom, and sister are still the most important people in my life.

PORTFOLIO CHECKLIST

In your portfolio, you should now have the following:

1. a Branching prewriting exercise
2. a First Draft. The first draft should have the transitional words and phrases underlined. Word order patterns should also be marked.
3. a Second Draft. The second draft should have your compound sentences double-underlined.
4. a Final Draft. Make sure you have at least two compound sentences.

PARTING SHOT

1. Holidays are often important times for families. Does your family have any special rituals connected with particular holidays?

2. Does your family practice any rituals which reflect your ethnic, cultural or national heritage? What are they?

3. Do you have any generational conflicts in your family?

GOALS IN REVIEW

In this chapter, you have learned about

- branching as a prewriting exercise
- the importance of transitions in a paragraph
- word order in sentences
- the compound sentence

PRACTICE CHAPTER TEST

Part I

Examine each of the following sentences and label each sentence with the number that represents its sentence type according to the following code:

1. Subject-Verb
2. Subject-Verb-Direct Object
3. Subject-Verb-Indirect Object-Direct Object
4. Subject-Linking Verb-Subject Complement
5. Subject-Verb-Object-Object Complement

_____ **1.** All of the clerks want a pay raise.

_____ **2.** Kelly struggles with her conscience.

_____ **3.** The doctor declared the patient dead.

_____ **4.** Harvey seems troubled by the news.

_____ **5.** Within a week, the bank sent Tyler his new checks.

_____ **6.** The college basketball tournament is a gold mine for television.

_____ **7.** Outside in the mud, the vehicle could not move.

_____ **8.** Quietly, quickly, and cleanly, Tracy removed the splinter from the boy's finger.

_____ **9.** The changes to the house are terribly unattractive.

_____ **10.** The workers called the management irresponsible.

_____ **11.** Norman loads crates at the dock for nine bucks an hour.

_____ **12.** The team elected Mario captain.

_____ **13.** Phyllis mailed Mary a bill for her rent.

_____ **14.** Late at night, the puppies howled at the moon.

_____ **15.** The flight attendant brought the captain some coffee.

Part II

Examine the following sentences. If a sentence is a simple sentence, mark it with an "S." If a sentence is a compound sentence, mark it with the letters "CP."

_____ **1.** The young director was excited about his new film, but he had not yet found a distributor.

_____ **2.** The musicians had trouble keeping their rhythm without their regular drummer.

_____ **3.** Despite her feelings of anxiety, Lyssa decided to enter the haunted house.

_____ **4.** Donny, the star athlete on the football squad, could not pass his chemistry class, so he was dropped from the team.

_____ **5.** The dust on the table annoyed the hotel guests; consequently, the housekeeper was fired.

_____ **6.** Marian could not understand her family's reaction to her decision.

_____ **7.** This encyclopedia set used to cost over $2000; now the same encyclopedia can be found on the Internet for free.

_____ **8.** Justine would love to hike in the mountains this weekend, but she has to work overtime instead.

_____ **9.** The doctor assisted the elderly woman in coping with her husband's death by recommending grief counseling.

_____ **10.** Jonathan could attend a private school in another state; however, he loves the weather in Buffalo too much to leave.

CHAPTER 3

Work

CHAPTER GOALS

In this chapter, you will learn about

- conducting a personal interview as a prewriting strategy,

- writing a cover letter and résumé,

- agreement, and

- complex and compound-complex sentences.

Work is the theme of this chapter. Almost everyone has to find paid employment at some time in his or her life, and for most people, a great portion of their lives will be spent working. Work, of course, is a way to make money, but often, work is much more than just that. Work is a way for people to find personal fulfillment, to connect with the world, and to improve their quality of life. People's career choices frequently exert tremendous influence over their lives—both inside the workplace and at home.

OPENING SHOT

QUESTIONS ABOUT THE PICTURE

1. The workers in the picture are working with their hands, using skills and techniques that must be learned and practiced over a long period of time. Is such skill and craftsmanship still valued?

2. Can small family businesses survive in today's modern world?

3. What kind of work environment are you most comfortable in: a small, intimate setting, or a larger, more business-like one?

4. Do you have to go to college to have a job that can support you?

READING

Questions to Consider

1. What role does work—paid employment—play in your life?
2. How does work affect the other parts of your life, such as family, school, and friends?

Words to Watch

prestigious	marked by honor; held in high regard
gyration	the act of turning around or revolving
quirks	an abrupt twist; a peculiar trait
start-up company	a new business
amnesty	an act of pardon for a large group; release from liability for a crime
apprentice	learning by practical experience
eclectic	composed of a variety of parts drawn from different sources
flextime	a work schedule in which workers can pick their own hours within a certain time range

To Work We Go

George J. Church

1 Harmanjit Singh and Keetha Mock would seem to have just about nothing in common. Singh, 25, is a bachelor, a graduate of the prestigious Indian Institute of Technology and a computer programmer for Lucent Technologies in California's Silicon Valley. Mock, 39, is a divorced mother of three in Pontiac, Mich., and a former welfare client who until last Christmas never worked steadily. But in their diversity, they exemplify one reason for the amazing length and strength of the U.S. boom. Despite all the recent gyrations of the stock market, the longest economic expansion in U.S. history has not only created incredible numbers of

new jobs but also brought into the labor force the most varied sorts of new workers to fill those jobs and keep the economy humming.

2   For the past two years or so, experts, beginning with Federal Reserve Chairman Alan Greenspan, have proclaimed the ability of labor supply to meet job demand to be impossible. There would not be enough workers available, they warned, to keep growth at the blistering pace of the late 1990s. To maintain output, employers would be forced to swipe workers from one another by bidding up wages. So inflation would rise as production slowed down. In effect, goodbye to the golden days.

3   Yet the economy has rolled merrily along, doing what supposedly could not be done. True, the sudden March flare-up in consumer prices—far larger than could be blamed on gas-pump inflation—indicated that labor costs may at last be starting a troublesome rise. Yet employment figures for the same month made it clear that the U.S. is a long way from running out of workers. Somewhere, somehow, employers found 416,000 people to add to payrolls in March, the most in any month in four years. Even after subtracting temporary Census hiring and adjusting for seasonal quirks, job gains continued the hot—some thought unattainable—pace of 1999. And it was not done by putting the officially unemployed back to work. The jobless rate—4.1% in March—has barely moved since September 1999, when it was 4.2%.

4   Obviously, the hot economy has prompted many people who had not thought of taking a job to look for one, and caused bosses to search for employees among men and women who had not traditionally been counted in the U.S. labor pool. Who are these people? Herewith a sampler:

Immigrants

5   Silicon Valley and other high-tech employers are bringing into the U.S. 115,000 computer programmers, engineers, scientists, and the like each year under H1-B visas (these allow people with special skills that the economy needs to enter the U.S. outside regular immigration quotas). But employers insist they need more, and bills are moving through Congress to raise the limit to as many as 195,000. Among others, roughly half of all recent alumni of the six-campus Indian Institute of Technology are said to be working in the U.S., including Harmanjit Singh and about 24 others from the New Delhi campus' 40-strong graduating class of 1997. "Nowadays start-up companies are visiting the I.I.T. campuses to recruit people," says Singh. "They lure them with stock options. They know that Indians are willing to work hard for an amount of money that may seem small to Americans but is unheard of in India." Singh was headhunted by a consulting company that got his name from a friend already in the U.S. "They phoned me, and after a 20-minute interview they sent me the paperwork for a visa," he says.

6   Less skilled immigrants are filling so many of the jobs that Americans traditionally disdain—dishwasher, gardener, construction day laborer, house cleaner, nanny—that portions of the economy have become heavily dependent on them. Restaurants alone employ 1.4 million immigrants, who make up almost 14% of all their workers. Christina Howard, senior

legislative representative of the National Restaurant Association, says eateries will need to add 2 million more jobs by 2010, and "we are absolutely looking to immigration" to help meet the goal.

7   The AFL-CIO has done a complete about-face on immigrants, from fearing them as low-wage rivals of American workers to viewing them as potential union members. The labor federation is even whooping up support for a legislative amnesty that would lift the fear of deportation from the estimated 6 million illegal immigrants now in the U.S. The Immigration and Naturalization Service has virtually stopped raiding businesses to look for undocumented workers. "It is much easier to find work now than ever before," says Josefina Diaz, a native of the Dominican Republic who cleans offices in midtown Manhattan. "It doesn't matter if you have a green card or not."

Women

8   The trend for growing numbers of females to work outside the home has been going on for decades, of course. But new recruits are still entering, or re-entering, the labor force. They include Keetha Mock and some 10,000 others helped by Kelly Services to come off the welfare rolls.

9   Mock, who grew up in a welfare home, had struggled for 17 years to support her family with no child support from her divorced husband. She had held a variety of short-lived jobs and had collected welfare for periods that added up to eight years. By last October, she had just about given up hope of employment, partly because she had not developed any skills in the 20 years since her high school graduation. After Oakland Community College contacted her for a training program it runs with Kelly Services, she missed her first interview, telling herself, "This ain't going to happen." A counselor, however, rescheduled the appointment and even drove Mock to it. The week before Christmas, Mock was hired as an administrative assistant at a General Motors truck plant in Pontiac, answering phones, setting up meetings and handling other secretarial duties. With fringe benefits, which she never got before, she earns about three times as much as she did in any previous job. Two sons, high school dropouts who Mock says have been "just laying around the house," have been inspired by their mother's success to snare jobs themselves. James, 19, is a porter at an Oldsmobile dealership, and Nathan, 18, is an apprentice cook at a restaurant.

10   Kathleen Shelby, a partner in FlexTime Solutions, a Maplewood, N.J., staffing firm that supplies interim workers in marketing, public relations and communications for corporations, reports considerable success in placing women who have been out of the work force for as long as 10 years. Most, she says, are mothers who dropped out because they could not put in the 50-hour week many companies now demand of full-timers, but are happy to work for shorter periods.

11   Younger mothers, some analysts say, are turning to work sooner after giving birth—though few as quickly as Chicagoan Gina Johnson, 18. Only two weeks after her second baby was born last May, she returned

to her job as shift manager in a fast-food restaurant, and she later landed higher-paying employment as manager of a card shop. Family members urged her to take more time off, says Johnson, who is single and engaged. But she told them, "I don't want anybody taking care of me." She gets baby-sitting help from the Daycare Action Council of Illinois but now can pay $30 a month of that herself.

The Young and the Old

12   Students have been holding down part-time jobs since education ceased to be a monopoly of the leisure classes, but employers are finding ways to get more of them to participate in the labor-short economy. For instance, United Parcel Service has an Earn and Learn program that offers part-timers an unusual benefit—student loans and tuition assistance. More than 8,000 students are currently enrolled in the program.

13   Several officials of A.A.R.P. and of employment agencies say they are finding work for more and more people over 55, though some of the prospects say this is true only for those with technological backgrounds. But the just enacted law that allows Social Security pensions ages 65 to 69 to earn unlimited amounts without loss of benefits ought to prompt more seniors to work, or to work longer.

14   Carl Camden, executive vice president, field operations, sales and marketing for Kelly Services, reports that "a fair number" of the temps Kelly supplies to employers are in their 60s, and "these are some of the most productive workers we have." But, he observes, "before the law was changed, many of them would ask us to keep very specific checks on how much money they earned"—and would stop working as soon as they hit the point at which they would begin to lose Social Security benefits.

15   For employers, finding and hiring new workers is often neither easy nor cheap. The Home Shopping Network has attracted an effective if eclectic mix of seniors, middle-aged women of all races, and teenagers to answer the 160,000 calls that pour in daily to its center in St. Petersburg, Fla. But new management had to turn the company upside down to do it.

16   To begin with, HSN spent $6 million renovating facilities at the 59-acre campus, including the employee cafeteria. It set up a program with a local high school that is expected to give 30 to 50 students part-time jobs at the call center, and figures at least some will stay with HSN after they graduate. It is pushing flextime to the max. It already offered some 40 different full-time or part-time schedules, and now it is starting a pilot program that will allow employees to draw up their own schedules around a core of required hours. Lisa Letizio, senior vice president of human resources, thinks this will be especially attractive to mothers who want to put in fewer hours while their children are small, gradually working longer hours.

17   Then there's money. In January, HSN raised starting pay from $6 to $7, and later this year it will offer health insurance to all its workers, including the 40% who are part-time. That is an unusual but no longer

unheard-of deal. There are reports of some fast-food restaurants also extending benefits to workers, including part-timers, who did not get them before. And wage hikes are cropping up in other places. Tony Vallone, owner of six upscale restaurants in Houston, was paying only minimum wage to his dishwashers and kitchen prep-workers 18 months ago. Now the dishwashers get an extra $2 an hour and the prep people $3 extra— and they all share in a 401(k) investment plan that was formerly limited to higher-paid workers.

18   So far, such reports are too sketchy to prove that the long-dreaded bidding war on wages has begun. But they do indicate that employers will have to push harder than ever to raise productivity to offset the wage and benefit increases they will be forced to grant. The vastly underrated American work ethic that prompts the most oddly assorted people to snap up jobs when offered a chance has kept the boom boiling longer than anyone expected. But from now on, putting them on the payroll is not likely to be as cheap.

PREPARING TO WRITE

Conducting an Interview

If you are looking for a job, you might hear that job seekers need to do their homework, but what exactly does this mean? It means that you need to know about yourself and the job you wish to get.

Knowing about yourself means being aware of how your education, job skills, and employment history can help get you where you want to go. Regarding your education, you might answer the following questions: What level of schooling have you completed? What are your eventual goals in school? What specialized courses or programs of study have you been in? As for your job skills, what have you learned to do that is marketable in the workplace? Can you type? Do you know how to use a computer? What special equipment do you know how to operate? When you consider your job history, what kinds of jobs have you had, how long did you hold them, and what skills did you learn from doing them?

You will want answers to these questions and others when you prepare to write a cover letter and résumé. But what you have done is only part of the process. You have to know about where you want to go.

What will your next job be? Will it be one that leads to a career, or is it just a way to earn money while you're in school? Eventually, of course, you'll want a career—a form of employment that gives you a strong measure of personal satisfaction as well as a paycheck—but many students spend their college days working in jobs that pay the rent and tuition, with the idea that they will move into a career later on.

When you think about the job you want—either for the short term or the long haul—you'll need to know more about the job. The first question a lot of students ask is, "How much does it pay?" This is a valid question, for money does matter, but it shouldn't be the first one. After all, you might never get the job if you don't ask some other questions first, such as "What education, training or job skills are needed to get this job?", "How hard is it to get a job like this?" or "How might this job change in the future?"

Preparing Yourself to Write

To answer questions like these, you might try several approaches. One simple approach is to head to a career counseling center. Many colleges and universities have such places, often located within the campus library. If your college or university does not have a career center, your local public library is likely to have materials related to job and career searches.

Ask a counselor or librarian for assistance in finding information about your chosen career. Usually, career centers or libraries can supply you with information such as how many people work in a certain job, what workers in the job earn, where in the country your chosen career is most plentiful, what type of education and job training are needed to get such a job, and how difficult it is to become employed in your chosen job or career. You can even find out which trade schools, colleges, or universities do the best job of preparing people for that career.

Another approach to investigating your career is to speak with people who are already in the kind of job or career you have chosen. Speaking to someone who is actually doing the job can give you a much better, more specific idea of what the job is like and how to get such a job. Also, you might learn important information about employment conditions where you live, and any special problems people have finding such jobs in your area. You might find how people feel about their jobs after working in them for ten or twenty years—whether they have received the kind of job satisfaction that often matters more in the long run than pay or benefits.

When you conduct a **personal interview** with a person who works in the field that you are interested in, prepare yourself ahead of time. A personal interview is much like a conversation, except that one person (the interviewer) is asking questions of another for a purpose. That purpose, in this case, is to get specific information about a job or career. Here are some tips for conducting a successful personal interview:

1. Set up the interview ahead of time. Don't assume that someone can talk to you whenever you are ready. Call ahead first, even if the person you are interviewing is a close friend or relative.

2. Ask if you can tape record your interview. Tape recorders can help relieve you of the burden of taking a lot of notes during an interview. Many people, however, may be uncomfortable being taped. If so, have a notepad and a pen handy. *Do not record interviewees over the telephone or in person without their knowledge and explicit*

approval. Even if you are planning to tape the interview, bring along paper and pen in case the person being interviewed changes his or her mind.

3. Prepare a written list of questions ahead of time. Don't plan on being able to remember them during the interview because you're likely to forget one or two of the questions you meant to ask. Look at the questions in *Reporting on the Personal Interview* to see the kinds of questions that you will want to ask.

4. Use the questions to keep the interview on track. An interview has a purpose: You need to get certain information. Sometimes that's not what the person being interviewed wants to talk about. Keep referring to your questions to make sure you learn everything you need to know.

5. Don't forget to say "Thank you" when the interview is done. After all, this person has done you a favor by giving his or her time to help you learn about a job or career.

Reporting on the Personal Interview

After you conduct a personal interview, you will need to gather together the information you learned from the interview. Write a four-part report in which you cover the following areas.

1. Personal information. Write the name of the person who is interviewed, the person's job title, for what company or business the person works, where the person works, how long he or she has been working at this particular job, and how long the person has been working in his or her career.

2. Factual job description. Record what the person's job responsibilities are and what the requirements are for having such a job. What education or training does the person have? What special job skills does he or she possess? How will this job change in the future? How much does the job pay, what are the benefits, and how much job security is there? What is the job environment like? How much travel is involved? What kind of clothing does the person have to wear to the job, such as a business suit, a uniform, or more casual attire?

3. The interviewee's emotional response. How does the person feel about his or her job? What does the person like? Dislike? Is the person glad he or she has this job? What is the person's overall emotional response to the job and the general career field?

4. The interviewer's emotional response. After having conducted the interview, are you still interested in pursuing a job in this field? Does the job sound appealing or not? Why or why not?

The following is a report of a personal interview conducted by a student named Virginia who interviewed a professional architect.

Report of Interview with Nicholas Janson

1. I interviewed Nicholas Janson, who is a senior architect at the firm of Ford & Associates here in San Diego. Mr. Janson has worked for this firm for twelve years, and he's been in the architecture business in one capacity or another for over eighteen years.

2. Mr. Janson specializes in commercial developments. His duties are to work with a team at the firm to create plans and sell them to development companies. Mr. Janson has a bachelor's degree in architecture, and the specialized job skills he possesses include using computers to create his designs—a skill he learned on the job as computer applications in architecture were quite different when he went to college. As a senior architect, Mr. Janson's income is between $65,000 and $70,000 a year with full benefits. He has good job security, but he notes that for younger architects, both the security and the money are not as good. He does not travel much anymore, which he is thankful for. His work environment is very professional. He wears a tie every day. He seldom wears his suit coat except when entering and leaving the office.

3. Mr. Janson likes his job a lot, but he also advises that his situation is better than average. He notes that many architects make less money and have less job security. He also commented on the fact that many of his projects do not allow for much creativity. Business parks and shopping malls are more concerned about cost, and concerns about appearances are minimal. Only a few of his projects have involved much genuine creativity, and this has been the cause of some professional frustration. He also finds that he has to be a salesperson as much as an architect—firms compete for the

business. He is happy though and is glad that he pursued his dream to be an architect.

4. I felt that Mr. Janson had a great job, but I'm a little scared about what could happen if I became an architect and didn't find a situation as good as Mr. Janson's. He mentioned that many architects make less money and do even more routine work than he does, yet he already feels unhappy that he can't be more creative. That definitely makes me think I need to investigate this job field more.

Prewriting

Do one or more of the following to prepare for the Chapter Writing Assignment.

1. Take stock of your education, job skills, and job history. If you need to, look back through old transcripts, job offers, and other employment-related materials you may have. Organize your materials into categories by jobs which you have held.

2. Visit a career center, either at your local public library or at your college or university. Investigate a career of your choice, learning about its growth potential, educational or job training requirements, and the best ways of finding employment in the field.

3. Conduct an interview with a person who actually holds the kind of job you are interested in doing yourself. Learn about the job, its requirements, the personal satisfaction people get from doing the job, and how that job may change in the future. Write a report of the interview.

CHAPTER WRITING ASSIGNMENT

Choose one of the following writing assignments. Instructions in the chapter will guide you through the writing process. At different points in the chapter, you will be asked to produce more work on this assignment. By the end of the chapter, you will complete your final draft.

1. Write a cover letter and a résumé for yourself. Direct the cover letter and résumé to get a job for which you are currently qualified.

2. Write a profile of the kind of education, training, and work experience you will need to get a job in your chosen career field. Then, detail how you can plan to get from where you are today to where you need to be.

3. How important is pay to you in deciding on a career, as opposed to other issues such as job satisfaction, working conditions, or possible advancement? Support your answer by using examples from your own knowledge and experience.

4. In George J. Church's article, "To Work We Go," he argues that the job market is so tight that employers have to offer extra incentives to prospective employees. Do you think that Church's view is accurate or not? Explain, using specific examples.

WRITING LESSON

Cover Letter and Résumé

When applying for a job, you might be asked to submit a cover letter and a résumé. Although some employers might have a format they want you to use, your prospective employer may not. In such a case, you will want to follow some basic guidelines.

Writing a Cover Letter

A cover letter is a letter that accompanies your résumé. It is a way of introducing yourself more personally to an employer. The cover letter helps the employer get a sense of what specific aspects of your work experience and education are important and relevant to a job.

An employer will likely read the letter before ever seeing you, so the letter makes a first impression. As in social situations, first impressions go a long way toward establishing positive or negative impressions about a person.

To write an effective, professional-looking cover letter, follow these simple guidelines:

1. Use 8½" × 11" white typing paper. Use a good quality, not erasable bond paper. If you are typing, make sure the ribbon has plenty of ink left in it to make sharp, clear letters. If you are using a computer, choose a font style that is formal and clean, such as Times Roman or Courier; avoid fancy fonts or italics because they are inappropriate in a business setting. Choose a good font size, such as 11 or 12 point. Anything smaller is too difficult for many people to read easily, and font sizes larger than 12 point look unprofessional.

2. Use one-inch margins on the top, right, left, and bottom margins.

3. Single-space your typed lines.

4. Use a block format, in which all lines begin flush against the left margin. Instead of indenting new paragraphs, insert an extra blank line between paragraphs.

The cover letter consists of the following parts.

Heading.   Many businesses and professionals use pre-printed letter-heads. Most likely, however, you do not have your own letterhead. Instead, you need to include your address in the upper left-hand corner of the letter. Insert the date, written in month-day-year fashion, underneath the address.

Inside address.   This is the address to which the letter is being sent. If possible, the letter should be addressed to a specific individual, not just to a job title. Sometimes this might take a little extra effort on your part, but it is well worth it. The job title should appear underneath the addressee's name and the mailing address goes under the job title.

The greeting.   The typical way to greet the recipient is to use the word "Dear" followed by the letter recipient's name. Generally speaking, do not use a person's first name, but use last names and titles, such as "Dear Mr. Frakes," "Dear Ms. Nizet," or "Dear Dr. Ellis." If you do not know the name of the letter recipient, address the letter to the job title, as in "Dear Director of Human Resources." In formal letters such as a cover letter, the greeting usually ends with a colon, not a comma.

Dear Mr. Frakes:

Dear Ms. Nizet:

Dear Dr. Ellis:

Dear Director of Human Resources:

Body.   This is the most important part of your letter. In the body, you must accomplish several tasks, but most importantly, you want to make a good impression on the reader. When you write the letter, be sure to keep a professional tone, be as specific as possible, avoid padding the letter with generalizations and "feel good" statements, and keep the letter as error-free as possible.

You need to be specific about which job you are interested in and how you learned about the job. Explain why you believe your education and experience qualify you for that job. Although the résumé accompanying your cover letter repeats some of the same information, keep in mind that your cover letter is essentially *highlighting* those aspects of your résumé that will be relevant for the job.

Write about the particular company you are applying to and why you are interested in working for them. This is done not simply to compliment an employer, but to let the employer know that you have done your homework about them. Any employer who knows you care about working for them will be more likely to hire you.

Keep the letter to a single page. If your letter is too long, cut out any unnecessary words and unimportant information. Your letter should be brief but packed with meaning. Remember that you are writing to impress your prospective employer.

Closing. The closing is the formal end of the letter. The closing begins with a parting statement, followed by a comma. Then, skip several lines and type your name as you sign it on official documents. This leaves a blank space in which to write your signature.

In a formal setting, the following parting statements are generally accepted:

Cordially,	Respectfully,	Respectfully yours,
Sincerely,	Sincerely yours,	Yours truly,

Below is a sample of a cover letter written by a community college student looking for employment as a data processing specialist.

3258 Francisco Lane
El Cajon, CA 92104

March 20, 2000

Donna C. Lawless
Director of Personnel
Giganto Corporation
2198 Lincoln Street, Suite 36
Syracuse, NY 14558

Dear Ms. Lawless:

Your advertisement in the March 17, 2000 edition of Good Jobs Employment Weekly indicates that you are looking for a data processing specialist with at least two years of experience. I would like to apply for that position.

As the attached résumé shows, I have worked in the data processing field for over three years. During that time I have been employed by two firms. At Worldly Travel, I gained experience working on PC-type computer systems and their related software; while working for Worldly Travel, I helped them develop more efficient systems for handling the paperwork related to recording travel expenses, reimbursements, and distributions. At Celestial Awakenings Mattress Stores, I continued to work with computers, and I expanded my knowledge of business systems, including accounting practices and inventory tracking.

In addition to my work experience, I have taken night classes at San Diego Mesa College, a local community college. During that time I have pursued my education both in general education fields and in the fields of business and accounting. I plan to continue my education until I receive a bachelor's degree in business.

I am quite interested in working for Giganto Corporation. Not only does Giganto have a fine reputation as an employer, but I recognize that Giganto is still diversifying its business. There is tremendous room for growth, and I wish to be a part of it.

If I can provide information not specified on the résumé, I shall be glad to do so. I am available for an interview at your convenience. I can be reached either at the address above or by phone at (619) 555-7685.

Sincerely,

Kelly M. Ponce

Kelly M. Ponce

Writing a Résumé

A résumé is a list of your educational background, work experience, and other achievements that employers might be interested in. The purpose of the résumé is to help an employer learn how well qualified you are for a particular job. A résumé often is presented with a cover letter, and it serves to give in greater detail some of the information presented in the cover letter.

The résumé should be handled much like the cover letter in its physical presentation, with a good, clean professional appearance being the top priority. In addition to the requirements of the cover letter, résumés often make greater use of underlining or bold letters as a way to set apart different pieces of information.

A typical résumé includes each of the following categories:

Personal information. Personal information includes your name, address, and at least one phone number. Do not include your social security number; you only give your employer that information after you have been hired. You also should know that discrimination in job employment based on gender, race, creed, or religion is prohibited by the federal government, so you generally do not include that kind of information. For jobs with physical health requirements, such as a police officer or fire fighter, you might need to include information such as your height, weight, and general state of health.

Job objective. This is usually included if you have a specific job for which you are applying. Many résumés, however, do not include a specific job objective, especially if they are accompanied by a cover letter.

Educational experience. Give this information in reverse chronological order—that is, your most recent educational experience first. Go back no further than high school. For résumés made for jobs which require a bachelor's degree or higher, most do not include high school. Mention the degree or certificate that you earned, your major or general course of study, the name of the institution, and where it is located. You might want to list any academic honors earned.

Military experience.   If you have served in the military, include that information as well. List dates served, the branch of the military, your highest rank, your specific job, and a brief description of your duties. If you have been discharged, mention the type of discharge you received.

Work experience.   List your employers in reverse chronological order. Give the name of your employer, the location, the title of the job you held, and a brief description of your duties.

Special skills.   List any special skills you have, such as fluency in a foreign language. If you have developed work-related skills which do not appear either under education or work experience, such as the ability to use specific computer software programs or applications, list those as well.

References.   You can choose to include references in your résumé, or you may simply write "References available upon request." If you include references, be sure to list at least three people—not family members—who know you and who can comment either on your work experience, your education and training, or your character. For each person, list a name, a job title, and either an address or phone number, or both. Make sure that you contact the person first to get his or her permission to be a reference.

Remember that the presentation of your résumé is important. An employer must be able to clearly read and understand your résumé. On the following page is a sample of a résumé for a community college student looking for work as a data processing specialist.

Kelly M. Ponce

3258 Francisco Lane   (619) 555-7685
El Cajon, CA 92104

Education

1996–98:   **San Diego Mesa College** 7250 Mesa College Drive San Diego,
             CA 92111 Concentrating on courses in Business and Accounting.

1992–96   **St. Mark's High School** 698 Cobble Drive Fairfax, CA 93555
             Took college preparatory courses

Work Experience

1997–now   **Celestial Awakenings Mattress Store** 164 33rd St. San Diego,
CA 92103 (619) 555-8599   Clerk—Data Processing

Currently I am working in the accounting services department, where I use PC computers daily to track orders, inventories, billings, and supplies.

Supervisor: Cesar Padilla

1996–97   **Worldly Travel** 7962 Monte Mar Road, Suite 123 San Diego,
CA 92112 (619) 555-4512   Clerk—Data Processing

Worked in the accounting services department handling travel expense reports, reimbursements, and distributions. Developed a new routing system for paperwork that was more time and cost efficient.

Supervisor: Annette Heinz

References

Richard W. Frakes. Professor. Department of Business Services. San Diego Mesa College, CA 92111. (619) 555-2964

Diane M. Steilen. Owner. Celestial Awakenings Mattress Store. 164 33rd St. San Diego, CA 92103. (619) 555-8599

Irvin Wagner. 5869 Brenner Road Fairfax, CA 93548. (213) 555-5632

Writing an Alternative Résumé

There is more than one way to write an effective résumé. An alternate form can be used if you are applying for a job that will require more information about your work experience and job skills, with less emphasis on your educational background. All of the elements previously described can be included, but in a different order, in which you place job experience and work skills first.

An alternative résumé could use the following order:

1. Summary of professional experience, including specific skills acquired
2. Professional job history
3. Conferences and/or special training sessions attended
4. Formal education

On the following page is a sample of an alternative résumé.

Kelly M. Ponce
3258 Francisco Lane
El Cajon, CA 92104
(619) 555-7685

Professional Summary

- Four years of experience working with professional environments as a data processing clerk.
- Three years' experience of having responsibility for handling daily account transactions.
- Direct experience with:
    * Windows 95/98/2000
    * Excel
    * Word
    * Adobe Acrobat

Recent Professional History

1997–now   **Celestial Awakenings Mattress Store** 164 33rd St. San Diego,
              CA 92103 (619) 555-8599   Clerk—Data Processing

              Currently I am working in the accounting services department, where
              I use PC computers daily to track orders, inventories, billings, and
              supplies.

              Supervisor: Cesar Padilla

1996–97   **Worldly Travel** 7962 Monte Mar Road, Suite 123 San Diego,
              CA 92112 (619) 555-4512   Clerk—Data Processing

              Worked in the accounting services department handling travel
              expense reports, reimbursements, and distributions. Developed a
              new routing system for paperwork that was more time and cost
              efficient.

              Supervisor: Annette Heinz

Education

1996–98:   **San Diego Mesa College** 7250 Mesa College Drive San Diego,
              CA 92111 Concentrating on courses in Business and Accounting.

1992–96   **St. Mark's High School** 698 Cobble Drive Fairfax, CA 93555
              Took college preparatory courses

Writing the First Draft

When Virginia conducted her interview, she discovered that the field of architecture was not as lucrative or as glamorous for everyone as she had initially thought. Still, she wanted to continue to pursue her interest in the field. She decided to do Question #1 and write a cover letter and résumé directed to applying to an architectural firm for work as an assistant or intern. This is the first draft of her cover letter:

2650 Conrad Avenue
San Diego, CA 92133

March 20, 2000

Jared O'Neil
O'Neil Architects
12th Floor
8865 5th Avenue
San Diego, CA 92120

Dear Mr. O'Neil:

I am writing in response to your ad in the newspaper last week about a job. It said that the job was for an assistant. I hope to become an architect someday and would very much like to work in that field.

I am a very hard worker. I have worked at several jobs in the past few years. I started as a cashier at a local fast food restaurant called Abbey's Burgers. After six months, I moved to retail. I worked at a local boutique called Mon Cherie's for a little while. It closed so I moved to a large department store chain. I still work there part-time while I attend school.

While my work experience contains no experience in architecture, I am planning to transfer to San Diego State University and major in architecture. I have already had a number of classes in architecture at a nearby community college.

I really want to become an architect after college, so I'd like to see the business from the inside. Your firm is located near my home, so it would be convenient for me. Please call me as soon as you can. I can be reached either at the address above or by phone at (858) 555-4334.

Sincerely,

Virginia Fuentes
Virginia Fuentes

Virginia Fuentes

2650 Conrad Avenue   (858) 555-4334
San Diego, CA 92133

Education

1998–2000:   **Grossmont College** 8800 Grossmont College Drive, El Cajon,
CA 92020 Concentrating on courses in Architecture.

1994–1998   **John Tyler High School,** 657 Park Circle, Lawrence, CA 93555
Graduated with a diploma

Work Experience

1998–now   **Pickham's** 52 Grace St. El Cajon, CA 92023
(619) 555-9652   Sales Associate

Sell clothes and do inventory.

Supervisor: Kathleen Rogers

1998   **Mon Cherie's** 8743 Girard Ave. La Jolla, CA 92137
(619) 555-2176   Sales Associate

Sold clothes. Store is now closed.

Supervisor: Michelle Roy

1996–1997   **Abbey's Burgers** 900 Beach Blvd. San Diego, CA 92112
(858) 555-9443   Cashier

Took orders, handled money.

References available upon request.

Now that you have completed your prewriting assignments and learned about the structure of a cover letter and a résumé, you are ready to write your first draft in response to one of the questions in the Chapter Writing Assignment. Complete this draft before beginning the Grammar Lesson.

GRAMMAR LESSON

Agreement

The subject and verb of a clause, or a pronoun and the word it refers to, must be of the same person and number. This is called **agreement.** Fortunately, in English, unlike many other modern languages, nouns that do not refer specifically to a gender-bearing object (such as a person or animal) usually do not carry gender. That is, while a man is a "he" and a woman is a "she," a table, a glass, and an automobile are all described as "it." (There are exceptions to this rule, such as the practice of referring to ships as "she.")

The key question of agreement for nouns is whether the noun is singular or plural. Most nouns change their form only when they change from singular to plural. In most cases, changing a noun to a plural involves adding -s or -es to the singular form. This not true for all nouns, of course. The plural of "man" is "men," the plural of "syllabus" is "syllabi," and the plural of "foot" is "feet." Most fluent speakers of English have a firm grasp of these irregular plural forms. If there is ever a problem, a dictionary can easily show a reader the plural form of an irregular noun.

Subject-Verb Agreement

Verbs change their form according to the person and number of the subject. To understand this, you need to know that there are three points of view or persons: **first person, second person,** and **third person.** The first person stands for "I"; the second person stands for "You," and the third person stands for the "He," "She," or "It" form. When the number is plural, these become "We," "You," and "They," respectively. The following is a sample conjugation of the regular verb "walk."

	Singular		**Plural**	
1st person	I	walk	We	walk
2nd person	You	walk	You	walk
3rd person	He, She, It	walks	They	walk

As this conjugation shows, the form of the verb does not change except in the case of the third person singular form, when an "s" is added. This is true for all regular verbs. Irregular verbs, such as the verb "be," do not follow this pattern.

	Singular		**Plural**	
1st person	I	am	We	are
2nd person	You	are	You	are
3rd person	He, She, It	is	They	are

Determining agreement for **collective nouns** and **collective pronouns** can be difficult. Collective nouns and collective pronouns refer to groups that function as a single unit. Examples of collective nouns include the following words: *board, class, committee, couple, faculty, gang, group, jury, platoon, squad, team, unit.* When these or other collective nouns are used to show a group or collection of people acting as one, the nouns are considered singular.

> The platoon <u>runs</u> through sand as part of its training.
> The board <u>votes</u> to increase the funding for the pilot project.
> The class <u>sits</u> quietly while waiting for the test results.

Examples of collective pronouns include the following words: *anybody, anyone, anything, everybody, everyone, everything, neither, no one, nobody, nothing, somebody, someone, something.* You might recognize these words from Chapter 1 as the type of pronouns called "indefinite pronouns." When the pronouns listed above are used, the subject is considered to be singular.

> Anybody <u>is</u> eligible to try out for the play.
> Everybody <u>wants</u> to lead a healthier life.
> Somebody <u>falls</u> victim to that prank every year.

There is a small group of collective pronouns that can be singular or plural. These include *all, any, more, most, none,* and *some.* If what the pronoun stands for is plural, then the pronoun is plural. If it is singular, the pronoun is singular. Examine the following sentences.

> All of the *horses* need to be fed. (*horses* is plural, so "All" is plural)
> All of the *water* is polluted. (*water* is singular, so "All" is singular)
> Some of the *soldiers* were wounded. (*soldiers* is plural, so "Some" is plural)
> Some of their *unhappiness* was caused by themselves. (*unhappiness* is singular, so "Some" is singular)

These pronouns create one of the rare instances when agreement is <u>not</u> determined by examining the simple subject only.

A special circumstance exists when the paired words *either/or, neither/nor,* and *not only/but also* are used. The noun or pronoun which is closer to the verb determines the number.

> Either the players or the coach <u>has</u> to be held responsible for the loss.
> Neither the bull nor the cows <u>have been interested</u> in breeding.
> Not only the enlisted men but also the lieutenant <u>was disciplined</u> for unruly behavior.

Note: Typically, sentences sound better if the plural noun comes second.

Not only the lieutenant but also the enlisted men <u>were disciplined</u> for unruly behavior.

ZOOM-Ⓝ PRACTICE

Write five sentences describing what you did yesterday at work or at home. Then, circle the subjects and verbs in each of the sentences. Check them for agreement.

EXERCISE 3.1

Some of the following sentences contain subject-verb agreement errors. Rewrite each sentence that has an error. If a sentence is correct, mark it with a "C."

she
Somebody in management claims ~~they~~ thought of the idea first.

1. The jury were picked from a large group of citizens.

2. The pack of dogs are in the kennel for safekeeping.

3. The members of Congress is scheduled to get a pay increase.

4. Many of the lions is now in a circus or zoo.

5. Everyone are suspects in this case until proven otherwise.

6. The squad of soldiers are approaching the target area.

7. Neither player want to be on the second-string squad.

8. The Marine Corps are considered to be the most exciting military service.

9. The gang of thugs are surrounded by the police.

10. Most of the class are passing with flying colors.

Pronoun-Antecedent Agreement

Pronoun-antecedent agreement is similar to subject-verb agreement. Since by definition a pronoun is a word that substitutes for a noun, an **antecedent** is whatever that noun is. Read the following sentence:

Trisha told Ben that he was welcome to use the telephone.

"Ben" is the antecedent of "he." Because Ben is a third-person, male, singular noun, the appropriate pronoun is "he." In other words, you can substitute the word "Ben" for "he" in the sentence without making any other changes:

Trisha told Ben that Ben was welcome to use the telephone.

Of course, this sentence does not flow as well as first one. That is why we use pronouns—to avoid unnecessary or awkward repetition of nouns.

As with subjects and verbs, many errors in using the correct pronoun occur when the antecedent is a collective noun or pronoun. Remember that in formal English, many indefinite pronouns are considered *singular*, such as the following:

another	each	everyone	nobody	somebody
anybody	each one	everything	no one	someone
anyone	either	many a(n)	nothing	something
anything	every	much	one	
each	everybody	neither	other	

Everyone wanting to see the show must purchase <u>his or her</u> ticket ahead of time.
<u>Each</u> of the women should check <u>her</u> physician's background.

These common indefinite pronouns are always considered plural.

both	many	several
few	others	

<u>Both</u> of the truckers knew <u>they</u> had to get their permits renewed.
<u>Many</u> of the employees had insurance coverage, but <u>several</u> did not because <u>they</u> had coverage from their spouse's employer.

These common indefinite pronouns are considered singular or plural depending on their antecedents:

all	more	none
any	most	some

If the antecedent is plural, the pronoun is plural. If the antecedent is singular, the pronoun is singular.

Some of the shop workers felt they had no options but to strike. (The antecedent of "they" is "some," which is a pronoun related to the plural "shop workers.")

Some of the water in the reservoir may be contaminated, so the workers have to remove it as a precaution. (The antecedent of "it" is "some," which is a pronoun related to the singular "water.")

If you are having difficulty determining the proper pronoun for an antecedent, check which *verb* is being used with the antecedent. Many times, especially for native speakers of English, choosing the correct subject-verb agreement occurs more easily than correct pronoun-antecedent agreement.

Incorrect: Each of the supervisors has to turn in their paperwork by 5:30 each day.

Notice that this sentence correctly uses the singular verb "has" with the singular pronoun "each," but uses the incorrect pronoun "their."

Correct: Each of the supervisors has to turn in his or her paperwork by 5:30 each day.

DON'T LOSE FOCUS!

Excessive use of "he or she" or other such constructions which incorporate both genders of the third person singular tend to be awkward when used frequently. To avoid the problem of the exclusive use of "he," many writers prefer to write sentences using the third person plural.

Original:

Each supervisor must turn in his or her paperwork by 5:30 each day.

Revised:

All supervisors must turn in their paperwork by 5:30 each day.

EXERCISE 3.2

Examine the following sentences for pronoun-antecedent errors. Fix sentences that are incorrect. If a sentence is correct, mark it with a "C."

it
Much of the job involved physical skills, but ~~they~~ also required mental discipline and knowledge.

1. Any student who wishes to graduate this May must get their application into the Admissions Office by April 10.

2. Each of the tools was put back into their proper place.

3. Many of the problems in the workplace have its roots in the area of human relations.

4. Although anyone can sign up for the course, they will need to have a good understanding of computers to succeed.

5. Many an employee has wanted their boss fired.

6. In major league baseball, neither the players nor the manager can be certain that they will still be with the team at the end of a losing season.

7. Some of the paychecks were temporarily lost, but it has been found in a box in the closet.

8. Many of the products consumers love most have its beginnings in the space program of the 1960s.

9. Nobody should have their pay docked without reason.

10. Each of the immigrant laborers sends money back to their families in their native country.

Pronoun Consistency

When you write, you want to make sure that your use of pronouns is consistent. If you start a sentence using a third person pronoun, do not shift to another point of view.

Original: When a <u>woman</u> becomes pregnant, <u>you</u> should make sure <u>you</u> see a doctor to start a program of prenatal care. ("Woman" is third person, but "you" is second person.)

Revised: When a <u>woman</u> becomes pregnant, <u>she</u> should make sure <u>she</u> sees a doctor to start a program of prenatal care. (Now the sentence is consistent, with all third person nouns and pronouns.)

EXERCISE 3.3

Examine each of the following sentences. If a sentence contains inconsistency in the use of pronouns, fix it. If the sentence is correct, mark it with a "C."

> *they*
> *When workers want to take a break from the assembly line, ~~you~~ have to get permission from the foreman.*

1. When people go to the theater to see a movie, we often pay too much for food and soft drinks.

2. When one applies for a job, you should make sure you dress properly.

3. We as a society need to understand the effects of stress, and then they need to do something about removing it from their lives.

4. The paychecks you receive each Friday already have taxes removed, but each worker can also have additional amounts deducted if you wish.

5. When a person is hired, he or she must first attend an orientation meeting.

6. The goal for each of us is to ensure that one has the proper training and equipment needed to do our jobs.

7. When one is tired, they often make mistakes.

8. I try to do the best that you can.

9. Joe likes to work hard until you are done.

10. If one searches for a career that meets your interests, they will find that the money will be there too.

GRAMMAR REVIEW

In the following sentences, find and correct problems with subject-verb agreement errors, pronoun-antecedent agreement errors, or pronoun consistency errors. Keep verbs in the present tense. If a sentence is correct, mark it with a "C."

1. Many a doctor has discovered that their diagnosis was terribly wrong.

2. If an employee wishes to change departments, they must file an application with the personnel department.

3. Ray, along with Will and Sela, travel extensively on the job.

4. Everyone who cares to can check their listing in the new directory before it is published.

5. After one has seen Mount Rushmore, you feel immense pride in your country.

6. Have either of your brothers used this new computer?

7. Anyone who sells insurance for a living must decide if they want to focus on corporate or personal accounts.

8. Each of the engineers who work on this project must undergo a background check before they can begin.

9. The crew of laborers are being taken to the work site by bus.

10. Each mechanic has a license which they received after a lot of classroom work and practical experience.

Applying the Grammar Lesson

In order to demonstrate your understanding of agreement, underline the subjects and verbs in the first ten sentences of the first draft of the Chapter Writing Assignment. Circle the pronouns and their antecedents.

Here is how Virginia applied the lesson to the first draft of her cover letter:

2650 Conrad Avenue
San Diego, CA 92133

March 20, 2000

Jared O'Neil
O'Neil Architects
12th Floor
8865 5th Avenue
San Diego, CA 92120

Dear Mr. O'Neil:

I am writing in response to your ad in the newspaper last week about a job. It said the job was for an assistant. I hope to become an architect someday and would very much like to work in that field.

I am a very hard worker. I have worked at several jobs in the past few years. I started as a cashier at a local fast food restaurant called Abbey's Burgers. After six months, I moved to retail. I worked at a local boutique called Mon Cherie's for a little while. It closed so I moved to a large department store chain. I still work there part-time while I attend school.

While my work experience contains no experience in architecture, I am planning to transfer to San Diego State University and major in architecture. I have already had a number of classes in architecture at a nearby community college.

I really want to become an architect after college, so I'd like to see the business from the inside. Your firm is located near my home which would be convenient for me. Please call me as soon as you can. I can be reached either at the address above or by phone at (858) 555-4334.

Sincerely,

Virginia Fuentes

Virginia Fuentes

Virginia Fuentes

2650 Conrad Avenue   (858) 555-4334
San Diego, CA 92133

Education

1998–2000   **Grossmont College** 8800 Grossmont College Drive, El Cajon, CA 92020
Concentrating on courses in Architecture.

1994–1998   **John Tyler High school,** 657 Park Circle, Lawrence, CA 93555
Graduated with a diploma.

Work Experience

1998–now   **Pickham's** 52 Grace St. El Cajon, CA 92023
(619) 555-9652   Sales Associate

Sell clothes, and do inventory.

Supervisor: Kathleen Rogers

1998   **Mon Cherie's** 8743 Girard Ave. La Jolla, CA 92137
(619) 555-2176   Sales Associate

Sold clothes. Store is now closed.

Supervisor: Michelle Roy

1996–1997   **Abbey's Burgers** 900 Beach Blvd. San Diego, CA 92112
(858) 555-9443   Cashier

Took orders, handled money.

References available upon request.

Writing the Second Draft

Now that you have completed the Grammar Lesson, you are ready to write the second draft for your Chapter Writing Assignment. Complete this draft before beginning the Sentence Lesson. Respond to the revision questions as you work on your rewrite.

Revision questions

- Does your topic sentence respond directly to the question you have chosen? If you are working on Question #1, are your résumé and cover letter focused toward applying for a specific job?
- Have you incorporated specific information that you received during your personal interview that could be helpful to you? Have you remembered to include specific details about your own experience?
- Have you used language that is appropriate for professional writing, and avoided being too casual or familiar?
- Examine your paragraph. Are all of your subjects and verbs in agreement? Are all of your pronouns and antecedents in agreement? Do you have pronoun consistency? Correct any errors you find.

After responding to the revision questions, Virginia rewrote her cover letter and résumé. She realized that her letter was too casually written, and that some of her comments would appear unprofessional. She also decided to include more specific details about how her education would be helpful to an architect's business.

2650 Conrad Avenue
San Diego, CA 92133

March 20, 2000

Jared O'Neil
O'Neil Architects
12th Floor
8865 5th Avenue
San Diego, CA 92120

Dear Mr. O'Neil:

I am writing in response to your ad in the *San Diego Union-Tribune* for the job of architect's assistant. The ad indicates that this position requires no degree, but familiarity with business and architecture is desired. I believe I am qualified for this position.

I have held several jobs in the business world in the past few years. I have experience handling money as a cashier at Abbey's Burgers. I have also worked in the retail business, first at a local boutique called Mon Cherie's, and now for a department store chain, Pickman's, where I have been a sales associate for the last two years.

While my work experience contains no experience in architecture, I have taken fifteen units of architecture classes at Grossmont College. I will be transferring to San Diego State University next fall, and I plan to major in architecture. My classes have included Introduction to Architecture, Theories of Architecture, and Computer Drawing.

I am aware that your firm has been involved with several important projects in the local area, including the remodeling of the Seaside Mall. My career goal is to become an architect, and I believe that working for your firm would provide me with invaluable experience.

I would be happy to answer any questions you may have. Please contact me either at the address above or by phone at (858) 555-4334.

Sincerely,

Virginia Fuentes

Virginia Fuentes

Virginia Fuentes

2650 Conrad Avenue   (858) 555-4334
San Diego, CA 92133

Education

1998–2000   **Grossmont College** 8800 Grossmont College Drive, El Cajon, CA 92020
Concentrating on courses in Architecture.

1994–1998   **John Tyler High School,** 657 Park Circle, Lawrence, CA 93555
Took college preparatory courses. Received diploma.

Work Experience

1998–now   **Pickham's** 52 Grace St. El Cajon, CA 92023
(619) 555-9652   Sales Associate

Sell clothes, arrange merchandise, perform regular inventory checks.

Supervisor: Kathleen Rogers

1998   **Mon Cherie's** 8743 Girard Ave. La Jolla, CA 92137
(619) 555-2176   Sales Associate

Sold clothes. Store closed in June 1998.

Supervisor: Michelle Roy

1996–1997   **Abbey's Burgers** 900 Beach Blvd. San Diego, CA 92112
(858) 555-9443   Cashier

Took orders, took customer payments and made change. Handled both cash and credit card transactions.

References

Lisa Wilson. Associate Professor. Architecture Department. Grossmont College. 8800 Grossmont College Drive, El Cajon, CA 92020 (619) 555-3800.

Michelle Roy. Former owner of Mon Cherie's. 4533 Fay Avenue, La Jolla, CA 92137 (619) 555-5664.

Mark Cogan. 4521 Hope Avenue. El Cajon, CA 92018 (619) 555-1215.

SENTENCE LESSON

Complex Sentences

In Chapter One, you learned that simple sentences express one main idea. In Chapter Two, you learned that compound sentences consist of two or more ideas, both of equal importance. The third type of sentence combines a less important (dependent) idea with a main (independent) idea. Take a look at the following.

While Terri was walking down the street, a fire alarm sounded.

This sentence consists of the dependent clause "While Terri was walking down the street," and an independent clause, "a fire alarm sounded." This type of sentence is called a **complex sentence.** Complex sentences have one main idea expressed in an independent clause, and one less important idea expressed in a dependent clause.

Dependent clauses can usually be identified by the presence of a subordinate conjunction at the start of the clause. A **subordinating conjunction** is the connector that achieves this unique relationship between the less important idea and the main idea. The following is a list of common subordinating conjunctions.

after	in order that	until	which
although	once	what	whichever
as	provided that	whatever	while
as if	since	when	who
because	so that	whenever	whoever
before	than	where	whom
even if	that	whereas	whomever
even though	though	wherever	whose
how	unless	whether	why
if			

When a dependent clause starts a sentence, it is followed by a comma. If the dependent clause appears after the main idea (independent clause), you do not use a comma.

Even though Mary got a pay raise, she was unhappy at her job.

Mary was unhappy at her job even though she got a pay raise.

In the first sentence, the comma appears after "raise" because the subordinating conjunction at the start of the sentence creates the dependent clause. In the second sentence, the subordinating conjunction appears in the middle of the sentence after the independent clause, so no punctuation is needed.

DON'T LOSE FOCUS!

One danger in recognizing dependent clauses is that sometimes dependent clauses that begin with the relative pronoun "that" actually drop the word, leaving it implied. In the following sentences, the dependent clauses are in italics:

Tammy knew *Robert was a scoundrel.*

Tammy knew *that Robert was a scoundrel.*

Both sentences are complex sentences. In the first sentence, "that" is implied, and in the second, "that" is stated explicitly. The "that" can be implied when the dependent clause functions as the direct object of a verb.

Professor Fowler learned *his prize graduate student was actually plagiarizing research.*

(The dependent clause tells what Professor Fowler learned.)

Wilma discovered *her blouse had been ruined by the dry cleaners.*

(The dependent clause tells what Wilma discovered.)

Ellen promised *she would write every week.*

(The dependent clause tells what Ellen promised.)

ZOOM-IN PRACTICE

Without consulting the list of subordinate conjunctions, write down as many of them as you can think of in two minutes. There are over thirty on the list. You should be able to think of at least fifteen.

_____   _____   _____

_____   _____   _____

_____   _____   _____

_____   _____   _____

_____   _____   _____

_____   _____   _____

_____   _____   _____

_____   _____   _____

_____   _____   _____

_____   _____   _____

_____   _____   _____

EXERCISE 3.4

If the italicized clause in each sentence is a dependent clause, write "D" next to it. If it is independent, write "I" next to it. For each dependent clause, underline the subordinating conjunction.

Alfredo left his job *because he felt unappreciated and underpaid.*
                                                                    D

1. *When Jerome left the interview,* he had a good feeling that the job would be his.

2. If you decide to take this job, *you will have to move to Canada.*

3. The people *who work in Human Resources departments* generally have strong personal relationship skills.

4. *The difference between having a job and having a career is one* that is important for college students to understand.

5. *Before he worked on commercial vessels,* Elden was in the Navy.

6. *As we learned how to handle the safety equipment,* we could see the dangers involved in the job.

7. Because his job only pays the minimum wage, *Paul is looking for a second job.*

8. My first job was working as a dishwasher at a restaurant *which was very popular among young people.*

9. Richmond felt *that he could no longer work and study at the same time.*

10. *Since my job at the campus radio station has been fun,* I plan to look at getting a career in the radio industry.

EXERCISE 3.5

Add an independent clause to each of the following dependent clauses, thereby creating a complex sentence.

After the strike was over, the employees were jubilant.

1. Because Rod, the office manager, was trying to cut down

   on expenses, _____

   _____.

2. _____ before

   the time clock struck five in the afternoon.

3. Although the sales people had all been notified of the

   change in the prices, _____

   _____.

4. If Stephanie does not get this new account, _____

   _____.

5. _____ that the

   promotion would go to Victor.

6. Unless business is conducted in an ethical fashion, _____

   _____.

7. _____ until

   Greg found a new job working in the fast food industry.

8. _____ when Diane

   transferred to a new division in Milwaukee, Wisconsin.

9. Because Martin forgot to sign his timecard _____

   _____.

10. _____ after a loud

    discussion was heard in the shop foreman's office.

Compound-Complex Sentences

You have been introduced to simple, compound, and complex sentences. There is one additional sentence type: the compound-complex sentence. A **compound-complex sentence** has more than one independent clause and at least one dependent clause. As such, the compound-complex sentence uses the coordination of ideas found in compound sentences, and the subordination of ideas found in complex sentences. The following sentence is compound-complex:

> Darnel, who felt guilty, tried to apologize to Alicia; however, she would not listen.

The sentence contains three clauses: The main ideas (the independent clauses) are underlined, and the less important one (the dependent clause) is double underlined:

> Darnel, who felt guilty, tried to apologize to Alica; however, she would not listen.

EXERCISE 3.6

Examine each of the following sentences and determine if it is a compound-complex sentence. If it is, put a check mark next to it. If not, leave the sentence blank.

√ *Labor Day, which celebrates working people, occurs in early September in the United States, but in many other countries, Labor Day is on May 1.*

1. Until the team starts to win, the coach's job will be in jeopardy, and the fans will be in an uproar.

2. Mr. Carlson, who works in the office downstairs, has told me that he intends to retire this year.

3. Although Nathan believes in ghosts, he does not believe in leprechauns; he is undecided about Santa Claus.

4. Because of the cost, Hank decided not to buy the machinery.

5. The box that was in the garage only has old papers in it, but Julie decided to hang on to it anyway.

6. The nurse practitioner saw the patient who had strep throat because the doctor had to attend to another patient.

7. Even though Stanley liked the book, he decided not to see the movie adaptation; he said that good books seldom made for good movies.

8. The circus clown frightened the younger children, but the older children adored her.

9. J.R. worked on his new Jeep in the driveway, but he forgot that the parking brake was not set.

10. If Leanne finds Marty, she will tell him not to worry about the money, but he'd better show up on Saturday with his pet Chihuahua.

Sentence Review

Examine each of the following sentences. Mark whether the sentence is a simple sentence (S), compound sentence (CP), complex sentence (CX), or compound-complex sentence (C-C).

1. Doug, who graduated from UCLA with a degree in chemical engineering, has started his own company.

2. Without saying very much, Clint Eastwood's characters manage to convey strong, clear messages to the bad guys.

3. The exit signs were clearly marked; nevertheless, when the fire broke out, the crowd panicked and could not find the doors.

4. The foreman could not find the right man for the job, so he hired the right woman.

5. My father always said that no one ever got rich working for someone else.

6. Whoever was painting the back fence forgot to finish the job.

7. The zoo has a great reputation for saving animals, but they were unable to prevent the death of Fido, a rare barking parakeet from South America.

8. Although she trained for the Olympics all her life, Ann never competed in one, for the boycott of the 1980 Olympics in Moscow killed her dreams.

9. After waving good-bye to his family at the airport, Victor boarded the plane to Oregon, never to return home again.

10. The student who discovered the mistake in the test was given an automatic A.

Applying the Sentence Lesson

In order to apply the lesson to your writing, identify all of the complex and compound-complex sentences in your second draft by underlining the complex sentences and double-underlining any compound-complex sentences. Then consider whether or not you have enough variety in your sentences. Examine Virginia's second draft results.

2650 Conrad Avenue
San Diego, CA 92133

March 20, 2000

Jared O'Neil
O'Neil Architects
12th Floor
8865 5th Avenue
San Diego, CA 92120

Dear Mr. O'Neil:

I am writing in response to your ad in the *San Diego Union-Tribune* for the job of architect's assistant. The ad indicates that this position requires no degree, but familiarity with business and architecture is desired. I believe I am qualified for this position.

I have held several jobs in the business world in the past few years. I have experience handling money as a cashier at Abbey's Burgers. I have also worked in the retail business, first at a local boutique called Mon Cherie's, and now for a department store chain, Pickman's, where I have been a sales associate for the last two years.

While my work experience contains no experience in architecture, I have taken fifteen units of architecture classes at Grossmont College. I will be transferring to San Diego State University next fall, and I plan to major in architecture. My classes have included Introduction to Architecture, Theories of Architecture, and Computer Drawing.

I am aware that your firm has been involved with several important projects in the local area, including the remodeling of the Seaside Mall. My carrer goal is to become an architect, and I believe that working for your firm would provide me with invaluable experience.

I would be happy to answer any questions you may have. Please contact me either at the address above or by phone at (858) 555-4334.

Sincerely,

Virginia Fuentes

Virginia Fuentes

Writing the Final Draft

Rewrite your second draft, making sure that you have at least two complex sentences and one compound-complex sentence. (Have these sentences in your cover letter if you're responding to Question #1.) This will be your final draft. Respond to the revision questions as you work on your rewrite.

Revision questions

- Does your paragraph have a strong sense of structure, with a beginning, middle, and end? If you wrote a cover letter, does the letter itself also have a sense of beginning, middle, and end?

- Have you provided effective transitions as you move from one idea to another?

- Have you included enough specific details? If you wrote a cover letter, have you made sure that you mentioned specific job skills or training that you have?

- Is the cover letter written in appropriate language? Make sure your language is not too casual or familiar.

- Have you eliminated any unnecessary words?

- Do you have at least two complex sentences and one compound-complex sentence? If not, rewrite so that you do.

Hand in the final draft, with the materials from your prewriting, first draft, second draft, and any other materials you created in the process of writing this assignment.

When Virginia did her final rewrite, she remembered to include a reference to her résumé in her cover letter. She worked to polish her cover letter, removing any unnecessary words. Mostly, she revised her cover letter and résumé with an eye towards making her application more appealing to a potential employer.

2650 Conrad Avenue
San Diego, CA 92133

March 20, 2000

Jared O'Neil
O'Neil Architects
12th Floor
8865 5th Avenue
San Diego, CA 92120

Dear Mr. O'Neil:

I am writing in response to your ad on March 17, 2000, in the *San Diego Union-Tribune* for the job of architect's assistant. The ad indicates that this position requires no degree, but familiarity with business and architecture is desired. I would like to apply for this position.

I am familiar with the workings of the business world. In my first job, I handled money as a cashier at Abbey's Burgers. I have experience in retail business, first at a local boutique, Mon Cherie's, and now for Pickman's, where I have been a sales associate for the last two years.

While my work experience contains no direct experience in architecture, I have taken fifteen units of architecture classes at Grossmont College. I plan to transfer to San Diego State University next fall and major in architecture. At Grossmont College, my classes have included Introduction to Architecture, Theories of Architecture, and Computer Drawing.

I am aware that your firm has been involved with several important projects in the local area, including the remodeling of the Seaside Mall. Since my goal is to become an architect, working for your firm would provide me with invaluable experience. I would be most grateful for the opportunity to work at O'Neil Architects.

I would be happy to answer any questions you may have. Please contact me either at the address above or by phone at (858) 555-4334.

Sincerely,

Virginia Fuentes

Virginia Fuentes

Virginia Fuentes

2650 Conrad Avenue   (858) 555-4334
San Diego, CA 92133

Education

1998–2000   **Grossmont College** 8800 Grossmont College Drive, El Cajon, CA 92020
Concentrating on courses in Architecture.

1994–1998   **John Tyler High School,** 657 Park Circle, Lawrence, CA 93555
Took college preparatory courses. Received diploma.

Work Experience

1998–now   **Pickham's** 52 Grace St. El Cajon, CA 92023
(619) 555-9652   Sales Associate

Sell clothes, arrange merchandise, perform regular inventory checks.

Supervisor: Kathleen Rogers

1998   **Mon Cherie's** 8743 Girard Ave. La Jolla, CA 92137
(619) 555-2176   Sales Associate

Sold clothes. Store closed in June 1998.

Supervisor: Michelle Roy

1996–1997   **Abbey's Burgers** 900 Beach Blvd. San Diego, CA 92112
                   (858) 555-9443   Cashier

                    Took orders, took customer payments and made change. Handled both cash and credit card transactions.

References

Lisa Wilson. Associate Professor. Architecture Department. Grossmont College. 8800 Grossmont College Drive, El Cajon, CA 92020 (619) 555-3800.

Michelle Roy. Former owner of Mon Cherie's. 4533 Fay Avenue, La Jolla, CA 92137 (619) 555-5664.

Mark Cogan. 4521 Hope Avenue. El Cajon, CA 92018 (619) 555-1215.

✔ PORTFOLIO CHECKLIST

In your portfolio, you should now have the following:

1. a report of your personal interview

2. a First Draft. The first draft should have the subjects and verbs of the first ten sentences underlined. The pronouns and their antecedents should be circled.

3. a Second Draft. The second draft should have your complex sentences underlined and compound-complex sentences double-underlined.

4. a Final Draft. Make sure there are at least two complex sentences and one compound-complex sentence.

PARTING SHOT

1. Examine how the two women are dressed. Which one seems better prepared, and why?

2. Some work environments allow for more casual dress, while others demand more formal clothing. Which environment would you prefer, and why?

3. What difficulties have you ever faced when applying for a job?

GOALS IN REVIEW

In this chapter, you have learned about

- conducting a personal interview
- writing a cover letter and a résumé
- agreement between subjects and verbs and between pronouns and antecedents
- complex and compound-complex sentences

PRACTICE CHAPTER TEST

Choose the right word in each of the following sentences.

1. The number of dolls in her collection (exceed, exceeds) one hundred.

2. There (are, is), according to economists, a chance that a recession could be right around the corner.

3. One of the many factors that led to the business's failure (was, were) the change in consumer demand.

4. (Do, Does) either of your sisters plan to work in the restaurant business?

5. Some of the profit from recent years (was, were) reinvested in the company.

6. Some of the managers in the home office (do, does) not seem to understand the problems we have here.

7. Anyone who wants to work here must have a drug test before (they, he or she) can be hired.

8. At a recent conference for women-only regarding sexual harassment in the workplace, each woman had an opportunity to discuss (her, their) feelings about the issue.

9. Many of the field laborers (are, is) from Mexico or Central America.

10. Neither the foreman nor the line workers (were, was) able to stop the accident.

11. The business decided not to tell (its, their) employees about the safety hazard.

12. Each electrician was required to have (his or her, their) own tools.

13. Every woman in the military (want, wants) respect for a job well done.

14. When the average man thinks of retirement, (they imagine themselves, he imagines himself) on a beach or golf course.

15. Neither of the two artists could explain (his, their) own work.

Examine each of the following sentences and label whether each is a simple (S), compound (CP), complex (CX), or compound-complex (C-C) sentence.

_____ **1.** The bank was closed down after the regulators found problems with their accounting.

_____ **2.** Unless you have a much better job offer, you should keep your job for now.

_____ **3.** Brett Favre is my favorite football star, and I wish that I could watch him play in person.

_____ **4.** The workers received a raise; however, the new raise did not even cover inflation.

_____ **5.** The electoral college system should be abandoned.

_____ **6.** The foreman, Mr. Hamm, was a fearsome presence on the line, but he actually was a pleasant person in private.

_____ **7.** Reno, which is in Nevada, is actually west of Los Angeles.

_____ **8.** To no one's surprise, Rick turned down the job offer even though the pay raise would have been substantial.

_____ **9.** Shelly could not believe that Scotty had found a new job.

_____ **10.** Jacklyn applied for the position yesterday; however, Estelle, who works in the Detroit office, has already been offered the job.

4

Multicultural America

CHAPTER GOALS

In this chapter, you will learn about

- a prewriting strategy called brainstorming,
- moving from the general to the specific in your writing,
- verbs, and
- sentence fragments, run-on sentences, and comma-spliced sentences.

The theme of this chapter is Multicultural America. Today, the United States has a broader range of ethnic groups, religions, languages, traditions, and cultures than at almost any time in its past, and it may have more diversity than any other country in the world. Issues relating to this wide range of cultures influence people at work, at school, at home, and at play.

OPENING SHOT

QUESTIONS ABOUT THE PICTURE

1. How do sports encourage people to embrace diversity?

2. What advantages are there to being exposed to cultural diversity?

3. Are women more likely than men to be open to racial and ethnic diversity?

4. The players in the photograph are playing soccer, a sport whose popularity in other countries is much greater than in the U.S. What other sports can you think of that have been imported to the U.S., and what sports that started here are now played elsewhere?

READING

Questions to Consider

1. How closely related are race and identity?
2. How necessary are racial labels?
3. If a person has parents of different races, how does that person identify himself or herself racially?

Words to Watch

queue	a line of waiting people or vehicles
eclecticism	made up of elements from a variety of sources
baristas	people who serve food and drinks in trendy restaurants, often from behind counters
multiethnic	of many ethnicities
shrine	a place of devotion to a venerated person or object
polyglot	a mixture or confusion of languages
demographic	characteristics of human population segments
pundit	a learned person
caste	a social class separated from others by distinctions of hereditary rank, profession, or wealth
miscegenation	marriage involving persons of different races
paradox	a seemingly contradictory statement that might be true
hue	color
argot	a specialized vocabulary
ossified	to have become bone; to be set in a rigid pattern
spurious	lacking authenticity or validity; false
epistemology	the study of the nature of knowledge
chimera	an imaginary monster made of grotesquely different parts

Beating the Wrap
Romesh Ratnesar

1   One of the more interesting cultural phenomena in Washington, D.C., these days is the success of a shiny new California-based eatery called WrapWorks. More than six months after the restaurant's opening, queues of customers, the faithful and the curious, spill outside its tall glass doors every noonday. The food is fast and neat, and intriguing in its eclecticism: Japanese soba noodles, Kung Pao chicken, blackened catfish mixed with mango salsa, all rolled into technicolor tortillas. The cheerful and many-hued baristas insist that you not call these snacks burritos. "Wraps" is the preferred term, the proper de-ethnicized label for such resolutely multiethnic fare. As patrons order their Thai peanut chicken and Chinese salad wraps, they often marvel at the food. They should. This is more than a triumph of good cheap eats; it's a triumph of the melting pot, an edible shrine to cross-culturalism, the new soul food for a happily polyglot society.

2   All at once, multiracialism has become an American fashion, commercially chic. In April, 21-year-old golf superstar Tiger Woods revealed that he does not consider himself black, but rather "Cablinasian," a blending of his Caucasian, black, Indian, and Thai blood. "I'm just who I am," he said. Newspapers rattled off demographic figures showing that the number of multiracial children in the U.S. has quadrupled since 1970, that the rate of black-white marriages has risen threefold in the last thirty years, that as many as 100 million Americans can claim mixed lineage. *Newsweek* pointed out that, in addition to Woods, stars like Keanu Reeves, Mariah Carey, and Johnny Depp boast "ambiguous or mixed ethnicity." Pundits hailed the dawning of a new age in American race relations, where the old rigid classifications of black and white give way to "many shades of beige." A Nike ad shows a succession of children of various races, each declaring "I am Tiger Woods." We are all Tiger Woods now.

3   The Office of Management and Budget will determine this summer whether to add a new "multiracial" category to the racial classifications listed on the U.S. Census forms—currently limited to "white," "black," "American Indian or Alaskan Native" and "Asian or Pacific Islander," plus an option for respondents of Hispanic origin. Supporters of the measure sensibly ask why millions of American children born of parents of different races should be forced to choose between them. But African American and Asian interest groups howl that the multiracial option will lower the number of Americans who situate themselves within the time-honored castes, and might encourage mixed-race citizens to flee their "blackness." (And yellowness and redness.) "If you look black," says one University of Virginia professor, "you are black." This reasoning, of course, is precisely what African Americans fought against for most of this century, when many states held onto "one-drop" miscegenation laws that barred anyone with a hint of black blood from intermarrying. But more than consistency is at stake now. Things like federal housing dollars and legislative redistricting rest upon a cold

racial calculus. Numbers matter. And multiracialism, paradoxically, is leaving transracial solidarity in tatters.

4   If given the choice, I will check the "multiracial" box on the Census survey three years from now. For years, I've selected the "other" option on official forms; there is nothing demonstrably inaccurate about identifying myself as "Asian or Pacific Islander," but that has never seemed satisfying enough. My skin color is dark brown, but a slight angle at the corner of my eyes, or a touch of lightness in my hue, betrays me. My father is an ethnic Tamil from Sri Lanka; my mother is a Malaysian of Chinese descent. So I am linked genealogically to mainland China as well as to the Indian subcontinent. Which is to say, as an American, not by much.

5   The riches that an interracial background bestows are modest ones, as quiet and simple as an old story retold, or a traditional meal recreated. They are treasures, in short, not so different from those shared by any other family, in any other place. That I come from mixed-race parents means that I sometimes eat with chopsticks, and sometimes with my hands; that I'm given the occasional second glance when I buy groceries with my mother; that I feel little pressure to date within a single race. Beyond that, it means nothing. It does not shape how I perceive the world or, beyond a cursory level, how the world perceives me. It does not influence how I work, or what I write, or whom I love. It is not destiny, nor religion, nor identity. In response to the resistance from traditional minority groups, the champions of multiracialism have stepped up their campaign. There are mixed-race magazines and web sites. Multiracial student associations have sprouted on college campuses like Brown, Wesleyan and Berkeley—Harvard boasts two, one for half-black and one for half-Asian students. They employ the familiar argot of race and identity that has done so much, in recent times, to brighten the color line. "I'm not going to sacrifice my identity for the black community," a biracial Brown sophomore told the Boston Globe. Says the president of the Association of Multi-Ethnic Americans: "This same one-drop rule is being used by minorities to keep power and rights at the expense of my community."

6   But what "community" is that? The great promise of America's multiracial citizens is that, as their numbers grow, they might render our ossified categories of race meaningless. Yet many multiracialists seem intent on doing just the opposite—inventing some spurious experience, some artificial epistemology, that all multiracial people inherit, as if a child born to one black and one white parent holds some inviolable connection with a child born to yellow and white parents, or like me, to brown and yellow ones. Rather than exposing the chimera of identity politics, this movement strengthens it, devising another illusory home in which the purported unprotected can find refuge and be whole.

7   Alas, surveys show that few Americans would choose to identify themselves as multiracial if offered the choice. So the ugly sniping among minority groups will probably subside. Hungry Washingtonians will still flock to WrapWorks. Tiger Woods will go back to just being a superb athlete. I saw him play once: he was a freshman at Stanford, already something of a novelty on campus. He hit his first drive that spring day

more than 300 yards, dead center, and then proceeded to play what I'm sure was one of the worst rounds of his life. He bogeyed the first five holes. He cursed and ranted and flung his clubs. He wheezed from pollen. He seemed very mortal and very young—and, for that, a lot like us. After the tenth hole, his shoulder hurting, Tiger quit. Everyone sighed disappointedly. Then I watched as his black father and Asian mother drew close, putting their arms around their son, shielding him.

PREPARING TO WRITE

Brainstorming

One of the most common activities that writers do to collect ideas is to brainstorm. When you **brainstorm,** you are writing down all of the ideas that come into your head about a given topic.

The point of a brainstorming activity is this: not all of your good ideas are lying on the surface of your thoughts, just ready for you to use. Although it is common for some people to describe computers as being like brains (or brains being like computers), in many ways the comparison is *not* true. When you use a computer, for example, you can create a file and write anything in that file you wish. You can then save that file, and the next time you look at it, the file will be the same as when you last saved it. This is not true for the thoughts stored in your brain. How wonderful it would be if each time you heard a good idea, you could store it safely in your mind under the heading of "Good ideas" and retrieve it whenever you needed a good idea. However, that's not how your brain works.

In truth, the human brain can do funny things, such as distorting memories or forgetting things altogether. That's when brainstorming can help. Brainstorming works by the process of free association. **Free association** means that you make connections between two things in your head, sometimes based on a logic that only you follow because it is based on your own personal experience, beliefs, or knowledge. The benefit of free association is that it can lead you into ideas you never knew you had, or that you did not realize were connected with other ideas.

Brainstorming, then, is a way for you to generate ideas quickly that you might not get if you just sat at a desk and pondered, hoping for an idea to strike you. Aimless day-dreaming seldom produces effective ideas for writers, but directed brainstorming can.

Preparing Yourself to Write

In order to brainstorm most effectively, you must do the following:

1. Set a timer. You should always brainstorm for a set period of time— it does not work well as an open-ended activity. You need to feel

the push of time, but you don't want to be constantly checking your watch. Instead, set a timer, such as a kitchen clock or a digital watch timer. Set the time for five minutes at first, until you get used to brainstorming. Once you're used to this activity, you can push for longer times, such as ten or fifteen minutes.

2. Don't stop. While the timer is going, you should be constantly working to write down ideas. That's when free association works best—when you're not editing your own thoughts. You should feel free to jot down any ideas you come up with, no matter how "bad" they seem at the time. Leave the judgments for after the brainstorming session.

3. Focus on a topic. You cannot brainstorm about "anything." That quickly becomes "nothing." Instead, you should have a predetermined topic. Sometimes that topic is given to you by an instructor, it might come from a writing assignment, or it could be something you are already interested in. No matter what the source, you always want to brainstorm about something specific.

4. There are two ways to brainstorm: by making a list or by mapping. A list is a vertical recording of words or short phrases. You make a list by starting at the top of a page, writing down the topic, and then working down from the top, writing separate items on each new line. Mapping is done on a blank sheet of paper with the topic at the center. After a brainstorming session, the paper might appear chaotic, with words and phrases all over the page. Then, however, you can take a pen or pencil and draw circles and lines that connect different ideas together. Figure 4.1 shows an example of brainstorming by listing. Figure 4.2 shows an example of brainstorming by mapping. Examine each of the figures so that you can brainstorm in both ways on your own.

Race and Sports

Jackie Robinson—first black major leaguer
Jesse Owens
Sports help stop racism
People play together
Everyone has a chance
Foreign players in baseball now
Golf has Tiger Woods—very popular player
Tennis'—Williams sisters
Athletes only care about winning, not race
Sports can help society—see different
    people working together
Many races in many sports
A lot of money in sports too
Endorsements go to the best players now,
    not just the white players

FIGURE 4.1 Sample of Brainstorming by Listing

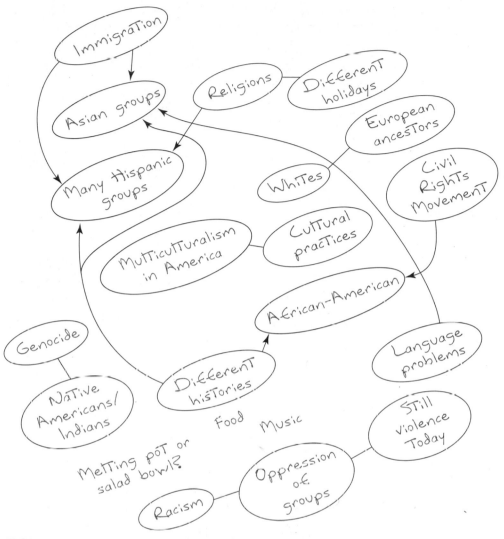

FIGURE 4.2 Sample of Brainstorming by Mapping

Prewriting

Now that you know how to brainstorm, do a brainstorming session on the subject of Multicultural America or on a question from the Chapter Writing Assignment. Start off by brainstorming for five minutes. Decide beforehand whether you are going to make a list or a map. When you're done with the brainstorming session, review the results, looking for interesting and original ideas.

After you have completed your brainstorming session, examine the results. What kinds of connections did you make? Did any new or unexpected ideas come to mind as you were brainstorming? If you wish to explore a topic further, brainstorm again, focusing on your new topic. This will give greater depth to your exploration for writing ideas.

Brainstorming

CHAPTER WRITING ASSIGNMENT

Write a 100- to 200-word paragraph in response to one of the following writing assignments. Instructions in the chapter will guide you through the writing process. At different points in the chapter, you will be asked to produce more work on this assignment. By the end of the chapter, you will complete your final draft.

1. How prevalent is racism today? Use examples from your own personal experience, education, or knowledge.

2. In your opinion, how can this country best deal with racial conflict? Explain, being as specific as possible.

3. Are younger people rather than older people likely to be more open to racial and ethnic diversity? Explain, being as specific as possible.

4. In his essay "Beating the Wrap," Romesh Ratnesar argues that people of mixed-race ancestry should not identify themselves as belonging to one race or another, but as "multiracial." Do you agree or disagree? Explain, being as specific as possible.

WRITING LESSON

Being Specific, Not General

One of the biggest traps writers can fall into is being overly general in their writing. What does "general" mean? General statements refer to *types* of things rather than *specific examples* of things. General statements avoid details; instead, they work on the level of ideas and concepts rather than facts, statistics, or examples. General statements are not of themselves bad or inaccurate. However, writers who rely only on general statements seldom make a convincing point when they write. The following is an example of an overly general piece of writing:

Racism is really bad. After all, racism is just all about hatred, anger, and ignorance, and that is just wrong. It's not right for people to be racist about people they don't know about, or even about people they do. Basically, racists don't like other people who are different from themselves because they can't think of any way to be other than the way that they are. People who are racist in this country really have a lot to learn about other people and I think it would be a good idea if people stopped being racist, opened their eyes, and started to learn more

about people who are different from themselves. I think this country

would be a lot better place and people would be a lot better people if

this would happen.

This paragraph is filled with overly general statements. Almost every sentence avoids being specific. Examine the paragraph. Notice that words like "racism" and "racist" are general statements which refer to the concept of prejudice based upon race. However, the author avoids illustrating or giving examples of racism or racists. The author also uses a number of terms showing value judgments, such as "wrong," "better place," and "better people" without really defining those terms. The overall effect is a piece of writing that is superficial, insubstantial, and unconvincing on the most basic levels.

Here is the same paragraph, only rewritten to be more specific:

Racism is a blight on the moral life of this country. Racism itself is

the stereotyping of any group of people based on their ethnicity, culture,

or appearance, and then thinking about that group negatively. Racism

fosters hatred, anger, and ignorance; it is based on beliefs that are not

true. Looking at people as members of a group strips them of their

individuality. For example, studies have shown that in certain big cities,

members of certain racial groups, particularly African-Americans, are

more likely to be pulled over by the police for traffic citations. This could

be based on the police officers' view that African-Americans are more

likely to be committing a crime. The officer doesn't pay attention to the

individual. The officer just looks at the car and pulls the black driver

over. Even more serious is the use of deadly force against people of

color. Anyone who saw the videotape of the beating of Rodney King, or

who heard about the shooting of unarmed Amadou Diallo 19 times by

New York police officers can scarcely believe that racial prejudice did not

play a role. Of course, not all police officers are racists, and there are

racists other than police officers. Still, the number of explicitly racist organizations, such as the KKK and Aryan Nation, and racist web sites on the Internet is exploding, offering propaganda to the unsuspecting and confirmation to the already prejudiced. Americans of all colors need to step back and think about the mindset that leads to racism and racist activity, and to fight against the onslaught of ignorance and fear this mindset represents.

This paragraph is better because it uses more specific details to make its case. The use of facts and examples, such as the Rodney King case and the shooting of Amadou Diallo, helps to make more concrete the idea of violence based on racial prejudice. The definition of racism as "stereotyping" in a negative fashion and the "stripping away of individuality" help a reader get a better sense of what the author is writing about. Also, referring to racist groups and racist web sites also helps to give more details about the extent of organized racism.

When you write, you want to make sure that you support general statements with specific details. As discussed in Chapter One, a paragraph will usually begin with a topic sentence that is more general than the rest of the paragraph. But the main part of the paragraph, where you present your support, should contain as many specific details as possible. Remember, details can consist of facts, statistics, examples, and personal experience. Using details will help make your writing stronger and more effective.

Writing the First Draft

Mark, who did the sample brainstorming by mapping, had different thoughts about racism and what he wanted to say about it. As he looked over his brainstorming, he realized that most of what he had written down had to do with race and sports. He decided to write his paragraph in response to Question #2 because he saw sports as an activity that heals racial problems.

I think that sports have done an awful lot to solve the problems of racism in this country. If nothing else, sports have been a way for different people to play together and learn about each other. There have been a lot of African-Americans who became famous for what they did in sports at times when race was really a problem, like Jesse Owens and Jackie Robinson. Other athletes in other sports have also done similar things. Athletes serve as role models too. Look at Michael Jordan. He's one of the most popular athletes ever. I think it's a real sign of how far we've come in this country that Jordan, an African-American, was so incredibly popular. Not only was he a fabulous basketball player, probably the best ever, but he also was paid to endorse all kinds of products, which showed his popularity with all fans, black and white. Of course, racism is still with us in different ways, but sports is one place to go to where no one is thinking about that.

Now that you have completed your prewriting assignments, you are ready to write your first draft in response to one of the questions in the Chapter Writing Assignment. Complete this draft before beginning the Grammar Lesson.

GRAMMAR LESSON

Verbs

What's happening? How are you? The answers to these questions and many others involve using verbs. As you saw in Chapter One, verbs come in two types: action and linking. As you have seen in Chapters Two and Three, verbs work with subjects to create the sense of what is happening in a sentence.

With action verbs, there is a sense of *doing*. Someone may be sleeping, laughing, or even just thinking.

Mary Beth **sleeps** in late every Saturday.
Buck **laughed** at Reed's joke.
Irving **thought** hard about his fate.

With linking verbs, there is a sense of *being*. Linking verbs join the subject with the subject complement—the noun, pronoun, or adjective on the other side of the linking verb that renames or describes the subject. Someone's professional status, the color of a car, or the taste of food can all be described using linking verbs.

Joseph Conrad **is** one of the few great writers in English who learned English as a foreign language.
Terence's first Mercedes **was** silver.
The pot roast **tasted** awful because Jenny added too much salt.

Verb Tense

Besides indicating the action or state of being in a sentence, verbs also indicate or reflect the proper time. Verbs change their form as a way of showing different **tenses.** There are several different tenses, but most are related to the three simple tenses: the past, present, and future.

PAST

	Singular	**Plural**
1st Person	I looked	We looked
2nd Person	You looked	You looked
3rd Person	He, She, It looked	They looked

PRESENT

	Singular	**Plural**
1st Person	I look	We look
2nd Person	You look	You look
3rd Person	He, She, It looks	They look

FUTURE

	Singular	**Plural**
1st Person	I will look	We will look
2nd Person	You will look	You will look
3rd Person	He, She, It will look	They will look

These forms are likely to be quite familiar to you. Even if you never thought of verbs in this way, you can see that most verbs do not change from person to person (such as from the first person or "I" form to the second person or "You" form), or from singular to plural. The one exception in the present tense is the third person singular, or "He, She, It" form. In that form, an "s" or "es" is added to the word.

Verbs that behave in this predictable fashion are called **regular verbs.** Regular verbs are easy to **conjugate** (or change into their appropriate form) because they follow a consistent pattern. They always keep the same form in the past tense by adding the letters "-ed," and they add the word "will" to the verb to create the future tense. If you are unsure about the form of a verb, consult your dictionary. If a verb is regular, a dictionary will not show any additional forms. That means that the expectation is that the past tense and the past participle will both end with -ed and the present participle will end with -ing. For example, the dictionary entry only shows the root form of the verb: "look." Thus, the verb "look" would be conjugated as follows:

Present Tense	**Past Tense**	**Past Participle**	**Present Participle**
look	looked	looked	looking

Irregular verbs, on the other hand, are verbs that do not follow a consistent pattern. In fact, there are many different ways for verbs to be irregular. Some only undergo minor changes in spelling or punctuation; others change their appearance entirely. Look, for example, at a conjugation of the verb "be" in the present tense:

PRESENT

	Singular	**Plural**
1st Person	I am	We are
2nd Person	You are	You are
3rd Person	He, She, It is	They are

There is no easy way to predict how a verb might be irregular. If a verb is irregular in the past tense, a dictionary will show the different forms that the verb takes by showing the past tense, the past participle, and the present participle. For example, the forms of the verb "begin" might appear in a standard dictionary entry as follows:

begin (v) began, begun, beginning.

Or, if the dictionary you are using shortens the words to show only the parts that change, the entry might look like this:

begin (v) -gan, -gun, -ginning.

EXERCISE 4.1

Fill in the blank with the proper past tense form of the verb in parentheses. Consult a dictionary if necessary.

Holly <u>took</u> *the wrong turn at the intersection. (take)*

1. Darlene _____ Jason a red tomato from her garden to take back to his grandmother. (give)

2. Once Greg Louganis _____ from a high dive and nearly killed himself when his head struck the board. (dive)

3. Without even trying, Bob _____ one of the most feared professors on campus. (become)

4. Alexandra _____ a distinct resemblance to an image from a Reuben's painting. (bear)

5. The child _____ out with laughter while watching cartoons on television. (burst)

6. Art _____ the hole in the wrong spot, so he had to fill the old one back up with dirt. (dig)

7. When the Teamsters _____ the shipping company, many businesses suffered. (strike)

8. Even though this movie _____ at 7:30 p.m., I still don't think we'll make it home before eleven. (begin)

9. Thanks to Yoko's careful attention, the new fruit trees _____ quickly. (grow)

10. Samantha _____ from her bed feeling that nothing could stop her from succeeding. (arise)

EXERCISE 4.2

Using a dictionary, change the following verbs into their past, past participle, and present participle forms.

Present	Past	Past Participle	Present Participle
bite	*bit*	*bitten*	*biting*
break			
bring			
build			
buy			
come			
cut			
drink			
fall			
fight			
forget			
get			
hit			

Present	Past	Past Participle	Present Participle
lay			
lie			
read			
see			
sleep			
stink			
swim			
take			
teach			
tear			
think			
throw			
wear			

Verb Tenses

The three basic times describe the following actions:

Present:

Janice *picks* the dead leaves off of her houseplants. (an action in the present)

Colleen's minivan *is* very comfortable. (an on-going action or state of being)

I *talk* with the supervisor each morning. (a habitual action)

In Shakespeare's famous tragedy, the ghost of Hamlet's father *commands* Hamlet to take revenge for his murder. (the literary present)

A penny saved *is* a penny earned (a general statement of an idea or truth)

Past:

Alex *broke* the lamp in the bedroom. (an action completed in the past)

Future:

> Next week, Chauncey *will enroll* at Gonzaga, a private college in Spokane. (an action that will take place in the future)

However, when you are attempting to describe events, matters can be more complicated. The **perfect tenses** help to make more precise distinctions in time.

Present Perfect:

> I *have lived* in my house for over five years. (an action that started in the past and continues into the present)

> According to my five-year-old son, he *has destroyed* the evil demons which lurked under his bed. (an action that started in the past and has been completed)

Past Perfect:

> Martha *had* already *started* the videotape of Casablanca when Kevin showed up at her door with an invitation to a party. (an action that started in the past before another action in the past)

Future Perfect:

> Tony *will have had* plenty of practice as quarterback before the start of next Friday's game. (an action that will be completed sometime in the future before another action)

Also, all six of these verb tenses can be presented in the progressive form. The **progressive tense** is formed by using the verb "to be" as a helping verb with the present participle (the -ing form) of the main verb. Progressive tenses are used to show an action in progress, no matter which time—past, present, or future—is used.

> Miriam *is having* trouble with her car. (present progressive)

> The night watchman *was inspecting* the doors to be sure they were locked. (past progressive)

> The clown *will be arriving* on top of a fire engine at noon. (future progressive)

> The caddie *has been having* trouble with his back all day. (present perfect progressive)

> The attorneys *had been hoping* for an out-of-court settlement, but the case went to trial instead. (past perfect progressive)

> The surgeons *will have been operating* for eight hours by the time a new team can be ready to assist. (future perfect progressive)

DON'T LOSE FOCUS!

Students sometimes fail to recognize the proper verb tense of a sentence because of the use of contractions. Contractions, which involve removing syllables when two words are joined together, hide the presence of helping verbs. For that reason, the helping verbs are not as obvious.

With contraction:

John's gone down to the creek to fetch a bucket of water.

Without contraction:

John has gone down to the creek to fetch a bucket of water.

Remember, oral language is usually more casual than written language, so you might discover while writing the presence of verb forms that you are not often aware of when you speak.

ZOOM-IN PRACTICE

Write for five minutes about a person whom you admire. Then, circle each verb. Find a better, stronger, more specific verb. Use the present tense.

EXERCISE 4.3

Identify the tense of the underlined verb in each of the following sentences.

Mr. Whitson has never been to a Cinco de Mayo celebration.—Present perfect

1. The detective sensed Conrad had been lying about his relationship to the rich widow, but now he had proof.

2. Beulah will laugh when she reads this.

3. Starr had hoped that no one would discover his ties to organized crime.

4. Oliver is reading that Stephen King novel voraciously.

5. I've seen what kind of damage that machine can do.

6. Up until last December, Maggie was still trying to reconcile with her father, but then she gave up.

7. The baseball writers will elect Tony Gwynn into the Hall of Fame after he <u>retires</u>.

8. Mother <u>will be sewing</u> patches onto pants all day long if you don't take better care of your clothes.

9. Terry <u>bought</u> the new dress in spite of her tight budget.

10. The team <u>will have been traveling</u> for twenty straight hours before they finally return home.

11. You <u>will have saved</u> half a million dollars before you retire if you start investing now.

12. I <u>have been looking</u> everywhere for the perfect holiday gift for my father.

EXERCISE 4.4

Write twelve sentences of your own in which you use each of the simple, perfect, and progressive tenses at least once each. Underline the verb and label its tense in each sentence.

1.

2.

3.

4.

5.

6.

7.

8.

9.

10.

11.

12.

Verbals

There is a special group of words, called **verbals,** that take the form of verbs but function as nouns or adjectives. Verbals that function as nouns are **gerunds** (the -*ing* form of a verb) and **infinitives** (the *to* form of a verb).

Learning a foreign language can be difficult. ("Learning" is a noun because it names an activity.)

The child likes to read books based on cartoons. ("to read" is a noun because it names an activity.)

An infinitive can also function as an adjective or an adverb.

The man to see about your toothache is Dr. Jack. ("to see" is an infinitive functioning as an adjective modifying "man.")

The lion paused to sniff the wind. ("to sniff" is an infinitive functioning as an adverb modifying "paused.")

Other verbals, called **participles,** act as adjectives. Participles can appear in two forms: **present participles** (the -*ing* form of a verb) and the **past participle** (the -*ed* form in regular verbs).

Speaking softly, the vampire soothed his next victim's nerves. ("Speaking" is a present participle functioning as an adjective modifying "vampire.")

The tired father watched his children play on the swings. ("Tired" is a past participle functioning as an adjective modifying "father.")

Remember: The gerund and the present participle have the same form, but have different functions. The gerund functions as a noun, and the present participle functions as an adjective. The importance of recognizing verbals is to be able to see that they are not verbs. If you see an infinitive or a participle not accompanied by a helping verb, then you have found a verbal.

EXERCISE 4.5

Underline any verbals in each of the following sentences.

I have always enjoyed going to museums.

1. Kamala decided to fly to Bombay in June.

2. The cultural arts fair was held in a open-air plaza to allow for more participants.

3. Singing loudly, the children showed a lot of enthusiasm.

4. Rodney decided to install a swinging gate.

5. The fishermen were using heavy line, but the struggling swordfish broke free anyway.

6. The woman to consult about your problem is not at work today.

7. Flying an airplane for the first time can be a surprisingly fun experience.

8. The crumbling wall could no longer hold up to the storm.

9. The detective stopped to examine the footprint.

10. Joking and laughing with TV reporters, the prisoner did not seem to care about his fate.

GRAMMAR REVIEW

Identify the verb tense of the underlined verb or verb phrase in each of the following sentences.

1. Jonathan was working on a new project which he hoped would make a ton of money.

2. By the time you read this note, Sonny will have been missing for over three weeks.

3. Reed is not coming to the wedding after all.

4. I know that I laid my books around here somewhere.

5. Whenever I hear about Paris, my memories begin to stir.

6. Gordon swears that he will read all of Shakespeare's plays over Christmas break.

7. The attorneys <u>have been</u> clear on this issue.

8. Yes, we <u>will be seeing</u> your grandparents this Thanksgiving.

9. The clerks <u>have been counting</u> the money and checking against the receipts all day.

10. Sarah <u>had</u> already <u>arranged</u> a ride when Damon volunteered to drive her to the airport.

11. When the season is over, Scott <u>will have attended</u> all eight Charger home games.

12. Ned <u>had been looking</u> for just that kind of suit, but the price was too high for him.

Applying the Grammar Lesson

In order to demonstrate your understanding of verb tenses, identify different verb tenses in your first draft. Underline each verb and write the name of the tense above the verb.

Here is an example of how Mark applied the grammar lesson to his first draft:

present   **present perfect**
I <u>think</u> that sports <u>have done</u> an awful lot to solve the problems of
                                                present perfect
racism in this country. If nothing else, sports <u>have been</u> a way for

different people to play together and learn about each other. There
present perfect   **past**
<u>have been</u> a lot of African-Americans who <u>became</u> famous for what they
past   **past**
<u>did</u> in sports at times when race <u>was</u> really a problem, like Jesse Owens
                                        present perfect
and Jackie Robinson. Other athletes in other sports <u>have</u> also <u>done</u>
                        present   **present**
similar things. Athletes <u>serve</u> as role models too. <u>Look</u> at Michael Jordan.
present   **present   present**
He<u>'s</u> one of the most popular athletes ever. I <u>think</u> it<u>'s</u> a real sign of how
        present perfect   **past**
far <u>we've come</u> in this country that Jordan, an African-American, <u>was</u> so
                        past
incredibly popular. Not only <u>was</u> he a fabulous basketball player, probably
                        past
the best ever, but companies <u>paid</u> him to endorse all kinds of products,
        past
which <u>showed</u> his popularity with all fans, black and white. Of course,
        present   **present**
racism <u>is</u> still with us in different ways, but sports <u>is</u> one place to go to
                present progressive
where no one <u>is thinking</u> about that.

Writing the Second Draft

After you have applied the grammar lesson to your first draft, you are ready to write the second draft of your Chapter Writing Assignment. Complete this draft before beginning the Sentence Lesson. Respond to the revision questions as you work on your rewrite.

Revision questions

- Does your topic sentence respond directly to the question you have chosen?

- Examine your paragraph. Does the paragraph begin with a general statement (your topic sentence), which is supported with specific details?

- Do you have at least three different, developed specific details in your paragraph? If not, add more.

- Are all of your verbs correct and in the appropriate tense?

After applying the grammar lesson, Mark rewrote his paragraph. He realized that he needed to be more specific with his use of details. Though he mentioned three athletes specifically in his first draft, he had not said very much about the first two. He also thought the paragraph seemed a little disconnected because the Michael Jordan example was not clearly related to the rest of the paragraph. He also worked to improve his topic sentence and remove any vague or unnecessary words.

Sports have done a lot to solve the problems of racism in this country. Different people come together in sports who might not otherwise learn about each other. There have been a lot of African-Americans who became famous for what they did in sports helping pave the way for civil rights. Jesse Owens competed and won against Nazis in 1936, Jackie Robinson integrated major league baseball in 1947. Their actions, and the actions of others like them, helping America change itself. How successful they were can be seen today in people like Michael Jordan. One of the most popular athletes ever which is a real sign of how far we've come. Jordan, an African-American, was incredibly popular not only as a basketball player, but also because of who he was one sign of his popularity with blacks and whites is that he made over $500 million in endorsements! Of course, racism is still with us in different ways, but sports is one place to go to where no one is thinking about that anymore.

SENTENCE LESSON

Fragments, Run-ons, and Comma Spliced Sentences

Previously, you learned that a complete sentence requires a subject and a verb, and that it must also express a complete thought. You also learned the difference between an independent clause and a dependent clause—namely, that a dependent clause does <u>not</u> express a complete thought. That is why a dependent clause requires the presence of an independent clause in order to form a complete sentence.

You might sometimes write sentences that do not fulfill the requirements of a complete sentence. When this occurs, you have written a sentence fragment. A **sentence fragment** is only part of a sentence. It is not, however, the whole. Sentence fragments are created in five ways:

1. The subject is missing.
2. The verb is missing.
3. The helping verb is missing.
4. The sentence is actually a dependent clause.
5. The sentence is actually a phrase.

Missing the Subject

The subject of a sentence answers the questions "Who or what is doing the action of the verb?" or "Who or what is being described or renamed by the verb?" Look at the following sentences.

Traveled to Egypt in a freighter.

Inside of a month was gone for good.

While Clarissa was packing for a trip to a dude ranch in Wyoming, slipped out of the house without a word.

In each of these sentences, the subject is missing. Look at the sentences with a subject:

Daniel traveled to Egypt in a freighter.

Inside of a month, *the money* was gone for good.

While Clarissa was packing for a trip to a dude ranch in Wyoming, *Horace* slipped out of the house without a word.

For many fluent speakers of English, missing a subject is not a common sentence error. Nevertheless, you must remain alert for this type of error, especially in a sentence that begins with a long phrase or clause that includes the same person as the subject.

After the couple fought for nearly half the night, broke up.

After the couple fought for nearly half the night, *they* broke up.

Missing the Verb

The verb of a sentence answers the question "What is happening?" A sentence without a verb either fails to state an action or to link together a subject with its complement. Look at the following sentences.

Morgan, the new kid on the block.

The waiter who was carrying our dinner.

Martin Luther King. A man of great distinction.

In each of these sentences, a verb is missing. Look at the sentences with a verb.

Morgan **was** the new kid on the block.

The waiter who was carrying our dinner **tripped.**

Martin Luther King **was** a man of great distinction.

As with the case of missing a subject, most fluent writers of English usually don't leave out a verb unless they are writing, as in the last example, short, choppy phrases that lack connections.

New Year's Eve. A time of champagne, dancing, and hope for the future.

New Year's Eve **can be** a time of champagne, dancing, and hope for the future.

Missing a Helping Verb

Some verb forms require helping verbs to work with main verbs, such as with the perfect tenses or the progressive tenses. If the helping verb is missing, the sentence is actually a sentence fragment. Look at the following sentences.

Margaret, standing in front of the fence for a long time.

The attorney join the suit against the firm.

The civil rights workers exposing the immorality of legal segregation in the South.

In each of these sentences, a helping verb is missing.

Margaret **has been** standing in front of the fence for a long time.

The attorney **might** join the suit against the firm.

The civil rights workers **were** exposing the immorality of legal segregation in the South.

An omitted helping verb is one of the more common ways that sentence fragments are created. This is common in sentences that begin with a subject, followed (erroneously) by a comma and then a present participle.

Edmund, looking through a hole in the wall.

Edmund **was** looking through a hole in the wall.

Another way to fix sentence fragments caused by a missing helping verb is to change the form of the verb itself by using one of the simple verb tense forms—past, present or future.

Edmund **looked** through a hole in the wall.

Creating a Dependent Clause

Another common mistake you may make is to confuse a dependent clause for a complete sentence. Look at the following sentences.

After Todd studied African-American history.

Because my car lacked good brakes.

Even though Anthony worked hard at his job.

Each of these examples is a sentence fragment because it is only a dependent clause. One way to know this is to check for the presence of a subordinating conjunction. Since each of these sentences begins with a subordinating conjunction—"After," "Because," and "Even though"—one way to fix these sentence fragments is to eliminate the subordinating conjunction altogether.

Todd studied African-American history.

My car lacked good brakes.

Anthony worked hard at his job.

Another way to fix the sentence fragments is to add a main idea to each fragment. The presence of the main idea makes the sentence complete.

After Todd studied African-American history, he wanted to learn even more.

I could not avoid the accident because my car lacked good brakes.

Even though Anthony worked hard at his job, he was not given a promotion.

Creating a Phrase

A phrase is a group of words that act as a unit but lack a subject and a verb. Sometimes sentence fragments are, in fact, phrases. Look at the following sentences.

During his tenure as a professor at Clarion University.

To help someone in a time of need.

Growing up with the types of privileges most other people can only imagine.

Each of these is a sentence fragment because they consist of a phrase only. Sometimes to correct a fragment of this nature, you can simply add the main idea.

During his tenure as a professor at Clarion University, Professor Shoemaker never once insulted a student nor spoke with disrespect to his colleagues.

My mother taught all of us children to help someone in a time of need.

Growing up with the types of privileges most other people can only imagine, Holland Brockton did not relate well to the experiences of the common person.

Sometimes a phrase can be written so that it becomes the subject of the sentence.

To help someone in a time of need is a virtuous act.

Growing up with the types of privileges most other people can only imagine prevented Holland Brockton from relating well to the common person.

(The phrase "During his tenure as a professor at Clarion University" cannot be made into a complete sentence this way because prepositional phrases cannot serve as the subject of a sentence.)

When the phrase begins with a participle, you can often form a complete sentence by changing the form of the verb and adding a subject.

Holland Brockton grew up with the types of privileges most other people can only imagine, which prevented him from relating well to the experiences of the common person.

EXERCISE 4.6

Examine each of the following sentences. If the sentence is a fragment, fix it. If the sentence is already correct, mark it with a "C."

Even though many Americans celebrate different heritages, all Americans have things in common as well.

1. Driving late into the night in order to be home for the holidays.

2. Jim Brown, one of the greatest football players ever.

3. To push hard for voter registration this year.

4. Simply finding out what went wrong.

5. Eddie Murphy. My kind of comedian.

6. Because her father had been so strict about her meetings with Evan.

7. Miss Emily, who knew about such things and did not approve.

8. Trouble without any other name to go with it.

9. When Marcus Clark wrote the book <u>For the Term of His Natural Life</u>.

10. Undoubtedly, because of all the publicity surrounding the scandal.

Run-On Sentences

A sentence fragment occurs when a sentence does not have everything it needs. However, there is such as thing as having too much. A **run-on sentence** happens when you combine two sentences without punctuating them properly. A run-on sentence (sometimes called a **fused sentence**) creates problems for the reader because it lacks either a stopping point or transitional words. Look at the following.

On Saturdays, my mother cooked soul food my family enjoyed these meals immensely.

This sentence is a run-on sentence because it combines two sentences without any punctuation:

<u>On Saturdays, my mother cooked soul food</u> <u>my family enjoyed these meals immensely</u>.

There are at least four different ways to fix a run-on sentence:

1. Use a period between the two independent clauses, creating two separate sentences.

2. Combine the sentences by using a comma and a coordinating conjunction.

3. Combine the sentences by using a semi-colon and, if desired, a conjunctive adverb.

4. Combine the sentences by subordinating one of the sentences to the other. If the first idea is the subordinate idea (dependent clause), add a comma at the end of it. If the first idea is the main idea (independent clause), do not add a comma.

Here is how the run-on sentence might look when corrected in each of these four ways:

1. On Saturdays, my mother cooked soul food. My family enjoyed these meals immensely.

2. On Saturdays, my mother cooked soul food, and my family enjoyed these meals immensely.

3. On Saturdays, my mother cooked soul food; in fact, my family enjoyed these meals immensely.

4. On Saturdays, when my mother cooked soul food, my family enjoyed these meals immensely.

Comma Spliced Sentences

A comma spliced sentence is like a run-on sentence in that two independent clauses are joined incorrectly. With a comma spliced sentence, the two independent clauses are joined with a comma, but without a coordinating conjunction.

Ahn wanted to go to the party at the youth center, her parents would not let her.

To fix a comma spliced sentence, your options are essentially the same as for the run-on sentence.

1. Remove the comma and use a period between the two main ideas, creating two separate sentences.

2. Combine the sentences by adding a coordinating conjunction after the comma.

3. Combine the sentences by removing the comma and adding a semi-colon and, if desired, a conjunctive adverb.

4. Combine the sentences by subordinating one idea to the other. If the subordinate idea comes first, keep the comma in. If you subordinate the second idea, remove the comma.

Here is how the comma spliced sentence might look when corrected in each of these four ways:

1. Ahn wanted to go to the party at the youth center. Her parents would not let her.

2. Ahn wanted to go to the party at the youth center, but her parents would not let her.

3. Ahn wanted to go to the party at the youth center; however, her parents would not let her.

4. Although Ahn wanted to go to the party at the youth center, her parents would not let her.

EXERCISE 4.7

Fix each of the following run-on and comma spliced sentences by adding a period to create two separate sentences.

David was studying for his bar mitzvah. H/*e had to learn how to speak Hebrew.*

1. Paul Robeson was an All-American football player at Rutgers University he also became a world-famous singer, actor, intellectual, and social activist.

2. The worst part of looking back are the regrets, the best part of looking forward is the hope.

3. The new sailor knew how to operate a navigational computer with ease he could not tie knots well.

4. Smiling sweetly, the actress called down to Romeo, the young actor had forgotten his cue.

5. Revolutionaries today are considered dangerous the country's founding fathers were all revolutionaries.

6. We do laundry every day the laundry basket always seems full.

7. The baby would not go the sleep, the parents were being driven crazy.

8. Paul brought flowers home for his mother she was very grateful.

9. The ambassador went to the official function reluctantly, she had hoped to avoid going.

10. The one-time ballet dancer was found homeless in the streets he had known some of the greatest stars of his time.

EXERCISE 4.8

Fix each of the following run-on and comma spliced sentences by using a comma and a coordinating conjunction to combine the ideas. Try to use each coordinating conjunction at least once.

so
Almost all cuisine in America comes from other countries, ^ learning to cook different foods has become an exploration of the world.

1. The jury was still out the lawyers for the defense were growing more confident.

2. The cows were being herded up the mountainside their clanging and mooing could be heard for miles.

3. Jared quit the basketball team, his grades had been suffering.

4. Lisa wanted a new, expensive stereo she asked her boss if she could work additional hours.

5. Victor could go to see his grandparents in Michigan for vacation he could go to the beach in Florida.

6. Martin found no peace in his home, he could not find it in the park.

7. The regatta began sailing on Tuesday, by Thursday Mitchell had to drop out.

8. The owner of the restaurant tried to vary his menu, then his regular customers started to leave.

9. Spike Lee is probably the most famous black film director in America I prefer movies made by John Singleton.

10. Alexandra appeared troubled, she was tossing her braids nervously and looking down at her feet.

EXERCISE 4.9

Fix each of the following run-on and comma spliced sentences by using a semi-colon and a conjunctive adverb to combine the main ideas. Try to use different conjunctive adverbs for each sentence.

;therefore,
Ethnic identities are becoming blurred nowadays ^ people will have to change their attitudes toward race and ethnicity in the future.

1. Ted worked hard on the farm to prevent crop loss the harvest failed anyway.

2. Watching the stars at night can be a peaceful experience star gazers should wear heavy, warm clothing in the winter.

3. It was the hottest day of the year, the community pool was packed.

4. The truck had broken down on the freeway, traffic was backed up for miles.

5. The ability to sing well is a true gift the ability to sing poorly is not.

6. Randall moved rapidly to close the deal he was able to get the best prices seen in over two years.

7. Appealing to a viewer's emotions is a powerful tool for advertisers they often make people fall in love with products just through their commercials.

8. Horses are majestic animals, not all of them are treated well.

9. Dr. Jacobsen's invention had the potential to make him very wealthy, the invention never actually worked.

10. Many artists believe that poverty is just a part of the artist's lifestyle other artists do become huge commercial successes.

EXERCISE 4.10

Fix each of the following run-on and comma spliced sentences by subordinating one of the ideas to the other.

Many Native American tribes are turning to gambling to make money/
because
∧ *other approaches have not been successful at wiping out poverty on reservations.*

1. One faction of the political party wanted to stay the course the other faction wanted a drastic change.

2. Einstein developed the theory of relativity, he developed the photon theory of light.

3. Three of the musicians waited on the stage, the fourth was still fighting his way through the crush of fans just off stage.

4. The story of Cinderella has been told in many languages and cultures it has different variations around the world.

5. The sisters had an intense hatred going back to their childhood they wound up trying to kill each other.

6. The prices for the dinner were quite high, the food was only average.

7. There was a breakdown in communications, the platoon was left stranded in enemy territory.

8. Our home's windows needed cleaning, Kenneth said he would clean them for $30.

9. Arlene moved to South Carolina she enrolled at a small, prestigious college.

10. The mobile home was on sale Roland was greatly interested in it.

Sentence Review

Examine the following sentences for sentence fragments. Fix any sentence fragments that you find. If a sentence is correct, mark it with a "C."

1. During the past ten years of difficulties, failures, and disappointments.

2. Toni Morrison, one of the greatest writers of our time.

3. Despite the presence of large numbers of hostile whites, James Meredith integrated the University of Mississippi.

4. After searching for his lost watch all night long.

5. The con man decided to leave town once he saw that the police were on to him.

6. To live and let live.

7. Working toward solutions to the problem of world hunger.

8. Jackie Robinson. More than just a great baseball player.

9. The combined efforts of many artists and technicians coming together in this film.

10. During the time that you were gone.

Examine the following sentences for comma splices or run-on errors. Fix the comma spliced and run-on sentences. Try to use each of the different correcting techniques at least once. If a sentence is correct, mark it with a "C."

1. You can start a savings account early, it will grow larger as you grow older.

2. While dog owning has its advantages, there are several problems you need to know about before buying a dog.

3. The work on the docks remained unfinished, the laborers had gone on strike.

4. Most athletes must exercise almost every day maintaining their good health is very important.

5. Work-related accidents were decreasing; therefore, additional safety regulations were not needed.

6. A marketplace in a foreign country can be exciting for tourists, there are a lot of things to be cautious about.

7. The computer program could not be adapted to the new computer, Hal had to scrap all of his plans.

8. The emotional qualities of the movie were undeniable the technical qualities were poor.

9. Abraham Lincoln's assassination brought many unintended effects, a government policy called "Reconstruction," intended to punish the southern states, was one.

10. Colin Powell was the first African-American to become the head of the Joint Chiefs of Staff, he served during the Persian Gulf War.

Applying the Sentence Lesson

In order to demonstrate your ability to identify and fix sentence fragments, run-on, and comma spliced sentences examine the second draft of your Chapter Writing Assignment and identify and fix sentence errors that you find.

Examine Mark's second draft with the sentence errors fixed. The places where the errors occurred are double-underlined, and the fixes are written in by hand, so that when Mark rewrites his assignment for the final draft, he can be sure to correct the errors. Note that Mark discovered two sentence fragments, one run-on sentence, and one comma spliced sentence.

Sports have done a lot to solve the problems of racism in this country. Different people come together in sports who might not otherwise learn about each other. There have been a lot of African-Americans who became famous for what they did in sports helping pave the way for civil rights. Jesse Owens competed and won against Nazis in 1936,/^Jackie Robinson integrated major league baseball in 1947. Their actions, and the actions of others like them, helping America change itself. How successful they were can be seen today in people like Michael Jordan ^ One of the most popular athletes ever which is a real sign of how far we've come. Jordan, an African-American, was incredibly popular not only as a basketball player, but also because of who he was ^ one sign of his popularity with blacks and whites is that he made over $500 million in endorsements! Of course, racism is still with us in different ways, but sports is one place to go to where no one is thinking about that anymore.

Writing the Final Draft

Rewrite your second draft, making sure that you have corrected all sentence fragments, run-on, and comma spliced sentences. This will be your final draft. Respond to the revision questions as you work on your rewrite.

Revision questions
- Does your paragraph have a strong sense of structure, with a beginning, middle, and end?
- Have you provided effective transitions as you move from one idea to the next?
- Have you moved from the general to the specific, including enough fully developed details to support your topic sentence?
- Does the paragraph employ the correct use of verbs?
- Have you corrected any sentence errors, such as fragments, run-ons or comma splices?

Hand in the final draft, with the materials from your prewriting, first draft, second draft, and any other materials you created in the process of writing this assignment.

When Mark created his final draft, he wanted not only to make sure that he had corrected errors, but that he had been as clear and specific as possible in his paragraph. He felt that one more example of a famous athlete breaking through racial barriers would help, so he went to the library and did a little research. What he found there helped him complete his final draft. He also deleted the sentence about how much money Michael Jordan made from endorsements, deciding to focus instead on the importance of race and sports.

Sports have done a lot to solve the problems of racism in this country. Americans come together to play sports who might not otherwise even know each other. For example, many African-Americans did amazing things in sports, which helped pave the way for civil rights. Jesse Owens competed and won against Nazis in the 1936 Olympic Games in Berlin, and Jackie Robinson integrated major league baseball in 1947. In 1961, Ernie Davis of Syracuse University became the first black to win college football's Heisman Trophy. The trails these athletes blazed helped today's athletes, like Michael Jordan. That Jordan is one of the most popular athletes ever which is a real sign of how far we've come in race relations. He is incredibly popular not only as a basketball player, but also because of who he is as a person. Thankfully, no longer is a person's race considered in whether or not that athlete is great. Of course, racism still exists, but sports is one place to go to where usually no one is thinking about that. People are just enjoying the game.

✔ PORTFOLIO CHECKLIST

In your portfolio, you should now have the following:

1. your brainstorming prewriting exercise.
2. a First Draft. The first draft should have all of the verbs underlined and their tense identified.
3. a Second Draft. The second draft should have any sentence fragments, run-on sentences, or comma-spliced sentences identified and corrected.
4. a Final Draft.

PARTING SHOT

1. What examples of racism have you witnessed?
2. What institutions in our society perpetuate racism?
3. What kinds of things has this country done to combat racism? How successful have these efforts been?

GOALS IN REVIEW

In this chapter, you have learned about

- brainstorming in two forms, listing and mapping, as a prewriting activity
- the power of using specific details in your writing
- verbs and verb tenses
- sentence fragments, run-ons, and comma spliced sentences

PRACTICE CHAPTER TEST

Part I

Identify the verb tense of the underlined verb or verb phrase in each of the following sentences.

1. Stevie <u>was playing</u> the new video game he received for his birthday.

2. By next Tuesday, Frank <u>will have been traveling</u> for over a year.

3. Tasha <u>is</u> not <u>waiting</u> for anyone.

4. Tyler <u>cried</u> about his missing blanket.

5. Whenever I <u>watch</u> that show on television, I think I'm wasting my time.

6. Jerry <u>will discover</u> that his study techniques are poor.

7. The workers <u>have tried</u> to get a raise for six months.

8. Cathy <u>will be visiting</u> her friends in San Francisco during her vacation.

9. The bank tellers <u>have been asking</u> all the customers for a picture identification.

10. Jordan <u>had</u> already <u>lost</u> his bid for re-election when he learned that he had been indicted on a bribery charge.

11. By the time Shawna graduates from college, she <u>will have taken</u> classes from almost every member of the physics department.

12. Leroy <u>had been hoping</u> to discover a new restaurant to eat at for lunch, but he could not find any he liked.

13. Huynh <u>was hoping</u> to get work at a Vietnamese grocery store.

14. Barlett <u>will have lived</u> in the house for eight years come next July.

15. Sharon <u>created</u> a mess she could not solve.

Part II

Examine each of the following sentences. If the sentence is a sentence fragment, mark it with the letters "FRAG," if it is a run-on sentence, mark it "RO," if it is a comma-spliced sentence, mark it "CS," and if it is correct, mark it "C."

_____ **1.** After turning in all of the evidence over to the police.

_____ **2.** The work stoppage was bad for everyone, however, the union felt that it had to be done.

_____ **3.** Football is becoming a more popular sport in other countries it still has a long way to go to surpass soccer in world-wide popularity.

_____ **4.** Amazed, Chris sat at his chair and began to compose a letter of protest.

_____ **5.** Renee, shocked to discover that the famous painting had been stolen in broad daylight.

_____ **6.** The electrical engineer lost his job he found a new one in an entirely new specialty.

_____ **7.** Marcel wanted to study piano, he persuaded his parents to give him lessons for his birthday even though they did not own a piano in their home.

_____ **8.** My mother likes to read the novels of Toni Morrison, my aunt prefers to read those of Terry McMillan.

_____ **9.** Terence wanted to move to Texas his wife agreed only as long as she could fly back home now and then.

_____ **10.** The Chinese New Year, which comes in spring.

The Media

CHAPTER GOALS

In this chapter, you will learn about

- a prewriting strategy called freewriting,
- avoiding wordiness,
- adjectives and adverbs, and
- misplaced modifiers.

The theme of this chapter is the media. The media include television, radio, movies, magazines, newspapers—all the different ways in which people receive and send pictures, words, ideas. In the contemporary world, the media seem present everywhere: at school, at home, at work, at play. While many people are fascinated and drawn to the media and their subjects, others are worried about the media's power—their ability to shape people's tastes, opinions, and desires.

OPENING SHOT

QUESTIONS ABOUT THE PICTURE

1. How are children affected by television?

2. What roles does television play in a family household?

3. How does television influence people's buying practices?

4. How does television interfere with or promote a person's growth and development?

READING

Questions to Consider

1. How much do the media—including television, magazines, radio, and newspapers—create or influence people's values?

2. How does the media's portrayal of families differ from the reality of families?

Words to Watch

au courant	current, up-to-date
mawkish	having an insipid, dull, or unpleasant taste
elegy	a poem or song expressing sorrow for someone who is dead
curmudgeonly	being like a crusty, ill-tempered old man
sado-necrophiliac	delight in cruelty combined with an erotic interest in the dead
insouciance	light-hearted unconcern

First Amendment First

John Derbyshire

1   On September 9, we had our annual block party in my suburban, lower-middle-class street. The event's showpiece was a talent show, the brainchild of our 10-year-old neighbor Siobhan. She herself performed three songs: "It Was Our Day," from the group B*Witched, and the Britney Spears numbers "What U See (Is What U Get)," and "Lucky."

2   For readers not au courant with the pop-music scene, the first of these songs is a mawkish elegy for a dead friend: "Heaven, heaven was calling you / Heaven, heaven needed you / I'll lay a rose beside you for ever." The second is a girl's protest against her boyfriend's possessiveness: "I know you watch me when I'm dancin' / When I party with my friends / I can feel your eyes on my back, baby / I can't have no chains around me." The third is about the inner loneliness of a

Hollywood star: "She's so lucky, she's a star / But she cry, cry cries in her lonely heart."

3   So there I was, sitting on a plastic chair on my neighbor's lawn, watching a 10-year-old girl singing about grief, sexual jealousy, and the hollowness of success. As I squirmed, I sank into reflections of the curmudgeonly kind: Is this all kids know nowadays? There used to be innocent songs that preteens could sing—I can remember a hundred of them. "Green Grow the Rushes-O" and so on. Now there are no topics, for anyone of any age, but sex and death.

4   Miss Spears had been in the newspapers that very morning; at the MTV Music Video Awards two nights before, the 18-year-old Britney had taken off everything but a few strategic spangles and performed the kind of dance for which lonely men in soiled raincoats used to pay extravagant door charges to ill-lit basement clubs. If I were to tell you I switched the thing off in disgust I would be guilty of a falsehood; but I am awfully glad my daughter Nellie (a 7-year-old whose contribution to the talent show was a faultless performance of Dvorak's "Humoresque" on violin) didn't see it. Yet even she already knows some Britney lyrics. They all do, preteens and pre-preteens. As parents say with a sigh, when you bring this up: It's the culture.

5   The culture came up often over the next few days. The following Monday the FTC released the report on the marketing of violence in the media. Meanwhile, the Senate Commerce Committee was holding hearings on the issue. Lynne Cheney showed up to urge show business to police itself, and to quote some lyrics from hip-hop star Eminem, who had won a major award at the MTV bash. One of Eminem's songs expresses the satisfaction a man feels at having raped and murdered his mother. Joe Lieberman went further before the committee, urging the FTC to step in and regulate media companies who would not tone down their products. Al Gore, on his way from one showbiz fund-raiser ($800,000) to another ($6.5 million), agreed.

6   What to make of all this? So far as public policy is concerned, there are three possible positions, identified here by those who take them.

7   My neighbors: it doesn't matter much, so there's no point in getting steamed. As an influence on the development of my children, my words and my example outweigh by a factor of hundreds anything Britney Spears does.

8   Mrs. Cheney: the media companies that promote creatures like Eminem should be shamed before the public, and thereby persuaded to mend their ways.

9   Gore-Lieberman and their trial-lawyer pals: Legislate, regulate, intimidate. Sure, there'll be some grumbling from Hollywood, but they will never defect to the party of the dreaded "Christian Right."

10   Most conservatives would sympathize with Mrs. Cheney; I greatly admire her myself. If, however, my neighbors are representative of the larger American public, as they probably are, then her program is a nonstarter. We must therefore choose between the first of the above options

and the third. Can there be any doubt which poses the greater threat to our ancient liberties?

11   What we are talking about here, remember, is sex and violence. The second of these gives me no trouble. I have never had much patience with the idea that children should be shielded from fictional violence. I would much rather my own children discover The Hunchback of Notre Dame as I did, in the thrilling sado-necrophiliac original, shot through with cruelty and lust, than via the lame jollity of the Disney version. Here I can appeal to the great storytellers of the past, who spared children very little. Check out the original "Cinderella," in which the ugly sisters get their eyes pecked out. Children take this stuff in stride. They may even, as Bruno Bettelheim argued, be helped by it. Certainly the evidence that exposure to graphic violence causes violent deeds is highly suspect: "Shooting the Messenger," a recent report by the Media Coalition (available on their website), persuasively refutes the kiddie-see, kiddie-do arguments.

12   Sex is more worrisome. As the doting father of little Nellie, I naturally spend a lot of time fretting about this. How will the vulgarity of our public entertainment shape her personality?

13   Our September 9 block party came on the anniversary of Elvis Presley's first appearance on the Ed Sullivan show 44 years ago. The following January, Sullivan had Elvis on for the third time; it was then that he issued his famous order for the singer to be shown only from the waist up, in order that the younger viewers might not be inflamed by the sight of his hip movements. We have traveled an awfully long way from Ed Sullivan to the MTV awards show. What is really surprising, though, is how little harm has been done. It needs some effort of imagination now to recall the alarm that Elvis raised at that time. Frank Sinatra called Elvis's music "the most brutal, ugly, desperate, vicious form of expression it has been my misfortune to hear." This comment reflected a widespread public attitude.

14   If, in 1956, you had asked any thoughtful American what consequences might follow from the abandonment of all customary restraint in entertainment, and from related phenomena like the attempted normalization of homosexuality, he would probably have said that the Republic could not survive such a transformation. Plainly these good people believed something that was, in fact, untrue: that the stability of society depended on the exclusion, by common consent, of certain things from the sphere of public display.

15   The insouciance of my neighbors in the face of today's popular culture is, therefore, quite reasonable. It's the culture—but it doesn't matter, it does no great harm.

16   To be sure, much mayhem has passed before our eyes since 1956. We have gone through Francis Fukuyama's "great disruption" with all its attendant phenomena: soaring rates of crime, bastardy, divorce, and so on. But we have come through to the other side at least; as Fukuyama himself points out, the indicators are trending downwards now, toward "re-normalization." And in all that happened, which was cause and which effect? Did Elvis—or Madonna, or Howard

Stern—have one-thousandth the influence on our culture that (say) the Pill had?

17   The world changes. As a conservative, I shall conserve what I can; but if I am to keep any influence over my children at all, some measured degree of acceptance is called for. There is a price to be paid for liberty, and Eminem and Britney Spears are the current coin in which that price must be paid. They will not be shamed, and they ought not to be banned: for if the guardians of our public virtue can outlaw hip-hop lyrics, you can be sure that "hate speech" will be their next target, and it is all too easy to imagine where that will lead. With the Second Amendment swirling down the drain, the survival of the First can no longer be taken for granted.

PREPARING TO WRITE

Freewriting

In Chapter 4, you learned about brainstorming, a prewriting activity based upon the idea of harnessing the mind's ability to create free associations among ideas. Another similar technique is freewriting. **Freewriting** tries, like brainstorming, to push ideas out of your mind and onto a sheet of paper. Freewriting is different from brainstorming: your thoughts are not chopped up into little words or phrases scattered on a page or down a vertical column. Instead, freewriting is more a "stream of consciousness" activity in which you write down your thoughts as fast as you possibly can.

The reason freewriting includes the word "free" is that you are free of concern or worry about *matters of correctness*. One of the great enemies of free association is the brain's tendency to edit or judge materials before they are allowed onto a page. A thought may strike your mind, but the next thing you might think is, "Oh, that's not very good, I can't write that down." This could prevent you from exploring the idea further. Be aware that you might have to go through several bad ideas to get to a good idea, but you'll never get there if you stop after the first bad idea.

Other concerns relate to spelling, grammar, and punctuation. However, worrying about these issues might stop your mind from exploring new ideas. Thus, freewriting should be done without concern for technical matters. Go ahead and make spelling errors—don't even bother to construct complete sentences. The point of a freewriting activity is to get ideas down on paper. Concern for correctness can come later.

Preparing Yourself to Write

In order to freewrite most effectively, do the following:

1. Set a timer. Just as you learned in the brainstorming instructions in Chapter Four, freewriting works best when it is done against the clock. The idea behind freewriting—of trying to put down on paper your thoughts as they come into your head—is completely undermined if you have an open-ended session, one in which you just keep going for as long as you want. In that case, you're likely to start thinking about "good" things to write and "bad" things not to write. Of course, the whole point of a freewriting session is to avoid thoughts like those. Set your timer for five minutes the first few times you are freewriting. With a little more practice, you can push the time to ten or fifteen minutes. Do not try to do longer periods of time because you'll end up in the same trap as an open-ended session: editing your thoughts before they wind up on paper.

2. Have a topic in mind. This will be your point of focus. A freewriting session that spends all of its time writing about irrelevant issues, such as planning your evening or wondering about an instructor's bad taste in clothing, is not much help. Keeping a topic in front of you will help keep your freewriting session productive.

3. Keep the pencil or pen moving throughout the entire session. Again, the point is to push yourself past the limits of what you already know you're thinking. If you run into trouble, write "I can't think of anything to say" over and over. If that doesn't work, trying repeating your topic over and over.

4. Don't think—write! That means you should not judge what gets written down on paper. When you freewrite, you are free to write as poorly as you want, using as many bad ideas as you can. That's the whole meaning of "free" in this activity. Don't worry about creating complete sentences or making sure that you're spelling everything correctly. You should have no concerns for technical correctness during a freewriting activity. This means no stopping to cross a word out, rewrite a phrase, or think about proper punctuation. Just keep writing whatever comes into your mind and worry about the quality of the ideas later.

5. Freewriting is to be done as you write normally—left to right along a line, not in a vertical column like a list, nor scattered around on the paper as in a mapping session. This should give your freewriting the appearance of "normal" writing. The benefit of this is that your use of language will be less choppy than in brainstorming. You'll draw more connections between one thought and another because your writing is apt to be more sequential, the ideas more connected.

6. After the timer marks the end of the session, you can read what you have written. Much of what you have done might not be helpful,

I Think The media is very responsible for how people Think about Things and how people wanT To have loTs of sTuff afTer all ThaTs how we learn abouT everyThing if you Think abouT iT I mean you learn abouT whaT's ouT There and whaT oTher people have and ThaT's really how people decide whaT To buy iTs Kind of silly in some ways I saw a commercial for pre-packaged coffee They made iT seem like counTing spoonfuls of coffee was so hard ThaTs rediculous buT I'll beT They sold a Ton of Those iT does seem like iT's always more, more, more and I can see how ThaT's caused a loT of problems for folks especially if you spend more Than you make

FIGURE 5.1 Sample of Freewriting Session

but, as you scan your freewrite, you'll find ideas cropping up here and there that might be the basis for further exploration.

In Figure 5.1, see an example of a freewriting session done by a student named Fanya in response to Chapter Writing Assignment question #1. Note that freewriting sessions should be handwritten rather than typed to allow for a smoother transition of thoughts to the page.

Prewriting

Now that you know how to freewrite, do a freewriting session on the subject of the Media or on a question from the Chapter Writing Assignment. Start off freewriting for five minutes. When you're done with the freewriting session, review the results. You might want to do a second freewriting session based on an idea that surfaced in your initial freewrite.

Freewriting Session

CHAPTER WRITING ASSIGNMENT

Write a 100- to 200-word paragraph in response to one of the following writing assignments. Instructions in the chapter will guide you through the writing process. At different points in the chapter, you will be asked to produce more work on this assignment. By the end of the chapter, you will complete your final draft.

1. How responsible are the media for fostering attitudes toward consumerism, attitudes that lead people to want more than they can have? Explain, using specific examples.

2. Have you ever seen a false depiction of yourself or your demographic group in the media? Did assumptions about your age, region, religion, lifestyle, appearance, or purchasing power ring false? Explain, using specific examples.

3. Respond to a recent editorial in a local newspaper or broadcast on a local television or news radio program. First, explain what the editorial said. Then, argue either for against the position in the editorial. Explain, using as many specifics as possible.

4. In his article "First Amendment First," John Derbyshire argues that media images do not influence children's behavior as much as the words and examples of their parents. Do you agree or disagree? Explain, using specific examples.

WRITING LESSON

Avoiding Wordiness

One of the hallmarks of good writing is that it does not bore its reader by using more words than necessary. Wordiness can produce more than boredom; wordy passages can confuse the reader. Keep in mind a simple maxim: Whatever does not add, detracts. Or, even more simply: Less is best.

There are several causes of wordiness. One of the most common is that a writer is unaware of what he or she is actually saying. If a writer fails to pay close attention to the words he or she uses, the writer risks being repetitious and vague. Wordiness involves failing to pay attention to the job each word does in a sentence.

As a writer, you need to make every word count. A general rule of thumb is to cut out any word that is not helping your writing.

Original:

Anita Hawkes, who has the job of being Director of Operations, had to answer criticisms and defend herself against charges that she was not competent.

Improved:

Anita Hawkes, the Director of Operations, had to answer to charges of incompetence.

Many excess words are used in the original sentence. The phrase "who has the job of" is unnecessary, since placing the job title after Anita Hawkes' name indicates that that is her job. The phrases "answer criticisms" and "defend herself against charges" are redundant. The phrase "she was not competent" can be reduced to "incompetence."

EXERCISE 5.1

Rewrite the following sentences, eliminating as many unnecessary words as possible.

The golf ball had a scratch on it which was such that the ball could not be used by the golfer for ordinary play.

The golfer could not use the scratched golf ball.

1. Due to the fact that he was going to move and relocate to Phoenix, which is in Arizona, he had to put his house up for sale and find a buyer.

_____

_____

2. Because she drove a smaller version of a van that was intended for family use, she was often called upon and asked by friends and neighbors to share riding space in her vehicle for their dependent minors.

_____

_____

3. It is clear at the present moment in time that the parts of cow flesh that are currently being warmed over hot coals is at the optimum point in time for being removed from the heat source.

_____

_____

4. In the month of January, Rebecca made the decision to fly in an airplane to Australia for a month of vacation, rest, and relaxation.

_____

_____

5. At the end of her oral presentation which she had to say in front of the class, Wilma was required to give a summary of her findings on the subject of illegal immigration.

_____

_____

6. Norm came to the conclusion that his life had been a less than successful enterprise up to that particular date in time.

_____

_____

7. The betrothed couple at the nuptial celebration gave their thanks and gratitude to their assembled and invited guests, family, and friends.

_____

_____

8. The patient started to feel dizzy and experience vertigo, and because of this, had to be seated in a wheelchair.

_____

_____

9. The workers who were employed by the company forced a job action and voted to strike against the company because of poor working conditions.

_____

_____

10. At home, where I live with a large number of family members, I feel comfortable and at ease, even if it is cramped and crowded.

_____

_____

Being Specific and Concise

One of the ways to avoid wordiness is to choose your words well. Wordiness is caused by vagueness. Careless writers avoid specific and concise terms, favoring more general ones instead. Use specific words whenever possible.

Original:

Mariah's new car was a blue-green type color.

Improved:

Mariah's new car was teal.

Often, there is a tendency to use vague terms—many times these are adjectives and adverbs—that do not themselves contain much meaning. Words such as *very, really, too, extremely, quite, many, a lot, definitely* add little meaning to sentences. Imagine a child being asked by Santa how good she was this year:

"Oh Santa, I've been very good."
"How good is that?" asks Santa.
"Very, very, very, very, very, very good!" the girl replies.

Of course, this is somewhat of an exaggeration, but much student writing is filled with words that could replaced by better, more accurate adjectives or adverbs:

"I've been saintly," the girl replies.

EXERCISE 5.2

Find words that better express the ideas behind the original, more general words or phrases. More than one answer is possible for each example.

ugly   grotesque

1. unhappy

2. interesting

3. definitely stupid

4. really smart

5. not talkative

6. exciting

7. attractive

8. very angry

9. good

10. bad

Avoiding Types

Another tendency of overly general writing is to identify types rather than specifics. Wordiness can be avoided if you know exactly what you are trying to communicate. Choose words that are as close as possible to what you mean.

Here are some examples.

General	Specific
the very quick runner	the sprinter
a sports celebrity	Tiger Woods
a difficult marital experience	divorce
an oral form of communication	talking
a major university	Harvard University
an exciting movie experience	watching *The Titanic*
a nice car	a Mercedes E320

EXERCISE 5.3

Find specific, concrete images and examples to replace the following general words.

an American hero <u>Charles Lindbergh</u>

1. a bad television show _____

2. an important book _____

3. a major life change _____

4. a hobby that many people enjoy _____

5. an award _____

6. a delicious meal _____

7. an important educational achievement _____

8. a problem with a car _____

9. a great comedian _____

10. an unfortunate occurrence _____

Combining Sentences

One way to eliminate wordiness is to combine sentences together to avoid the needless repetition of words.

Original:

The cat was black. The cat was purring. The cat was Monica's. The cat was under the bed.

Improved:

Monica's purring, black cat was under the bed.

The trick to combining sentences successfully is to find ideas or words in sentences that are repetitive. Then, you can essentially *fold* one sentence into another.

Original:

The floor of the basement was wet. It was also slippery.

In these sentences, the word "it" refers to "The floor of the basement," so that is where the repetition occurs.

Improved:

The floor of the basement was wet and slippery.

ZOOM-IN PRACTICE

Take each of these five phrases and reduce them to a single word.

a university-level teacher with a Ph.D. _____

body movements and actions intended to generate healthful effects on the body _____

a very famous actor or actress _____

a play that features a lot of singing _____

a multi-level apartment in which the bedroom areas are above the living areas _____

EXERCISE 5.4

Make a single sentence from each of the following groups of sentences by combining them.

Diane worked.

She worked in Tacoma.

Tacoma is in Washington.

She worked as a production assistant.

She worked for a local television station.

Diane worked as a production assistant for a local television station in Tacoma, Washington.

1. The team was a football team.
   The team was from the University of Nebraska.
   The team lost an important game.

   _____

2. Janice and Steve decided to take a walk in the park.
   The park was located in the center of town.
   They walked in the evening.

   _____

3. Amy usually gets fish when she eats out.
   Amy rarely orders steak.

   _____

4. The famous writer gave a talk.
   The talk was at the local library.
   The local library was crowded.

   _____

5. The photographs were of an orphanage.
   The photographs were in black and white.
   The photographs were very powerful emotionally.

   _____

6. Thomas was about to enter the classroom.
   The classroom was empty.
   Thomas remembered that he had forgotten his books.

   _____

7. This was the way it had to be, she said.
   She said that they would always be friends.

   _____

8. Many people nowadays seem to enjoy gourmet coffee.
   They are quite willing to spend a lot of money for a cup
   of coffee.

   _____

9. The youth of America have many opportunities for the future.
   They have many problems to overcome as well.

   _____

10. Jericho looked for his maps.
    He was desperate.
    He ransacked his glove compartment.

    _____

Using the Active Voice

You can write sentences using two voices: the **active voice** and the **passive voice.** These terms refer to ways sentences are constructed. Take a look at the following pair of sentences:

Active voice:

Ryan threw the football.

Passive voice:

The football was thrown by Ryan.

In the active voice sentence, the sentence follows the word pattern of Subject-Verb-Direct Object. "Ryan" is the subject of the sentence, and he is also the doer of the action, which is the verb "threw." The "football" is the direct object because it is the receiver of the action.

However, in the passive voice sentence, these relationships are turned around. The subject of the passive voice sentence is "football" even though it is still the receiver of the action. The verb is now a verb phrase, "was thrown." Ryan, the doer of the action, is now at the end of the sentence in a prepositional phrase. In fact, the sentence can be rewritten to remove Ryan completely:

The football was thrown.

The passive voice has two main problems: it is wordier, and the doer of the action is often removed. A passive voice sentence puts the emphasis on the receiver of the action.

There are times, such as when the doer of an action is unknown, when you might want to use the passive voice to emphasize the receiver of the action. For example:

The victim had been strangled.

To know if a sentence is written in the passive voice, look at the form of the verb. The passive voice uses a verb phrase that includes using a form of the verb "to be" as helping verb, and the past participle of the main verb.

to be	+	past participle
was		thrown
had been		strangled

EXERCISE 5.5

Rewrite each of the following sentences by changing them from passive voice sentences to active voice sentences. In some sentences, you may need to supply the doer of the action when you shift to the active voice.

The television was turned off by the irate parent.

The irate parent turned off the television.

1. Children are influenced by media images.

   _____

2. Society's demand for easy, non-threatening entertainment has caused the steady decline in the quality of television programming.

   _____

3. The kidnappers were told that their request to appear on television was denied.

   _____

4. The secret was leaked to the press.

   _____

5. Due to the success of their show, the actors were given a large pay raise.

   _____

6. The candidate for mayor was shown in an unflattering pose by the newspaper.

   _____

7. The tabloid was sued by the actress for printing lies about her.

   _____

8. The sportswriter was told never to enter the baseball team's locker room again.

   _____

9. The television audience was shocked by what the host had to say.

   _____

10. Cigarette commercials were banned from television many years ago.

   _____

Writing the First Draft

After Fanya completed her freewriting exercise, she looked over the results and decided to write a paragraph based on the phrase "needless goods." Her paragraph was written to respond to Question #1 from the Chapter Writing Assignment.

Television is constantly pushing the idea that I need to buy many things that actually aren't needed at all. These needless goods are often things that are supposed to save people time, but I think what they really do is make people lazy, and people wind up paying a lot for that laziness. I saw, for example, a commercial for pre-measured coffee so you don't have to count how many spoonfuls of coffee you're putting in the machine. That kind of thing is not needed. Anyone can count spoonfuls of coffee. Another thing is that all this is pushing people to buy more and more things as a way to find happiness. It's like they want people to see that if you have a lot of things you'll be happy—like the good cars, the best clothes, even deodorants. You'll meet the right guy or girl if only you have their product. It's not just commercials too. There are lots of shows that show how rich and famous people live, and that sets a goal for everyone else. If people could ignore the hype, and just pay attention to what they need, and have good sense, then they wouldn't have too many problems. But everywhere you look, the message is the same—buy, buy, buy!

Now that you have completed your prewriting assignments and learned about avoiding wordiness, you are ready to write your first draft in response to one of the questions in the Chapter Writing Assignment. Complete this draft before beginning the Grammar Lesson.

GRAMMAR LESSON

Adjectives and Adverbs

When you describe what something looked like, how fast or slow it was, what its color was, or how large or small it was, you use adjectives and adverbs. We use **adjectives** to describe nouns and pronouns, and we use **adverbs** to describe verbs, adjectives, and other adverbs.

Adjectives answer questions such as Which? What kind? What color? And How many? By doing this, they help the reader to imagine or understand better what is being described. As such, adjectives help the reader make distinctions. This means that they help the reader to distinguish one thing from another. Examine the following sentences.

The car was involved in an accident.
The <u>expensive</u>, <u>new</u>, <u>black</u> car was involved in a <u>fatal</u> accident.

The first sentence contains no adjectives. As such, the sentence is general and non-specific. We have absolutely no sense of what the car was like, nor do we have a sense of how serious the accident was. In the second sentence, the adjectives give the reader a more specific understanding of the car and of the accident as well.

Adjectives that answer the question "Which?" point out the distinguishing characteristic or position in an order of something.

Karen told the waiter that her <u>favorite</u> dessert was ice cream.
The <u>first</u> book on the shelf is autographed by the author.

Other adjectives answer the question "What color?"

The <u>purple</u> stain would not come out of the carpet.
The meat was now <u>gray</u>.

Some adjectives answer the question "What kind?"

Her <u>cotton</u> blouse shrank in the dryer.
The <u>large</u> size of his <u>tax</u> refund drew some <u>unwanted</u> questions.

Even other adjectives answer the question "How many?"

<u>Six</u> times a week Sukisha waters all <u>five</u> of her tomato plants.
Pedro bought a <u>dozen</u> rolls from the baker.

Adverbs answer questions such as When? How? How often? Where?
And To what extent? Adverbs make verbs come alive—speeding them
up or slowing them down, intensifying or lessening the effect of adjectives or other adverbs. Examine the following sentences.

Jacklyn tried to hide her contempt for the reporters.
Jacklyn <u>rarely</u> tried to hide her contempt for the reporters.

By simply adding the adverb "rarely," the meaning of the entire sentence has been changed. Other adverbs placed in the same position
would change the sentence in other ways as well:

Jacklyn <u>often</u> tried to hide her contempt for the reporters.
Jacklyn <u>carefully</u> tried to hide her contempt for the reporters.

Some adverbs answer the question "When?"

At the convention's opening session, Murray spoke <u>first</u>.
The commercial ran <u>late</u> in the evening.

Other adverbs answer the question "How?"

Dr. Zeman asked <u>quietly</u> about her friend's condition.
The mayor talked <u>passionately</u> about the new food program for the
homeless.

Still other adverbs answer the question "How often?"

Wayne used the new truck only <u>sparingly</u>.
The players <u>regularly</u> spent extra hours in the weight room.

Some adverbs answer the question "Where?"

Put the computer printer <u>here</u> on the desk.
Tommy's friend moved <u>away</u>.

Some adverbs answer the question "To what extent?"

The insurance policy only <u>partially</u> covered the damage.
The Padres <u>completely</u> dominated the Dodgers today.

EXERCISE 5.6

Indicate whether the underlined word in each sentence is an adjective (adj.) or an adverb (adv.).

> *adj.*   *adv.*   *adj.*
> *The* <u>award-winning</u> *documentary* <u>sympathetically</u> *depicted the* <u>difficult</u>
>
>   *adj.*
> *lives of* <u>migrant</u> *laborers*.

1. <u>Approximately</u> seventy percent of all incoming freshmen need some form of remedial math or English.

2. The <u>newest</u> shows on network television strive to give a greater sense of realism.

3. The closing of the asylum has left people wondering where the <u>mental</u> patients will go.

4. <u>Clearly</u>, the best movie of 1999 was *Shakespeare in Love*.

5. The news of her daughter's engagement was the <u>best</u> thing she had heard in months.

6. All of the <u>financial</u> news was good, for a change.

7. The audience cheered <u>wildly</u> as the opera singer walked on stage.

8. Martin was <u>seriously</u> depressed about losing his job as chief bottlewasher.

9. The BMW took the turn <u>too</u> quickly and plunged off the cliff.

10. Sean liked his mother's <u>red</u> pantsuit best.

The Form of Adjectives and Adverbs

Many adverbs are formed by adding the suffix -ly to an adjective. Here is a list of some common adjectives and their adverb counterparts.

Adjective	Adverb	Adjective	Adverb
close	closely	private	privately
critical	critically	public	publicly
entire	entirely	quick	quickly
false	falsely	slow	slowly
full	fully	soft	softly
heavy	heavily	thorough	thoroughly
important	importantly	various	variously
light	lightly	vital	vitally

Note: Remember that the presence of the "-ly" ending alone does not guarantee that a word is an adverb. Be sure to examine the word's function in the sentence.

DON'T LOSE FOCUS!

Do not use adjectives and adverbs merely to prop up poor word choices. For instance, one of the characteristics of bad writing is the tendency to overuse adverbs such as "very," "really," and "too." Instead, try to find better nouns, verbs, adjectives or adverbs to express your meaning.

Original:

That movie was really very bad.
The car was going really quick.
The speech went on too long.

Improved:

That movie was terrible.
The car was speeding.
The speech dragged on.

Good and Well

One of the more confusing pairs of adjectives and adverbs is "good" and "well." The trouble comes in two ways: first, in casual conversation, most speakers do not use the words properly. That creates trouble when speakers turn to writing and are unable to use the words correctly. The second problem is the word "well" can be used as both an adjective and an adverb, but the meaning of the word changes as it changes its part of speech.

Good. "Good" is usually an adjective. That means "good" is used to describe a noun or a pronoun.

> The baked ham tasted good. ("Good" describes the baked ham.)

> The good dog was rewarded with a biscuit. ("Good" describes the dog.)

Well. "Well" is used often as an adverb. That means "well" is used to describe a verb, an adjective, or another adverb.

> My grandparents played cards well into the night. ("Well" describes how long they played.)

> Mark did well on his calculus exam. ("Well" describes how Mark did on the exam.)

"Well" can also be an adjective. As an adjective, "well" means "a state of good health."

> Muffin is well now that she has come back from the veterinarian's office. ("Well" indicates that Muffin is enjoying a state of good health now.) Angelica does not feel well this morning because she has a temperature. (The negative "not" shows that Angelica feels sick, or "not in a state of good health.")

EXERCISE 5.7

Fill in each blank with either "well" or "good" as required.

The director and the actors worked well *together.*

1. It is _____ that you finally know the truth about Mr. Ed.

2. If you pass this class, remember to say that you did

   _____ in your class.

3. Jonathan feels _____ about getting a large pay increase.

4. Taya feels _____ now that the pills have broken her fever.

5. The food smells _____ in the kitchen.

6. The women's field hockey team played _____ in the championship game.

7. This semester, Sean did _____ in math but not in English.

8. Stanley lives _____ off the interest alone from his inheritance.

9. The rich oil magnate knew the politics of Washington

_____.

10. A parent who worries about his or her children's safety is a

_____ parent.

GRAMMAR REVIEW

Identify whether the underlined word in each sentence is an adjective or an adverb.

1. Non-fat milk is the <u>best</u> drink to have in the morning.

2. Lynda made it <u>quite</u> clear where she stands on that issue.

3. The radio-show host spoke <u>emotionally</u> about the latest foreign conflict.

4. The pictures on the wall were hung in a very <u>careless</u> fashion.

5. Her singing voice is <u>so</u> beautiful that I don't ever want to forget it.

6. We must focus <u>squarely</u> on the task at hand.

7. The <u>purple</u> stain on the sofa refused to come out.

8. The kids left their toys <u>outside</u>.

9. The <u>real</u> problem is the financing for the project.

10. Bo looked about the room <u>nervously</u>.

Fill in the blank with either "well" or "good" as appropriate.

1. Morgan did _____ on his test today.

2. It is _____ that you renewed your license so early.

3. Mary Beth is not feeling _____ today due to the flu.

4. Professional golfers must play _____ on Thursday and Friday or they will not make the cut for Saturday and Sunday.

5. The music selections for next week's party sound

_____.

Applying the Grammar Lesson

Examine the first draft of your Chapter Writing Assignment for your use of adjectives and adverbs. Put parentheses around the adjectives in your draft, and put square brackets around the adverbs.

Look at how Fanya marked her first draft:

Television is [constantly] pushing the idea that I need to buy (many) things that [actually] aren't needed at all. (These) (needless) goods are [often] things that are supposed to save people time, but I think what they [really] do is make people (lazy), and people wind up paying for that laziness. I saw, for example, a commercial for (pre-measured) coffee so you don't have to count how (many) spoonfuls of coffee you're putting in the machine. (That) kind of thing is not needed. Anyone can count spoonfuls of coffee. (Another) thing is that all this is pushing people to buy (more) and (more) things as a way to find happiness. It's like they want people to see that if you have a lot of things you'll be (happy)—like the (good) cars, the (best) clothes, even deodorants. You'll meet the (right) guy or girl if [only] you have their product. It's not [just] commercials [too]. There are lots of programs that show how (rich) and (famous) people live, and that sets a goal for everyone [else]. If people could ignore the hype, and [just] pay attention to what they need, and have (good) sense, then they wouldn't have [too] (many) problems. But everywhere you look, the message is the same—buy, buy, buy!

Writing the Second Draft

Now that you have completed the Grammar Lesson, you are ready to write the second draft of your Chapter Writing Assignment. Complete this draft before beginning the Sentence Lesson. Respond to the revision questions as you work on your rewrite.

Revision questions
- Does your topic sentence respond directly to the question you have chosen?
- Do you have any words that can be cut? Are there phrases that can be rewritten as a single word? Are there sentences that can be combined?
- Have you used specific and direct adjectives and adverbs? Have you avoided overused adverbs such as "very," "really," and "too"? Make sure you have as many specific details as possible to explain your ideas to the reader.

After identifying the adjectives and adverbs in her paragraph, Fanya rewrote her paragraph. In her second draft, Fanya tried to eliminate unnecessary words by combining sentences whenever possible and selecting her adjectives and adverbs more carefully. She made an attempt to tighten her paragraph by focusing more strongly on one single idea, and expressing that idea in her topic sentence, which is the first sentence of her paragraph.

Here is Fanya's second draft:

The media are constantly pushing us to buy needless goods, to the point where people forget what's really important in life. Commercials often push products that are supposed to save people time, but what they really do is make people lazy. People wind up paying a lot for that laziness. I saw, for example, a commercial for pre-measured coffee so you don't have to count how many spoonfuls of coffee you're putting in the machine. Anyone can count spoonfuls of coffee! This pushes people to buy more and more things as a way to find happiness. By buying the expensive car, the stylish clothes, even perfumed deodorants, they want you to think that then you'll be happy. With their product, you'll meet the right guy or girl. Everywhere you look—television, radio, billboards, even the Internet—there's so much of a push to buy things that no one can resist. It's not just

commercials either. Showing how rich and famous people live, you can

see them on television or in magazines. That sets goals for everyone

else which most of us can never hope to match. To ignore the hype

and have good sense, it can help you to avoid unnecessary purchases.

But it's not easy because nowadays, everywhere you look, the

message is the same—buy, buy, buy!

SENTENCE LESSON

Misplaced Modifiers

While you can easily see how adjectives and adverbs modify or describe other words in a sentence, you might not have realized that phrases or clauses can do the same thing. That is, phrases or clauses can act like modifiers—like adjectives or adverbs.

Confusion can happen when you fail to put the phrase or clause near the word that it modifies. When a phrase or clause modifies the wrong word, the result is a **misplaced modifier.** Misplaced modifiers can create a misunderstanding, sometimes an unintentionally humorous one.

> There was a report of an arson fire set in a downtown warehouse by the fire department.

> A treat that is always tasty, Miss Miller baked us her cookies.

> The reporter will talk to the football star who scored the winning touchdown during tonight's news broadcast.

Each of the sentences can easily be rewritten.

> The fire department reported the arson fire set in a downtown warehouse.

> Miss Miller baked us her cookies, a treat that is always tasty.

> The football star who scored the winning touchdown agreed to talk to the reporter during tonight's news broadcast.

EXERCISE 5.8

Rewrite the following sentences to correct the misplaced modifiers.

Diego made a speech to his class that was very passionate.

Diego made a very passionate speech to his class.

1. Glenn watched the scandal on his new television that rocked the nation.

   _____

2. Kecia wore a dress to her class that was very attractive.

   _____

3. Falling from the tree, Alejandro watched the leaves.

   _____

4. Jostling with other shoppers, the cart full of groceries was difficult for Laurie to handle.

   _____

5. Grazing on soft, fresh shoots of grass, the hunter aimed his gun at the deer.

   _____

6. Turning sour and spoiled, Fred discovered the milk that had been left outside.

   _____

7. My daughter found our lost dog driving around the neighborhood.

   _____

8. Pale with fear and anxiety, the plane took off with Angelica strapped tightly to her seat.

   _____

9. The passengers waited for the subway in the terminal that was to go to Central Park.

———————————————————————————————

10. The mowers worked outside while I tried to listen to classical music making a lot of noise.

———————————————————————————————

Similar to the misplaced modifier is the **dangling modifier,** in which the word to be modified is not in the sentence. To correct a dangling modifier, rewrite the sentence to include the word which is being modified.

Original:

Leaving early in the morning, the apartment complex was quiet.

Rejected at every turn, singles bars no longer seemed appealing.

After replanting the garden, the roses started to do much better.

Rewritten:

When Habib left early in the morning, the apartment complex was quiet.

Rejected at every turn, Douglas decided that singles bars no longer seemed appealing.

After we replanted the garden, the roses started to do much better.

EXERCISE 5.9

Rewrite the following sentences to correct the dangling modifiers.

Looking at every music magazine in the store, there were still no articles on my favorite rock band to be found.

Even though I looked at every music magazine in the store, I still could not find any articles on my favorite rock band.

1. As a child, my grandmother used to bake for me often.

———————————————————————————————

2. To avoid becoming overweight, stop eating sweets and fatty foods and exercise more.

_____

3. After working for days, Tonisha's essay was excellent and received the highest grade possible.

_____

4. Standing at the beach, the waves crashed onto the rocks with ferocious power.

_____

5. Nearly broke, a Christmas gift seemed out of the question.

_____

6. Having repaired the roof, the house looked perfect once again.

_____

7. After training for a year, the marathon was a rewarding experience.

_____

8. Frustrated, the game had become virtually an obsession.

_____

9. Exhausted from travel, Harold's patience had worn thin.

_____

10. To talk to the supervisors, a sign-up list is available in the office.

_____

Sentence Review

Rewrite the following sentences to correct any dangling or misplaced modifiers.

1. Close to death, the doctor knew something drastic needed to be tried for the patient.

_____

2. Lying down on the bed, Gabriela's headache only got worse.

_____

3. Fighting hard and ferociously, the battle was won by the Marines.

_____

4. To leave the country, a passport is needed.

_____

5. Barking wildly, the old man tried helplessly to control the dogs.

_____

6. Consuela gave a dress to her mother that was wild and daring.

_____

7. The customer signaled the waiter with a raised eyebrow.

_____

8. Working all night long, the problem with the computer was finally solved.

_____

9. After paying off the bills, the checking account was nearly empty.

_____

10. Simmering for hours, Jody showed me how to really make spaghetti sauce.

_____

Applying the Sentence Lesson

Identify and rewrite any dangling or misplaced modifiers that you may find in your Chapter Writing Assignment paragraph. Look at Fanya's second draft. Sentences with dangling or misplaced modifiers are underlined:

The media are constantly pushing us to buy needless goods, to the point where people forget what's really important in life. Commercials often push products that are supposed to save people time, but what they really do is make people lazy. People wind up paying a lot for that laziness. I saw, for example, a commercial for pre-measured coffee so you don't have to count how many spoonfuls of coffee you're putting in the machine. Anyone can count spoonfuls of coffee! This pushes people to buy more and more things as a way to find happiness. By buying the expensive car, the stylish clothes, even perfumed deodorants, they want you to think that then you'll be happy. With their product, you'll meet the right guy or girl. Everywhere you look—television, radio, billboards, even the Internet—there's so much of a push to buy things that no one can resist. It's not just commercials either. Showing how rich and famous people live, you can see them on television or in magazines. That sets goals for everyone else which most of us can never hope to match. To ignore the hype and have good sense, it can help you to avoid unnecessary purchases. But it's not easy because nowadays, everywhere you look, the message is the same—buy, buy, buy!

Writing the Final Draft

After you have identified and corrected all dangling or misplaced modifiers, rewrite your second draft. This will be your final draft. Respond to the revision questions as you work on your rewrite.

Revision questions

- Does your paragraph have a sense of structure, with a beginning, middle, and end?
- Have you included enough specific details and examples in your paragraph to support the topic sentence?
- Have you checked your paragraph further to cut unnecessary words, phrases, or sentences?
- Have you examined all of your modifiers to determine if each is the best possible word to convey your intended meaning?

Hand in the final draft, with the materials from your prewriting, first draft, second draft, and any other materials you created in the process of writing this assignment.

Fanya located four sentences with dangling or misplaced modifiers. In the process of preparing her final draft, she corrected those sentences.

Also, she looked for more ways to cut down on the use of unnecessary words, and she added details to better convey her meaning. Here is her final draft.

The media are constantly pushing consumers to buy needless goods, to the point where people can develop money problems. Commercials often push products that are supposed to save time, but what they actually do is make people lazy. People wind up paying for that laziness. For example, one commercial sells pre-measured coffee for people too busy to count how many spoonfuls of coffee they've used. Anyone can count spoonfuls of coffee! This pushes people to buy more and more things as a way to find happiness. They want you to think that when you buy the expensive car, the stylish clothes, even perfumed deodorants, you'll be happy. With their product, you'll meet the right guy or girl. Everywhere you look—television, radio, billboards, even the Internet—there's a push to buy things. It's not just commercials either. Television programs and magazines show how the rich and famous live, setting goals most of us can never hope to match. Ignoring the hype and having good sense can help you to avoid unnecessary purchases. However, it's not easy because all around, the message is the same— buy, buy, buy!

PORTFOLIO CHECKLIST

In your portfolio, you should now have the following:

1. your freewriting exercise.
2. a First Draft. The first draft should have the adjectives identified with parentheses and adverbs identified with squared brackets.
3. a Second Draft. The second draft should have dangling or misplaced modifiers underlined.
4. a Final Draft.

PARTING SHOT

1. Does the media promote violence?
2. Has television news become more sensational than serious?
3. What are the differences between news reporting on television and in newspapers or magazines?

GOALS IN REVIEW

In this chapter, you learned about

- a prewriting strategy called freewriting
- avoiding wordiness
- adjectives and adverbs
- misplaced modifiers

PRACTICE CHAPTER TEST

Part I

Circle the right word for each sentence.

1. You have to know your English grammar (well, good) in order to pass this exam.

2. The military rejected the latest design for a new jet fighter, saying that it flew too (slow, slowly) for its mission.

3. The book print was too (small, smally) for me to read.

4. My grandmother went in for an operation last week, but now the doctors say that she is doing (well, good).

5. The test is (to, too, two) hard for Jim.

6. Tania felt (certain, certainly) that this time all would be different.

7. The dinner smelled (well, good) to Uncle Henry.

8. The runner (final, finally) finished the marathon after running for eight hours.

9. The report notes that many managers make decisions too (quick, quickly), without consulting subordinates who may have helpful, first-hand knowledge.

10. Elden felt (angry, angrily) about the election results.

11. The team played very (well, good) in the preseason but faltered in the regular season.

12. The synthetic fabric felt (roughly, rough) against her skin.

13. The struggle went on for hours, with each combatant trying (desperately, desperate) to gain an advantage.

14. Marcia wants to go to the store, (to, too, two).

15. The candidate wanted to win the election (badly, bad).

Part II

Underline the dangling or misplaced modifier in each of the following sentences.

1. Hoping to create a diversion, an accident was staged by the robbers in front of the bank.

2. Returning to his home after being in the U.S. for three years, Kenya seemed suddenly strange and foreign to Barasa.

3. Ethnic neighborhoods appeal to immigrants which are still found in many of America's cities.

4. Mowing the lawn on a Saturday morning, life seems simple and pleasant.

5. Lovette hid the love letter underneath the mattress which was from Enrique.

6. The tests were given back to the students at the end of the period which the instructor had graded.

7. Walking through the rain, her shoes were ruined.

8. Hoping to promote multicultural awareness on campus, the Festival of Colors was started by the college president.

9. Tired of being dominated by outsiders, a movement to create a free Hawaii is gaining power among native Hawaiians.

10. The trouble at the beach was started by angry locals fighting with tourists which was shown on television.

6

Technology

CHAPTER GOALS

In this chapter, you will learn about

- a prewriting strategy called the Question Grid,
- subject-specific language,
- commas, and
- pronoun case.

The theme of this chapter is Technology. As the twenty-first century begins, technology is playing an increasingly large role in how we work, how we learn, and even how we play. As technology becomes more complicated, fewer of us understand how things work, yet we find ourselves relying increasingly on it, from computers, to cars, to medicines, and even to our entertainment. The good that can be done by technology—and the disturbing possibilities for the misuse of technology—have created much public discussion.

QUESTIONS ABOUT THE PICTURE

1. In what practical ways is technology an important part of your life?

2. Is there a mix of tradition and technology in your life?

3. In what ways to do you find technology de-humanizing?

4. How does technology separate you from your parents' generation?

OPENING SHOT

READING

Questions to Consider

1. Do you embrace technology or do you avoid it? Explain why.

2. What are some of the advantages of new technology? Think of some specific examples of new technologies and the benefits that have come from them.

3. What are the problems of new technology? Think of some specific examples of new technologies and the problems that have come with them.

Words to Watch

inept	lacking in ability; generally incompetent
contraption	a device or gadget
e-mail	electronic mail
snail mail	regular postal service mail
opt	to make a choice
tedious	tiresome; boring
rite of passage	a ritual associated with a crisis or change in a person's status (such as becoming an adult)
savvy	practical know-how

Stop the Clock

Amy Wu

1 My aunt tends to her house as if it were her child. The rooms are spot-less, the windows squeak, the kitchen counter is so shiny that I can see my reflection and the floors are so finely waxed that my sister and I sometimes slide across in socks and pretend we are skating.

2 Smells of soy sauce, scallions and red bean soup drift from the kitchen whenever I visit. The hum of the washing machine lulls me to sleep. In season, there are roses in the garden, and vases hold flowers arranged like those in a painting. My aunt enjoys keeping house, although she's wealthy enough to hire someone to do it.

3 I'm a failure at housework. I've chosen to be inept and unlearn what my aunt has spent so much time perfecting. At 13, I avoided domestic chores as my contribution to the women's movement. Up to now, I've thought there were more important things to do.

4 I am a member of a generation that is very concerned with saving time but unaware of why we're doing it. Like many, I'm nervous and jittery without a wristwatch and a daily planner. I am one of a growing number of students who are completing college in three years instead of four—cramming credits in the summer. We're living life on fast-forward without a pause button.

5 In my freshman year, my roommates and I survived on Chinese take-out, express pizzas and taco take-home dinners. We ate lunch while walk-ing to class. Every day seemed an endless picnic as we ate with plastic utensils and paper plates. It was fast and easy—no washing up. My girl-friends and I talked about our mothers and grandmothers, models of domesticity, and pitied them. We didn't see the benefits of staying at home, ironing clothes and making spaghetti sauces when canned sauces were almost as good and cleaning services were so convenient. A nearby store even sold throwaway underwear. "Save time," the package read. "No laundry."

6 We baked brownies in 10 minutes in the microwave and ate the frosting from the can because we were too impatient to wait for the brownies to cool. For awhile we thought about chipping in and buying a funky contraption that makes toast, coffee, and eggs. All you had to do was put in the raw ingredients the night before and wake up to the smell of sizzling eggs, crispy toast and rich coffee.

7 My aunt was silent when I told her about plastic utensils, microwave meals and disposable underwear. "It's a waste of money," she finally said. I was angry as I stared at her perfect garden, freshly ironed laun-dry and handmade curtains. "Well, you're sure wasting your time," I said defensively. But I wasn't so sure.

8 It seems that all the kids I know are time-saving addicts. Everyone on campus prefers e-mail to snail mail. The art of letter writing is long gone. I know classmates who have forgotten how to write in script, and print like 5-year olds. More of us are listening to books instead of read-ing them. My roommate last year jogged while plugged in. She told me

she'd listened to John Grisham's "The Client." "You mean you read," I corrected. "I didn't read a word," she said with pride.

9   My nearsighted friends opt for throw-away contacts and think the usual lenses are tedious. A roommate prefers a sleeping bag so she doesn't have to make her bed. Instead of going to the library to do research, we cruise the Internet and log on to the Library of Congress. Schoolkids take trips to the White House via the Internet and Mosaic. I heard that one school even considered canceling the eighth-grade Washington trip, a traditional rite of passage, because it's so easy to visit the capital on the Information Superhighway. I remember how excited my eighth-grade classmates and I were about being away from home for the first time. We stayed up late, ate Oreos in bed and roamed around the Lincoln Memorial, unsupervised by adults.

10   It isn't as if we're using the time we save for worthwhile pursuits like volunteering in a soup kitchen. Most of my friends spend the extra minutes watching TV, listening to stereos, shopping, hanging out, chatting on the phone or snoozing.

11   When I visited my aunt last summer, I saw how happy she was after baking bread or a cake, how proud she seemed whenever she made a salad with her homegrown tomatoes and cucumbers. Why bother when there are ready-made salads, ready-peeled and -cut fruit and five-minute frosting?

12   Once, when I went shopping with her, she bought ingredients to make a birthday cake for her daughter. I pointed to a lavish-looking cake covered with pink roses. "Why don't you just buy one," I asked. "A cake is more than a cake," she replied. "It's the giving of energy, the thought behind it. You'll grow to understand."

13   Slowly, I am beginning to appreciate why my aunt takes pleasure in cooking for her family, why the woman down the street made her daughter's wedding gown instead of opting for Vera Wang, why the old man next door spends so much time tending his garden. He offered me a bag of his fresh-grown tomatoes. "They're good," he said. "Not like the ones in the supermarket." He was right.

14   Not long ago, I spent a day making a meal for my family. As the pasta boiled and the red peppers sizzled, I wrote a letter to my cousin in Canada. At first the pen felt strange, then reassuring. I hand-washed my favorite skirt and made chocolate cake for my younger sister's thirteenth birthday. It took great self-control not to slather on the icing before the cake cooled.

15   That night I grinned as my father and sister dug into the pasta, then the cake, licking their lips in appreciation. It had been a long time since I'd felt so proud. A week later my cousin called and thanked me for my letter, the first handwritten correspondence she'd received in two years.

16   Sure, my generation has all the technological advances at our fingertips. We're computer-savvy, and we have more time. But what are we really saving it for? In the end, we may lose more than we've gained by forgetting the important things in life.

PREPARING TO WRITE

Question Grid

Asking questions of a topic is an excellent way to consider a number of different issues related to it, and your attitude towards it. One way to ask questions of your topic in an organized manner is to create a question grid. A **question grid** is a way to arrange questions and answers so they are easily read.

To create a question grid, use parallel vertical and horizontal lines. Along one side (the top, for instance) you arrange a series of questions. Along another side (the left side, for instance) you arrange a series of items related to your topic.

For example, take the issue of whether technology has helped or hurt society. Kenny arranged his grid as follows.

	Is it good or bad for society?	Is it cheap or expensive?	Helpful or more of a nuisance?	Will its effect on society last?
Cell phones and pagers	Bad—no one can get away from them	Too cheap—even teenagers can afford them	Nuisance—pagers and phones ring at awkward times	Creates too many ways to bother people
Music on CD-ROMs	Good—better quality music	Slightly expensive	Helpful—totally replaced albums because they never scratch or warp	Only superficial impact; doesn't change the music
Internet	Good—faster communication and more data easily found	Expensive at first (if you have to buy a computer); relatively cheap after that	Very helpful for students, researchers and people who want to play games or chat	Huge impact—affects how we learn about things, how we buy things, how we meet people

FIGURE 6.1   Kenny's New Technologies Question Grid

Preparing Yourself to Write

In order to prepare a question grid, you must first establish what your topic will be. Then, make up a list of questions. Figure 6.1 has four questions, but you may wish to ask even more. Don't feel limited by the size of paper—in fact, you might want to use an $8\frac{1}{2}'' \times 11''$ inch sheet *sideways* so that you can get more questions on the sheet along the horizontal line.

How could you best develop the questions and the items to be examined? First, you might read more about your topic in a library. Find relevant articles in magazines or newspapers. Reading them can be an excellent way to educate yourself about a topic. If you already have a specific topic—say, for instance, that you decided to write about the Internet—you could narrow your topic even further to aspects of the Internet, such as free speech on the Internet, computer crimes and fraud, or copyright and privacy issues.

Once you have a topic and some items, decide which questions would be relevant. In Figure 6.1, the questions relate to the *value* of the item and its effects on society. However, you might choose an entirely different direction. For example, you might want to ask more personal questions, such as how you use a certain technology, or how you feel about its place in the world. You might ask questions about something's usefulness, or what impact it will have on other, older technology. Essentially, the questions are yours to determine.

Prewriting

Now that you know how to do a question grid, create one of your own using the subject of Technology, or you may look ahead to one of the questions in the Chapter Writing Assignment. Either use the question

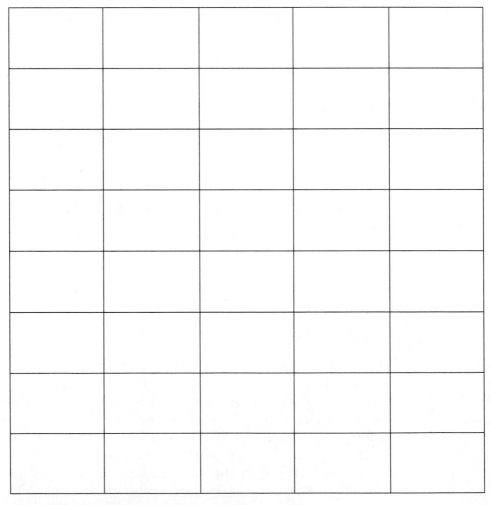

FIGURE 6.2   Question Grid

grid in the book or take a blank 8½″ × 11″ sheet of paper, and draw a grid, using vertical and horizontal lines (again, you might want to turn the sheet on its side, so that the horizontal lines are longer). Decide which questions are relevant for your topic, and write them across the horizontal line at the top of your sheet. Then break your topic down into specific items that you can examine, and list them along the vertical line on the far left margin.

Once you have laid out your grid, fill in your answers for each item and each question. Take time when you are finished with the question grid to review the results before beginning to draft your writing assignment.

CHAPTER WRITING ASSIGNMENT

Write a 100- to 200-word paragraph in response to one of the following writing assignments. Instructions in the chapter will guide you through the writing process. At different points in the chapter, you will be asked to produce more work on this assignment. By the end of the chapter, you will complete your final draft.

1. Have technological advances made daily life better or worse? Explain, using specific examples.
2. Do you consider yourself more of a technophile (someone who embraces technological advances) or a technophobe (someone who avoids or fears technological advances)? Explain, using specific examples.
3. Choose a recent technological invention or product and argue whether its effects will be more positive or negative.
4. Amy Wu, author of "Stop the Clock," suggests that technological advances have come at the expense of human relationships and traditional customs and practices. Argue for or against this position, using specific examples.

WRITING LESSON

Using Subject-Specific Language

Read the following passage.

When I went into the hospital emergency room, I found my father on a bed that had wheels on it that several people in strange clothes were pushing into a small area. There, a bunch of people stood around him, talking to each other using words I couldn't understand. An older woman, who I guess was the doctor, ordered that a needle be stuck into his arm. The needle was connected to a long, thin tube which came up to a plastic bag that was filled with something clear that was hanging from what looked a little like a coat rack. All sorts of machines were beeping and buzzing, and I had no idea if my father was going to be okay or not.

Although the passage relates a potentially dramatic event—a visit to a hospital emergency room—the writing itself lacks power. One reason is the lack of subject-specific language; that is, the writer does not express himself or herself very well because of an inability to name things properly and describe actions. **Subject-specific language** refers to the vocabulary or terms that one might expect to be used in a given situation, condition, or environment. In a hospital emergency room, we expect to see words such as the following:

gurney	physician	IV unit
smock	resuscitator	EMT (Emergency
nurse	hypodermic needle	Medical Technicians)

If the writer used more subject-specific language, the same passage might read as follows:

When I went into the hospital emergency room, I found my father on a gurney being wheeled into a room. There, the EMTs who brought him in and the emergency room nurses stood around him, exchanging directions and information. The physician on duty, an older woman, ordered them to start an IV immediately. An IV unit was brought over, and a needle was inserted into my father's arm. A resuscitator beeped and buzzed. I had no idea whether my father was going to be okay or not.

By using subject-specific language, the writer is able to more clearly draw a picture for the reader.

Using subject-specific language might take a little extra work—you might have to do some research to learn the proper names of things or procedures. However, that is better than having to fall back on vague descriptions that carry little meaning.

One way to ensure that you have subject-specific language is to explore the literature, such as books or magazine articles, that is available on a given topic before you begin writing. In that literature, you will find vocabulary words that relate to your topic. When you learn the subject-specific vocabulary, you can use these words in your writing, rather than struggling with uncertain or vague terms.

Kenny, the student who did the Question Grid in the prewriting exercise, came up with a list of terms used with the Internet:

Internet

World Wide Web	hacker
web site	virus
web page	download
e-mail	plug-ins
browser	HTML
search engine	hypertext
link	chat rooms
URL or address	

Remember, in writing, the point is to communicate your ideas to your reader. To do that, subject-specific language is essential.

ZOOM-IN PRACTICE

Write down ten words associated with one of the following topics:

cooking	gardening	clothing	physical fitness	jewelry

Writing the First Draft

After Kenny completed his Question Grid, he looked over the results and decided to write a paragraph based on the positive aspects of the Internet. His paragraph was written in response to Question #1 from the Chapter Writing Assignment.

The Internet has a more positive than negative influence on the world today. Some people think, because some web sites are devoted to sex, and some crazy people post instructions on how to build a bomb, that the Internet must be a bad thing. It's not. People, who use the Internet, are mostly using good. After all the Internet is simply a way to find information quickly. You can get on a computer in one part of the country and read a newspaper from another. You can tour museums in Europe without ever leaving home. If you want to leave home you can even buy airline tickets, hotel rooms, and rental cars right from your computer, before you go. Chat rooms normally aren't places, where sexual predators hang out but just places for people with similar interests to talk and exchange ideas. The number of people doing bad things on the web, is quite small compared to the total number of users. The Internet has overall been a real boost for the economy for shut-ins and for college students doing research. It's definitely good.

Now that you have completed your prewriting assignment, you are ready to write your first draft in response to one of the questions in the Chapter Writing Assignment. Complete this draft before beginning the Grammar Lesson.

GRAMMAR LESSON

Commas

The comma is a frequently misused punctuation mark. This is the unfortunate result of believing that a comma should be placed "wherever you pause." The trouble with that alleged "rule" is simple: people don't speak the same way and might pause at places where others might not.

Also, how long must a pause be to qualify for a comma? It is impossible to determine.

This Pandora's box of trouble can be avoided by learning that there are specific rules regarding the use of commas. A few of the rules require some judgment on your part, but most of the rules are clear and straightforward. In fact, you're probably familiar with most of them already, without even knowing it.

One way to learn how commas are used is to look at the different situations in which you might use a comma.

1. **Use a comma after an introductory word, phrase, or clause.**

Introductory words

Well, some people find that sort of thing entertaining.

Yes, we know about the computer virus that has infected the student lab.

Oh, I'm not sure about that.

Introductory phrases

After the party at Adam's house, no one felt ready to go home.

To understand how the system works, you have to use it yourself.

Showing no regard for his own life, the rescue worker entered the crumbling building to search for survivors.

Her purse stolen, Sara had no way to prove her identity to the security guard.

Introductory dependent clauses

Although the movie ran longer than normal, the audience did not seem to mind.

While the children played on the swings, the parents set up the picnic lunches.

Before the band could begin playing, they had to find their lead singer.

2. **Use a comma before a concluding element (such as a phrase or clause) if it qualifies, contrasts, or sends the logic of the sentence in a different direction.**

Ingrid often has trouble sleeping, but not tonight.

I find television boring, sometimes even numbing.

What mattered to her in a shoe was style, not comfort.

Reilly doesn't want to hear from him, unless it's to apologize.

Note: Some instructors will disagree with this last example. Many prefer that the writer not use a comma before a concluding dependent clause.

Reilly doesn't want to hear from him unless it's to apologize.

Place commas in the following sentences, using rules 1 and 2 as your guide. If a sentence is already correct, mark it with a "C."

Failing to understand the nature of the problem, Morgan shut the computer off.

1. His patience gone he started to yell at everyone around him.

2. Although few people have lived through a night on Mt. Everest Martin is one of them.

3. I try to bring joy into the world not troubles.

4. The boarder left the house because the landlady was too intrusive.

5. After all that has been said and done we have got to see this project through to the end.

6. Still much was left unsaid.

7. Dancing down the grocery aisles Carla created quite a scene.

8. Amazingly the jury declared the defendant "not guilty."

9. The gas tank empty the driver had to walk all the way to a service station.

10. Raising his voice Andrew announced his intentions.

3. **Use commas to set off nonessential elements, such as appositives, phrases, or clauses.** (An appositive is a word or phrase which renames another noun or pronoun.) The key word in this rule is "nonessential." This means that the element is not necessary in order to identify the noun or pronoun being described. If the information in the element is needed to identify the noun or pronoun, then the element is considered <u>essential</u> and it will take no commas.

Nonessential appositives

Puppo, my old friend, still lives in San Francisco.

The motorcycle gang, the 'Burban Bikers, stepped into the bar for a drink.

Spain, a poor country, suffers from many economic troubles.

Nonessential phrases

The lawyer, hoping to be elected as a judge, took a tough stance against crime.

Simon, disappointed for months, finally found his lost love.

Marilyn, showing a great deal of restraint, led the drunk to the door.

Nonessential clauses

Sergeant Durrell, who captured the intruder, was given special recognition.

Her husband, who works for the Internal Revenue Service, has a hard time keeping friends.

Santa Barbara, which lies along the coast north of Los Angeles, is a popular vacation destination.

DON'T LOSE FOCUS!

Knowing the difference between essential and nonessential elements is crucial in your use of commas. Essential elements take no commas; nonessential ones do. How can you best determine which you have? Examine the noun or pronoun being described by the element and determine whether you know exactly who is being spoken of in the sentence.

Sentence with a non-essential clause

Sergeant Durrell, who captured the intruder, was given special recognition.

Sentence with an essential clause

The soldier who captured the intruder was given special recognition.

In the first sentence, the subject "Sergeant Durrell" is specific; therefore, the clause "who captured the intruder" is a modifier (giving additional information about Sergeant Durrell). In the second sentence, the subject "the soldier" is too general. The reader does not know which soldier is being referred to. That's why the clause "who captured the intruder" is essential: it is essential in order to know *which* soldier is being given special recognition. In a sense, the clause names the soldier.

EXERCISE 6.2

Place commas in the following sentences, using rule 3 as your guide. If a sentence is already correct, mark it with a "C." Pay special attention to whether an element is essential or nonessential.

Doctor Nguyen, who studied at Berkeley, devised a computer model of the human immune system.

1. The pink Cadillac that Elvis bought his mother is still on display at Graceland.

2. The bum worn and haggard slumped down on the railroad tie.

3. Nicole's father who works in plastics wears good-looking suits to work.

4. The rowing team hoping for a small miracle watched as the other team's skiff overturned.

5. The researcher who worked inside the government lab was leaking secrets to a foreign country.

6. His wedding anniversary which is in early August is usually a very happy occasion.

7. The classic motorcycle belonged to Ricky Shoemaker a noted cycle enthusiast.

8. *Casablanca* my favorite movie is on television tonight.

9. The computer which defeated the chess grand master had a special design.

10. Of his three children, the one who lives in Canada seems the happiest.

---

4. **Use a comma, or a pair of commas, to set off an interrupting element.**

However, Martin is going to see the movie with his mother.

The examination, moreover, was held in the old music hall.

Amy, not Heidi, was the prom queen last year.

The book club decided to read a novel by Toni Morrison, the one from Oprah's book list, before next month's meeting.

The shopowner, I believe, was charged with fraud.

The answer, in reality, is not blowing in the wind.

5. Use a comma before a coordinating conjunction when it joins two independent clauses.

I don't want do this, but I have to.

Karen's new computer does not work with her old printer, so she must buy a new one.

The soldiers and sailors were sent to a foreign battlefield, and their families worried about them.

Note: If there is one subject with two or more verbs, remember that you have only one clause, and no comma should be used before the coordinating conjunction.

Every evening the couple watches television and eats dinner on the living room sofa.

6. Use a comma to join three or more elements in a series.

The fashion designer had homes in Paris, New York, and Hong Kong.

The old drunk claimed that in his youth he had scaled the Himalayas, swum the English Channel, and dated Hollywood starlets.

In order to build that dam, the engineers must draw up plans, the electric company must find private financing, and the local politicians must vote to approve the project.

Note: Some instructors prefer that you not use a comma before the final element. Check with your instructor for his or her preference.

The fashion designer had homes in Paris, New York and Hong Kong.

7. Use a comma to join coordinate adjectives.

The loud, obnoxious, and rude neighbor ruined the perfect life on Maple Street.

The fashion model eagerly drank her daily ration of cold, non-fat milk.

The tired, hungry, and frightened refugees were led to the shelter by the Red Cross workers.

Note: Do not use a comma between modifiers that do not modify the same word.

The red velvet shoes were placed carefully in the thin cardboard box. ("red" modifies "velvet" which modifies "shoes"; "thin" modifies "cardboard" which modifies "box")

EXERCISE 6.3

Place commas in the following sentences, using rules 4 through 7 as your guide. If a sentence is already correct, mark it with a "C."

The software was only written, I'm afraid, for computers that are no longer in use.

1. The filing process was quick easy and efficient.

2. The birds were not native to the area but they adapted to it well.

3. However the reason for the technical errors was not clear.

4. The sailors decided in fact to declare a mutiny.

5. Grandma's long red cotton sweater is hanging in the hall closet.

6. The clerk locked the store's doors closed up the cash register and tallied the evening's receipts.

7. She was unable to travel to the opening of the new store or call the people who were expecting her there.

8. The war had made the soldier naturally cautious but he liked the thought of seeing a new land.

9. The squat dark vase will be perfect for holding those types of flowers.

10. The early morning sun woke Alex from his slumber.

---

8. **Use a comma to prevent misreading of the sentence.**

   To know more, students will need to read more.
   Those who do, do not always understand the frustration of those who don't.
   Seconds before, the audience started to applaud.

9. **Use a comma to separate a direct quotation from its formal introduction or formal conclusion.**

   Jerry said, "Be careful with that gun."
   "Not over my dead body," replied Shauna.

Note: If the formal expression (of who said the quotation) is *inside* the quotation, commas should appear on each side of the expression.

"I don't believe," commented Edward, "that I ever claimed to be perfect."

10. **Use a comma to separate the date from the year in a sentence, and following the year if it appears before the end of the sentence; to separate distinct parts of an address, such as street addresses, cities and states; and, to separate a proper name from letters indicating a degree or title.**

June 6, 1944, is a date that will always be remembered in American history.

Send this package to 2031 Steilen Drive, Anchorage, Alaska 99654.

The authors of this article are Julieanne Stevens, Ph.D., and Joseph Ho, M.D.

EXERCISE 6.4

Place commas in the following sentences, using rules 8 through 10 as your guide. If a sentence is already correct, mark it with a "C."

"This should be heaven," muttered Cassandra, "but it feels more like Brooklyn."

1. To understand Sarah Ann listened closely.

2. This letter was postmarked April 16 1999.

3. "Do you suppose" asked Bruce "that she would go out on a date with me?"

4. This happened on Friday February 13.

5. The drug samples were intended for Glenn Demlinger M.D.

6. September 7 1992 was one of the happiest days of my life.

7. Walter said "And that's the way it is."

8. To cook the skin must first be removed.

9. The client wanted the package sent to 344 Hollister Avenue Goleta California 93110.

10. "Eat anything you can find" smiled Linda.

GRAMMAR REVIEW

Place commas in the following sentences, using all the comma rules as your guide. If a sentence is already correct, mark it with a "C."

1. Mom I think I need your help.

2. The rock band frustrated and bored destroyed the hotel room.

3. The advertisements claimed moreover that the diet pills were safe.

4. The chief executive wanted his portrait done on canvas in somber tones not on velvet with fluorescent paints.

5. John who was directing the show decided who would make the cast and who would not.

6. Under the present system too many people can get away with fraud.

7. Locked out of his home the man tried to break in through a window.

8. "I can tell" sneered the evil warrior "that you have been training for this day."

9. 1984 was a fabulous year but 1991 was even better.

10. The suspect described as tall with curly black hair was last seen carrying a long silver case.

Applying the Grammar Lesson

Examine the first draft of your Chapter Writing Assignment to check for the proper use of commas. Consult the list of ten rules to ensure that you can justify each of your commas. Here is Kenny's first draft. He noticed a number of commas that needed to be removed, which he marked with a circle, and he noticed where he needed commas, which are marked with bold typeface and an underline.

The Internet has a more positive than negative influence on the world today. Some people think, because some web sites are devoted to sex, and some crazy people post instructions on how to build a bomb that the Internet must be a bad thing. It's not. People, who use the Internet, are mostly being good. After all, the Internet is simply a way to find information quickly. You can get on a computer in one part of the country and read a newspaper from another. You can tour museums in Europe without ever leaving home. If you want to leave home, you can even buy airline tickets, hotel rooms, and rental cars right from your computer, before you go. Chat rooms normally aren't places, where sexual predators hang out but just places for people with similar interests to talk and exchange ideas. The number of people doing bad things on the web, is quite small compared to the total number of users. The Internet has overall been a real boost for the economy, for shut-ins, and for college students doing research. It's definitely good.

Writing the Second Draft

Now that you have completed the Grammar Lesson, you are ready to write the second draft for your Chapter Writing Assignment. Complete this draft before beginning the Sentence Lesson. Respond to the revision questions as you work on your rewrite.

Revision questions
- Does your topic sentence respond directly to the question you have chosen?
- Examine your paragraph. Are there any general words or terms that could be replaced by more subject-specific language?
- Do you have enough specific, concrete examples to help your reader understand your ideas?
- Have you checked each comma against the ten rules?

After correcting for his use of commas, Kenny was ready to write more. In his second draft, he tried to use subject-specific language whenever possible. In his new sentences, he was more careful with his use of commas. He tried to improve on his paragraph by arguing more about the usefulness of the Internet. To that extent, he chose to make his second-to-last sentence his topic sentence, which then became the first sentence of his paragraph.

Here is Kenny's second draft.

The Internet has been a positive influence on the world because it has been a boost for the economy, for shut-ins, and for college students doing research. Although some people think the Internet is bad because some web sites are devoted to sex and some crazy people post instructions on how to build a bomb, people whom use the Internet are mostly being good. After all, its simply a way for people like you and I to find information quickly. Also, a lot of business is conducted over the Internet. Many traditional businesses offer online shopping. Other businesses, sometimes called "e-businesses" strictly operate online. For them who can't get around well due to physical illness, injury, or some other problem, the Internet can help. They can read newspapers from around the country or tour museums in Europe without ever leaving home. Those whom want to leave home can even buy airline tickets, hotel rooms, and rental cars right from the computer. Us students do a lot of research over the Internet. Not only are there newspapers and television networks with web sites, but also many college libraries make their offerings available over the Internet. The students themself benefit most by doing homework without actually being in the library. Overall, the Internet has made life a lot better for many people.

SENTENCE LESSON

Pronoun Case

Case refers to the different forms that pronouns take in a sentence depending on how they are used. There are three cases: subjective, objective, and possessive. If you look at how personal pronouns appear in these three cases, their uses will become clear.

Subjective	Objective	Possessive
I	me	my, mine
you	you	your, yours
he	him	his
she	her	her, hers
it	it	its
we	us	our, ours
they	them	their, theirs

The **subjective case** is used when pronouns act as the subject of a clause. The **objective case** is used when pronouns act as an object in a sentence. The **possessive case** is used when the pronoun acts to show ownership or possession of something.

For many fluent speakers of English, choosing the right case for a pronoun occurs instinctively. There are a few situations, however, when the question of which case to use may not be obvious.

Misuse of Case in a Prepositional Phrase

Some writers become confused when using pronouns in a prepositional phrase, especially if the phrase has more than one object joined with the word "and." In conversational English, there is tendency to use the subjective case in this situation. Remember, however, the objective case should be used because the pronoun is an object of the preposition.

Incorrect

Why don't we just keep this a little secret between you and I?

Correct

Why don't we just keep this a little secret between you and me?

Incorrect

To we students, the news of the fee increase came as a shock.

Correct

To us students, the news of the fee increase came as a shock.

Note: Even though this last example may sound awkward, notice that the word "us" is the object of the preposition "to." The pronoun must be presented in the objective case.

Misuse of Case with an Appositive

An appositive is a phrase made up of nouns or pronouns which modifies or renames another noun or pronoun. Remember to stay consistent with the pronoun—its case is determined by its function in the sentence.

Incorrect

The three players—Cory, Thomas, and him—were in trouble from the start.

Correct

The three players—Cory, Thomas, and he—were in trouble from the start.

Incorrect

The city council members told us (Yolanda and I) that we had no right to hear their deliberations on personnel matters.

Correct

The city council members told us (Yolanda and me) that we had no right to hear their deliberations on personnel matters.

Misuse of Case in a Comparison

Comparisons can lead to confusion about case if the comparison is not explicitly completed.

Incorrect

Skip is richer than me.

Correct

Skip is richer than I.

If you complete the sentence explicitly, the reason for using the subjective case is clear.

Skip is richer than I am.

Misuse of Case in a Subject Complement

Remember that subject complements are *not* direct objects. A direct object is something which is acted upon by a subject. Direct objects appear in sentences which have action verbs. Subject complements are joined or connected to subjects by linking verbs. Therefore, subject complements take the subjective case.

Incorrect

It was him who murdered the school dean.

Correct

It was he who murdered the school dean.

Incorrect

The driver who parked in the handicapped zone was her.

Correct

The driver who parked in the handicapped zone was she.

Incorrect

The substitute teacher will be me.

Correct

The substitute teacher will be I.

Note: In common usage, the subject and complement in the above sentence would likely be reversed.

I will be the substitute teacher.

DON'T LOSE FOCUS!

Comparisons in sentences can be confusing if you do not express their meaning explicitly. Examine the following sentences:

Cathy is not as interested in sports as him.
Cathy is not as interested in sports as he.

Both of these sentences can be considered correct, depending on the intended meaning. If the comparison is meant to refer to a compared level of interest in sports, then the second sentence would be correct, and thus could be written out more fully:

Cathy is not as interested in sports as he is.

However, if the comparison was meant to compare the level of interest in sports Cathy has to her level of interest in the male "he," then the first sentence would be correct, and could be written out more fully as:

Cathy is not as interested in sports as she is interested in him.

Writers should express their ideas explicitly if there is any chance of confusion in the comparison.

EXERCISE 6.5

Choose the correct word in the parentheses.

It was (they, them) who created the computer virus.

1. My sister can shoot basketballs better than (I, me).

2. It was (he, him) who told the police about my petty thievery.

3. Some easterners don't understand that (we, us) Californians have a serious side, too.

4. The boss told (we, us) employees that the project had to be finished by the end of the month.

5. Nicole couldn't decide if seeing you and (I, me) had been a mistake.

6. Tab, along with Jack and (I, me), went fishing at the lake.

7. The star player left tickets for his family and (she, her).

8. Nobody understands how (we, us) night people suffer in an 8 to 5 job.

9. Angelica doesn't go to sporting events as often as (I, me).

10. The mystery guest on the late show will be (she, her).

Who/Whom

In conversational English, the use of the word "whom" has virtually disappeared. When you are writing in college, however, you will be expected to know when to use "whom" properly. This is actually fairly simple if you remember that "whom" is the objective case of "who."

Subjective	Objective	Possessive
who	whom	whose

If you have to decide whether to use "who" or "whom" in a sentence, you can determine whether the pronoun is subjective or objective by substituting the more familiar words "he" or "him." If "he" would be correct, use "who," and if "him" would be correct, use "whom."

"This package should be mailed to (who/whom)?"

If you choose between "he" or "him," you should easily see that the sentence would correctly read:

"This package should be mailed to him."

Therefore, the correct version should be:

"This package should be mailed to whom?"

See how this technique works on the following sentences:

(Who/Whom) did she visit late at night?
(Who/Whom) put up the bail money for Dixie?
He does not care (who/whom) receives the credit for the project.

The correct sentences read:

Whom did she visit late at night?
Who put up the bail money for Dixie?
He does not care who receives the credit for the project.

The same rules apply for "whoever" and "whomever." These pronouns are used to refer to "whatever person." They can be used as subjects or objects, but not as possessives.

Whoever thought of mixing pickles with grape jelly was quite original.
You can place the blame on whomever you wish.

EXERCISE 6.6

Choose the correct word in the parentheses.

Good jobs in the telecommunications industry are available to anyone (who, whom) has enough training and practical experience.

1. (Who, Whom) left these pillows on the floor?

2. I want to talk with (whoever, whomever) is in charge of the sales campaign.

3. The leftovers can be eaten by (whoever, whomever) wants them.

4. To (who, whom) should this letter be addressed?

5. Lucy decided that (whoever, whomever) can pay the most should sponsor the event.

6. Mary Beth has already reserved the church for her wedding, no matter (who, whom) the unlucky groom is.

7. The new car was delivered to the woman (who, whom) purchased it last week.

8. The agent (who, whom) the scriptwriter called was not available for a meeting.

9. The hacker (who, whom) broke into the FBI's files was found guilty of felony crimes.

10. The artist was willing to paint a portrait for (whoever, whomever) was ready to pay him.

Misuse of the Possessive Pronouns

As you could see from the list of personal pronouns, some pronouns have two forms in the possessive case. Some possessive pronouns function as adjectives, and others function as subjects or subject complements. Here is a list of possessive pronouns and their functions:

Adjectives	Subjects or Subject Complements
my	mine
your	yours
his	his
her	hers
its	its
our	ours
their	theirs
whose	whose

In <u>my</u> opinion, the inheritance should be <u>mine</u>. ("my" modifies "opinion"; "mine" is a subject complement indicating ownership of the inheritance)

<u>His</u> was the winning ticket. ("His" is the subject while indicating ownership of the winning ticket)

The patent for the invention was <u>theirs</u>. ("theirs" is a subject complement indicating ownership of the patent)

It's clear that <u>hers</u> was the best application. ("hers" is a subject indicating ownership of the application)

Who's working on <u>our</u> problem? ("our" modifies "problem")

Note: The possessive "its" has no apostrophe. "It's" is a contraction for "it is" or "it has." Similarly, the possessive "whose" has no contraction. The word "who's" is a contraction for "who is" or "who has."

The train lost <u>its</u> caboose somewhere south of the junction. ("its" modifies "caboose")

<u>Whose</u> car is that? ("Whose" modifies "car")

The lovely singing voice was <u>whose</u>? ("whose" is a subject complement indicating ownership of the voice).

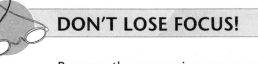

DON'T LOSE FOCUS!

Because the possessive case modifies a noun or pronoun, use it with gerunds (a verbal that has the -ing form of a verb). You do this because a gerund functions as a noun.

Incorrect:

The audience was annoyed by <u>him</u> talking throughout the movie.

Correct:

The audience was annoyed by <u>his</u> talking throughout the movie.

EXERCISE 6.7

Choose the correct word in the parentheses.

(*It's*, *Its*) *clear that computer technologies will affect the future of publishing.*

1. The search for artificial intelligence has had (it's, its) difficulties.

2. (Who's, Whose) responsible for this latest development?

3. Palm-sized computers will soon have (their, theirs) day in the public spotlight.

4. Congratulations on (you, your) inventing a new mousetrap.

5. The engineering firm offers (it's, its) employees good benefits.

6. Technology has made (its, it's) presence felt even in the kitchen.

7. I can't wait to find out (whose, who's) going to create the next great new advance in computer software.

8. They claimed that the idea for wireless computers was (their, theirs).

9. (Whose, Who's) going to remember the old-fashioned way of doing things in the future?

10. The change-over from using typewriters to using computers for word processing has had (it's, its) disadvantages, too.

Sentence Review

Choose the correct word in the parentheses.

1. (Our, Ours) is a special kind of love.

2. A message was sent for Robert and (I, me).

3. Even though the opportunity is (your, yours), I hope you consider other people's feelings as well.

4. The tennis player who won the tournament was (he, him), the aged teen idol.

5. The book was given to the librarian (who, whom) placed it in a bin to be shelved.

6. For (we, us) suburban dwellers, automobiles are essential.

7. The patterns were clear to Holmes, (who, whom) recognized the criminal's methods of operation.

8. The patient wanted an appointment with (whoever, whomever) the receptionist could find was available.

9. Clearly, you found the movie more appealing than (she, her) did.

10. The magazine that was (your, yours) was accidentally thrown away.

Applying the Sentence Lesson

Identify and rewrite any misused pronouns that you find in your Chapter Writing Assignment paragraph. Look at Kenny's second draft. Mistakes in pronoun case are underlined.

The Internet has been a positive influence on the world because it has

been a boost for the economy, for shut-ins, and for college students doing research. Although some people think the Internet is bad because some web sites are devoted to sex and some crazy people post instructions on how to build a bomb, people <u>whom</u> use the Internet are mostly being good. After all, <u>its</u> simply a way for people like you and <u>I</u> to find information quickly. Also, a lot of business is conducted over the Internet. Many traditional businesses offer online shopping. Other businesses, sometimes called "e-businesses" strictly operate online. For <u>them</u> who can't get around well due to physical illness, injury, or some other problem, the Internet can help. They can read newspapers from around the country or tour museums in Europe without ever leaving home. Those <u>whom</u> want to leave home can even buy airline tickets, hotel rooms, and rental cars right from the computer. <u>Us</u> students do a lot of research over the Internet. Not only are there newspapers and television networks with web sites, but also many college libraries make their offerings available over the Internet. The students <u>themself</u> benefit most by doing homework without actually being in the library. Overall, the Internet has made life a lot better for many people.

Writing the Final Draft

Rewrite your second draft, making sure that you have corrected all errors in the use of pronouns. This will be your final draft. Respond to the revision questions as you work on your rewrite.

Revision questions
- Does your paragraph have a strong sense of structure, with a beginning, middle, and end?
- Have you provided effective transitions as you move from one idea to the next?
- Have you checked your use of subject-specific language, making sure that each word used is appropriate and accurate?
- Have you examined your use of pronouns to ensure that they are all in the proper case?

Hand in the final draft, with the materials from your prewriting, first draft, second draft, and any other materials you created in the process of writing this assignment.

Kenny found several pronoun case errors in his second draft. In preparing his final draft, he corrected those errors. He also worked on trying to shorten his paragraph by eliminating unnecessary words, yet he still wanted to keep as many specific details in his paragraph as possible. Here is his final draft.

The Internet has been a positive influence on the world by helping businesses, shut-ins, and college students. Although some people think the Internet is bad because some web sites are devoted to pornography or bomb-building, people who use the Internet are mostly being good. After all, it's simply a way for people like you and me to find information quickly. For example, a lot of business is conducted over the Internet. Many traditional businesses, such as retail stores, offer online shopping. Other businesses, sometimes called "e-businesses," strictly operate online. For those who can't get around well due to physical illness, injury, or some other problem, the Internet can help them to read newspapers from around the country or tour museums in Europe without ever leaving home. Those who want to leave home can buy airline tickets, hotel rooms, and rental cars right from the computer. We students do a lot of research over the Internet. Not only are there newspapers and television networks with web sites, but also many college libraries make their offerings available over the Internet. The students themselves benefit most by doing homework without actually being in the library. The Internet has made life easier for many people.

PORTFOLIO CHECKLIST

In your portfolio, you should now have the following:

1. your Question Grid.
2. a First Draft. The first draft should have comma errors circled.
3. a Second Draft. The second draft should have pronoun case errors underlined.
4. a Final Draft.

PARTING SHOT

1. How has agricultural America changed because of technology?
2. How has technology separated—or joined—rural America from urban America?
3. Has technology improved our food and water supply, or corrupted it?

GOALS IN REVIEW

In this chapter, you learned about

- a prewriting strategy called the Question Grid
- subject-specific language
- commas
- pronoun case

PRACTICE CHAPTER TEST

Part I

Place commas in the following sentences.

1. New technologies will help create medical cures but they might also create new illnesses.

2. August 10 1991 is an important date in our lives.

3. I told you Joshua not to eat with your mouth open.

4. The operator asked "What city are you calling?"

5. Please take this frog away from me!

6. The satellite which was being used by a telecommunications company to route cell phone calls failed to work.

7. Ryan a giant of a man shops at special clothing stores.

8. Patrick Henry once said "Give me Liberty or Give me Death!"

9. After turning in for the night Gilbert hardly expected what happened next.

10. When I clean my house I do a very good job.

11. The steak was tough dry and burnt.

12. Basil rosemary and thyme are three common herbs used in cooking.

13. I wanted the family van not the sports car.

14. The president along with members of his cabinet smiled for cameras in the Rose Garden of the White House.

15. Send this package to 3464 Washington Place Chicago Illinois 32092.

Part II

Choose the correct word in the parentheses.

1. Yvette is stronger than (her, she).

2. This problem is just between Dorothy and (I, me).

3. The poet (who, whom) the college hired to deliver a lecture is nationally renowned.

4. The class in Black Studies is being taught by the man (who, whom) was an honored graduate of Baylor University.

5. The idea for the new name of the campus newspaper was (her, hers).

6. (It's, its) important to remember that America was formed by many different ethnic, religious and social groups.

7. The director said that (whoever, whomever) got the starring role would have to be willing to shave her head for the final, dramatic execution scene.

8. Patrick decided to learn Gaelic because (its, it's) the language of his ancestors.

9. We can't decide (who's, whose) to blame for this latest fiasco.

10. The newspaper referred to (his, him) vandalizing of a military computer network as an act of treason.

7

Health

CHAPTER GOALS

In this chapter, you will learn about

- asking questions as a prewriting strategy,
- choosing your words carefully,
- end punctuation and internal punctuation, and
- word usage.

Health is the theme of this chapter. The old saying "If you have your health, you have everything" is often best understood during times of illness or injury. All people have an interest in staying as healthy as possible, yet the lifestyle choices people make sometimes run counter to good health—eating too much, drinking too much alcohol, not exercising properly, not resting enough, not getting physical check-ups. These choices and others affect people's health.

OPENING SHOT

QUESTIONS ABOUT THE PICTURE

1. What role does exercise play in your life?

2. What are the benefits of physical exercise?

3. How can people who are not athletes participate in an exercise program?

4. What different kinds of physical activities can be good exercise?

READING

Questions to Consider

1. How healthy are you? How would you like to improve your health?

2. How does your emotional life affect your health? For instance, do you overeat when you are experiencing emotional turmoil or stress?

3. Have you ever been on a diet? If so, how well did it work?

Words to Watch

palpitation   a trembling or shaking

prestigious   having a level of respect, honor, or high standing

physiologist   a person who studies the biological functions of living organisms

pondering   reflecting with care or consideration

coincidental   happening or existing at the same time

predicament   a situation, especially an unpleasant, troublesome, or trying one

Emmy award   an award given for outstanding achievement in television

icon   an idol; one who is the object of a great attention and devotion

metabolism   the complex physical and chemical processes by which the body converts food into energy

FROM MAKE THE CONNECTION
Introduction
Bob Greene and Oprah Winfrey

1   It was the summer of 1992, and I was about to meet Oprah Winfrey. At the time, I was the fitness director for a new spa in Telluride, Colorado, and Oprah was one of our first guests. I wondered if I was the only person in America who had never seen "The Oprah Winfrey Show." But I certainly knew who she was. As I sat in my office waiting to meet her, I thought about the first time I had heard her name.

2   It was back in 1987, and I was in charge of a health and fitness program at a South Florida hospital. There was one particular week when we were flooded with calls about one of our weight-loss classes. The reason for this sudden interest, I soon found out, was Oprah's first significant weight loss and the show she did about it. She began that show by pulling out a wagon loaded with 67 pounds of fat to dramatize how much weight she'd lost. She had dropped the pounds by using the Optifast fasting and supplement system.

3   I was quite familiar with such diets, since we offered one at the hospital. But I firmly believed that a fasting and supplement program should be used as a last resort, and then only for a few select individuals—certainly not the average person trying to lose weight. These diets have many risks, including gall-bladder complications, heart palpitations, and feelings of depression, and the resulting weight loss is almost always temporary. I knew someone as popular as Oprah Winfrey could inspire a lot of imitators, and I didn't have a good feeling about it. I also didn't think Oprah could keep the weight off once she stopped taking the supplement and began eating real food again.

4   My instinct was confirmed the following year when she regained all the weight she lost, plus some. That story also made national news, and the hospital again received a large increase in calls. I was amazed that one individual could have such a tremendous impact on our industry. Yet, I felt bad for her, as I would for anyone who struggles with a weight problem. I find it hard to believe, but I remember daydreaming at the time that I would like to meet her. I thought, "I could really help her."

5   Now, two years later, here I was about to meet her. Shortly after leaving the hospital, I had moved to Colorado to help open the Doral Telluride Resort and Spa. It was an unusual move for me, leaving a prestigious program and accepting less money than I was used to, but I was drawn here. I had always wanted to live, work, and ski in a beautiful western mountain town. I had even considered working as a ski instructor after graduate school, but I knew it was probably time to grow up and use my degree.

6   As an exercise physiologist, I had worked in medical settings for about a decade, helping people lose weight and drastically change their lifestyle for health or medical reasons. In recent years, I found that most of my time was spent with administrative duties, personnel headaches, and paperwork. I really missed working one-on-one with clients.

7   When the spa opened, and I was asked to work with Oprah, I didn't hesitate. As I sat in my office pondering how all these seemingly coincidental events in my life had led up to the moment I once daydreamed about, I heard voices in the corridor. Someone was being given a tour. It was Oprah. I left my office to meet her.

8   When I was introduced to Oprah, I looked her directly in the eyes, as I always try to do when I speak to someone. "It's a pleasure to meet you," I said. But I couldn't help noticing how she quickly averted her eyes and looked straight down at the floor. I later thought, "Did I stare too directly? Is it a celebrity thing? Does she not want to be here?" Then

it dawned on me that this was the same reaction I get virtually every time I meet new clients who want to lose weight.

9   The feeling of embarrassment about their predicament is so great that they often avoid looking me in the eye. Moreover, they expect that I am passing judgment on them for being overweight, much like they do themselves. I guess I didn't expect such a reaction from Oprah Winfrey, who is the star of her own television show, and the winner of multiple Emmy awards, not to mention a worldwide icon. She was noticeably uncomfortable. But she had no reason to be. The truth is, especially at that moment, I had tremendous respect for her, as I do for anyone attempting the challenge of permanent weight loss.

10   Over long hikes and workouts, Oprah and I laughed, shared stories, and generally grew comfortable with each other. One day we were hiking along with her good friend Arleen and, in an attempt to learn something about me, Oprah asked, "So, Bob, where are you from?" I told her I grew up in New Jersey. "Oh, that's near Stedman," she said. I thought maybe she was confused. "No, you must mean Camden," I responded. "I don't know of a Stedman, New Jersey." Suddenly, Oprah broke up with laughter, but for the life of me I couldn't figure out why. Finally, when she was able to compose herself, she explained to me that Stedman was the first name of her boyfriend, Stedman Graham. She was simply bemused that she had met someone so unaware of her very public life. Arleen gave me a look like "You've been living up in these mountains too long." I got the feeling Oprah liked the fact that I knew so little about her life and that I didn't even own a television.

11   (I now know Stedman Graham quite well, and I have to say he was very supportive of Oprah during the difficult process of shedding the weight. So often, the important people in your life act to sabotage your efforts, usually in very subtle ways. This subtle sabotage is usually not malicious or even intentional, but can undermine even the most committed person.)

12   During her three-week spa visit, Oprah and I hiked many miles in the San Juan mountains and spent a lot of time in the gym. I figured she had lost about ten pounds, but I didn't want her to weigh herself, because I knew she would be disappointed if the scale didn't reflect a large weight loss. Oprah is a person who expects a lot of herself—perhaps too much. I'll never forget how after one week of training she said she wanted to run a marathon by the time she was 40. I knew she was going to be 39 that January and that she weighed approximately 233 pounds, and that she tapes two, sometimes three shows a day in addition to running her company. Most anyone would have thought she was just making idle conversation, but I took her seriously. I knew she could do it.

13   By the end of her stay, Oprah had lost between 10 and 12 pounds. Both she and I were thrilled with the results. I felt confident of her commitment to lose weight, but I also recognized the enormous task she had ahead of her to permanently change her life. As we parted, she

said, "You wait, I'll be back this fall and I'll be as cute as a button." I smiled and thought, what a fun three weeks.

14   Meeting Oprah, I learned four very important things about her:

- She was physically capable of exercising at the proper intensity levels.
- She basically knew how to eat healthy.
- She possessed the will and desire to make the changes in her life that would result in permanent weight loss.
- She was either unaware of, or greatly underestimated, the depth and complexity of the emotional issues that contributed to her being overweight.

15   Oprah is a source of inspiration in so many ways. She has been blessed with so many gifts, but a favorable metabolism is not one of them. In addition, for most of her life, she has used food to cope with stressful or painful events. These are the reasons she is such a great role model for people attempting to change their lives. For Oprah to maintain her weight at the level she desires, she must work extremely hard—much harder than the average person. She also must find healthier ways to deal with life's problems—in a life that sees problems on a daily basis. This is not to say that she always follows my program to the letter, but she realizes that when she does, she gets results quickly, and when she doesn't, it is her choice. She also knows that this new, healthier way of eating, living, and thinking has greatly improved the quality of her life. She now has control over her life, and you can too!

PREPARING TO WRITE

Asking Questions

In Chapter Six, you created a question grid in order to examine issues related to your writing topic. There is another way to ask questions about your topic that will be logical, clear, and helpful. This form of asking questions relies on a technique associated with journalism: Asking questions that begin with Who, What, When, Where, Why, and How.

When writing news stories, journalists try to answer these questions in their first paragraph, sometimes called *the lead*. Asking these same questions of your writing topic, however, can serve an entirely different purpose—showing you the many different ways that your topic can be explored.

The technique works when you create your own questions. The questions can suggest a writing topic. Perhaps the answer to a question leads to other questions that will suggest a writing topic. Sometimes the questions themselves might be unanswerable, or you might not know the answers right away. When that happens, you probably will want to explore your writing topic further. Pursuing answers to questions can open up a lot of possible writing topics you might not otherwise have been exposed to.

Consider, for example, the general subject of health. Imagine that the focus of your interest in health is on the importance of daily exercise. You might create the following lists of questions.

Who? Who are the experts? Who argues that exercise is important? Who knows what forms of exercise work best? Who benefits? Who, if anyone, cannot benefit from exercise?

What? What exercises are best? What exercises are not good? What is going on in the body during exercise? What happens after the exercise routine is over? What parts of the body are helped by what exercises? What is the general purpose of exercise?

When? When is the best time of the day to exercise? When should you stop exercising if you feel pain? When are you too young or too old to exercise? When will you see results from exercise?

Where? Where are the best places to go to exercise? Where should you avoid going to exercise?

Why? Why should you exercise? Why does exercise affect your overall health? Why are some exercises helpful and others not?

How? How does the body respond to exercise? How do certain exercises help create body mass while others help to lose fat? How long do you have to exercise? How difficult of an exercise routine do you need to do in order to see results?

No single short piece of writing could answer all of these questions. You might want to pick just one question and make that the focus of your writing. The point of asking questions, though, is to see how varied your writing topic could actually be, so that you eventually find something interesting and exciting to write about.

Note: Be sure that your questions are complete sentences. Short phrases are usually not enough to indicate your area of inquiry exactly.

Preparing Yourself to Write

In order to prepare yourself to answer these six questions, first take a sheet of paper, and along the left hand margin, write down "Who," "What," "When," "Where," "Why," and "How." Be sure to give yourself plenty of room to scribble down many questions.

Before posing questions, consider how well you know your topic. If you're already fairly familiar with it, you'll probably be able to begin answering the questions right away. If you're not, you will want to explore the topic further before beginning. Go to the library and look up magazine and newspaper articles. Find a book or two on your topic. Asking questions of a topic can lead you in many different directions, but you usually have to be familiar with the major issues related to your topic first, even if it is strictly from a personal point of view.

The following sample is a list of questions written to prepare to write Question #2 by a community college student named Makena.

Who? Who sabotages people's efforts? Who needs to stop other people from getting healthy? Who won't support getting healthy? Who will? Who needs the support of others?

What? What kind of behavior is support? What is not supportive? What do people want from others to make them non-supportive? What do you do or say to someone who isn't supportive?

When? When do food issues start? When do issues about support start? When is it too late to change? When does someone recognize that they have a problem?

Where? Where does one learn eating habits? Where can one un-learn them? Where is one most vulnerable—in one's own home? One's parents' home? At a restaurant? In private? At a friend's house?

Why? Why are some people not supportive of others? Why do people need support from others? Why is losing weight so difficult for many people? Why is losing weight important?

How? How does one lose weight? How does one get support for losing weight if others aren't giving it? How does support or lack of support help? How can families make people unhealthy? How can they make people healthy?

Prewriting

Once you have reviewed materials on the major issues related to the subject of health, or one of the questions from the Chapter Writing Assignment, take your sheet with the six question words along the left-hand margin and begin filling in questions. Make sure you have at least two questions for each, but preferably more.

CHAPTER WRITING ASSIGNMENT

Write a 100- to 200-word paragraph in response to one of the following writing assignments. Instructions in the chapter will guide you through the writing process. At different points in the chapter, you will be asked to produce more work on this assignment. By the end of the chapter, you will have completed your final draft.

1. How important is maintaining your health on a daily basis? Consider whether health concerns—such as diet and exercise—are something you are aware of constantly. Why or why not?

2. One of the points that Bob Greene makes in his introduction to <u>Make the Connection</u> is that friends and family sometimes sabotage people's efforts to live a healthier life. Why do you think this might be? Include specific examples of ways you have seen this happen.

3. Greene argues that emotional issues contribute to Winfrey's weight troubles. How can emotional problems contribute to someone becoming overweight? Explain.

4. Not all health problems are related to diet and exercise. If you have had such a problem, how did (or does) this problem affect the way that you lived your life?

WRITING LESSON

Choosing Your Words

One of the enemies of good writing is poor word choice. Selecting the right words to express your meaning is not simple. As a writer, you have to take into account several factors, such as **subject, purpose,** and **audience.**

Subject

Chapter Six discussed the importance of subject-specific language. As you remember, subject-specific language is the vocabulary necessary to communicate accurately about a given subject, so that the writer does not fall into the trap of being vague, abstract, and overly general. Knowing your subject, and knowing the vocabulary of that subject, will help you choose words that best express your meaning.

Purpose

The ultimate purpose of writing is communication, but within that broad task there exist several different purposes. Most instructors divide the purposes of writing into three simple ones: to entertain, to educate, and to persuade.

Writing to **entertain** sounds like creative writing, only. Indeed, writing to entertain can include writing novels, scripts, short stories, poems, or even song lyrics. However, writing to entertain is not limited to these forms. Even when you write for a class, you want the writing to be interesting. While you are usually not writing one-liner jokes, you should use language that involves the reader, either intellectually, emotionally, or even spiritually.

Writing to **educate** is common, particularly within school. Writing to educate situations include short answer tests, lab reports, and essay exams. When you write to educate, being clear and specific is of great importance. After all, explaining how something works, or why one event caused a whole series of consequences, cannot be done if the reader cannot follow your logical train of thought.

Writing to **persuade** is writing that convinces a reader to take some course of action, or to take the writer's side on some controversial issue. Since the ultimate purpose is persuasion, the writer needs to choose words that will convey ideas forcefully (without appearing stubborn or extreme). Like an attorney addressing a jury at a trial, the writer needs to be aware of the effect words have on an audience, and choose words that show the writer to be credible and knowledgeable.

Audience

An awareness of **audience** is the third, and sometimes hardest, aspect of choosing appropriate language. Sometimes, such as when you write to a friend, choosing language to fit your audience is easy because you know your audience so well. However, in school, you often do not personally know the person who will be reading your work. Instead, you must form an idea of a *general academic audience*. If you have a concept of a general academic audience, then you can write with confidence no matter who the reader will be. (Of course, always follow your instructor's specific requirements on how to write an assignment.)

Writing for a general academic audience usually requires the following:

- Using Standard American English or SAE. SAE is more formal than conversational English or dialects of English. SAE requires that you know and follow proper rules of grammar, punctuation, spelling, and usage. Some instructors may require formal English while others allow for more informal language. Know your instructor's requirements.

- Avoiding personal pronouns such as "I" or "you" unless you are recounting a personal experience or directing a specific passage to a specific reader. The third person pronouns (he, she, they) are considered preferable in academic writing.

- Avoiding contractions. In most academic writing, all words should be spelled out.

- Avoiding abbreviations, such as "NY" for "New York." Exceptions are made for a few standard abbreviations, such as "a.m." or "etc." If you plan to use an acronym (a word formed from the first letters of a series of words), such as "NASA," you may write out the name, followed by the acronym in parentheses, such as "National Aeronautics and Space Administration (NASA)." Use "NASA" thereafter.

- Avoiding slang, along with most colloquialisms (everyday nonstandard phrases or expressions), even if you believe the expression is well known. Simply put, academic writing has the expectation of more formal language.

- Avoiding your thesaurus! Sometimes, in an effort to make their writing appear "smarter" or more formal, some writers look through their thesaurus to uncover synonyms that sound "better." This can often lead to trouble. The main cause of trouble is that most synonyms are not *exact* synonyms. Each word carries the flavor of its own meaning, and a writer who is not careful about this risks selecting the wrong word. For instance, the word "woman," may appear in a thesaurus with such words as "lady," "girl," "dame," "matron," and "virgin." Clearly, these words do not all mean exactly the same thing, so they cannot be used interchangeably.

Ultimately, proper word choice can be highly subjective. You need to be aware of your word selection. Take into consideration subject, purpose, and audience. Close attention to detail is a key to writing well. Your words *do* matter.

ZOOM-IN PRACTICE

Write ten slang expressions that you know and their Standard American English equivalents.

Slang   Standard American English

_____   _____

_____   _____

_____   _____

_____   _____

_____   _____

_____   _____

_____   _____

_____   _____

_____   _____

_____   _____

Writing the First Draft

Makena, whose questions you have already seen, wrote the following paragraph for her first draft in response to Question #2 of the Chapter Writing Assignment.

Sometimes friends and family can get in the way of people who are trying to improve their health. I have a friend (Shara) who has a weight problem. She tried to cut back on eating, but her mother wasn't supportive at all. She say to Shara, Why arent you eating everything I give you? Dont let that food go to waste. Shara said "she didn't want to eat so much." and her mother actually got angry with her. Shara is having a hard time because: she wants to lose weight but she doesn't want to make her mother angry either. Sometimes it happens in other ways. When she and her boyfriend go to the movies, he always wants butter on the popcorn. Do you know how unhealthy that stuff is? Well, Shara wants her own popcorn without butter, and he told her she's "stuck up" now. Shara just wants two things; to lose weight and keep her friends. But it's like as if they're making her choose: that isn't right. I try to be supportive because I want her to be healthy, and I've always been pretty healthy myself. I eat lots of salads, fish, and chicken, and I try to stay away from fried foods, butter, and desserts. It seems to me that friends should help each other—that's what it's all about, right?

You are now ready to write your first draft in response to one of the questions in the Chapter Writing Assignment. Pay special attention to your choice of words. Complete this draft before beginning the Grammar Lesson.

GRAMMAR LESSON

Other Punctuation

The English language contains many punctuation marks in addition to the comma, which you learned about in Chapter Six. Punctuation marks can be divided into two categories: end punctuation and internal punctuation. End punctuation refers to marks used at the end of a sentence: a period, a question mark, or an exclamation point. Internal punctuation refers to punctuation marks that appear within a sentence.

End Punctuation

End punctuation marks are relatively simple and usually occur at the end of a sentence. One end punctuation mark is a period.

In 1976, Americans celebrated the Bicentennial with parades, fireworks and picnics across the nation.

Please remove your hat when you enter the church.

The butler asked when to serve the cigars and brandy.

Periods are also used in the formation of many abbreviations:

Mr., Sept., p.m., Inc., qt., Cal., F.B.I.

Most students have little trouble in the use of question marks or exclamation points, as well. Still, there are a few points to keep in mind. A question mark ends any direct question. No question mark is used for an indirect question.

Direct question

Miss Julie asked, "Is there a doctor in the house?"

Indirect question

Miss Julie asked if there was a doctor in the house.

Direct question with the quotation at the start of the sentence

"Is there a doctor in the house?" asked Miss Julie.

In the first direct question, there is a quotation—a rendering of the actual words Miss Julie used. Note that the question mark falls *inside* the quotation marks. In the indirect question, the sentence is a statement reporting what Miss Julie said, but not using her precise wording. Since the sentence is a statement, it ends with a period, not a question mark. In the third example, the question mark appears at the end of the quoted material, but a period still ends the overall sentence of which the quotation is a part.

Inexperienced writers tend to overuse exclamation points. Too frequently, they use exclamation points to convey excitement or intense emotion instead of using words which convey the meaning better. While exclamation points indicate excitement, if the words don't show that excitement, the result will be flat and unenthusiastic.

My day was fine.

My day was fine!

The presence of the exclamation point in the second sentence does little to elevate the level of enthusiasm. A better sentence might read:

My day was fabulous!

By using the word "fabulous," which carries a stronger emotion than the word "fine," the writer is able to convey excitement. This excitement is emphasized by the exclamation point.

Exclamation points may also be used with interjections:

Wow! That was the most incredible meal I've ever eaten!
Ouch! I stubbed my toe!

Exclamation points also appear frequently after sentences that convey a sense of command (called **imperative sentences**):

Catch the ball!
Help! Call an ambulance!

EXERCISE 7.1

Place a period, question mark, or exclamation point in each sentence where needed.

"Does this hurt?" asked the doctor as he pushed on the patient's abdomen.

1. Sandra complained, "I never have enough hot water in the morning"

2. "Can you really be too rich" wondered Merrilee as she scrubbed the floor

3. Golly I can't believe I just ate that entire fudge sundae

4. "Should I become a vegetarian" wondered Hank

5. The airline pilot wondered whether or not the landing strip had been cleared

6. Your aerobic workout sessions must last a minimum of twenty minutes

7. "Ouch" yelled the carpenter. "I just smashed my thumb"

8. Do the vitamins Sherry takes each day actually help to maintain her health

9. Meet me at the work site by 7 am or your job is in jeopardy

10. "Why buy something you don't like, even if it is cheap" asked Professor McLaughlin

---

Internal Punctuation

Internal punctuation is used inside a sentence. Besides the comma, the most common internal punctuation marks include colons, semicolons, dashes, parentheses, brackets, quotation marks, apostrophes, and hyphens.

Colons

The colon is used primarily in three ways: to introduce a list, to introduce a word or phrase that renames or amplifies an earlier part of the sentence, and to introduce a direct quotation.

Introducing a list

The following members of the board were in attendance: Janice Perkins, Amy Han, Camille Levinson, and Maya Wright.

Several artists influenced his work: Braque, Picasso, Duchamp, and Pollock.

The State Department declared these countries were harboring terrorists: Libya, Iran, Iraq, and the Sudan.

Renaming or amplifying

His act had only one flaw: it wasn't funny.

There in my palm was my last hope: a phone number.

The searchers faced a dilemma: call off the search for the night or risk placing themselves in danger.

Introducing a direct quotation

In my dorm room, I hung a poster with the following words: "If Ignorance is Bliss, 'Tis Folly to Be Wise."

An announcement was posted: "The position has been filled."

The words on the sign indicated a distinct lack of hospitality: "No dogs allowed."

DON'T LOSE FOCUS!

Do not fall into the common trap of placing a colon between a linking verb and a subject complement. If the sentence can be read through without interrupting the independent clause, do not add a colon.

Incorrect

My favorite summertime sports are: water polo and tennis.

Correct

My favorite summertime sports are water polo and tennis.

Incorrect

The winner of the lottery ticket was: my Uncle Ferd.

Correct

The winner of the lottery ticket was my Uncle Ferd.

Do not place a colon between an object and a preposition. A common error is to use a colon after the phrase "such as."

Incorrect

The professor had many annoying quirks, such as: his forgetfulness and his lack of good grooming.

Correct

The professor had many annoying quirks, such as his forgetfulness and his lack of good grooming.

EXERCISE 7.2

Add or remove colons in the following sentences as needed. If a sentence is already correct, mark the sentence with a "C."

The nurse suggested a simple remedy: more sleep.

1. The traveler prepared to fly to: Paris, Madrid, and Lisbon.

2. Hippocrates, the father of medicine, said "The life so short, the craft so long to learn."

3. There remained only one problem: a lack of money.

4. There in the doorway stood both my trouble and my salvation the pizza delivery guy.

5. There were four names on the list Robert M. Wright, Louis J. Hawkes, Norman Smiley, and Paul Stein.

6. Those in attendance included the Secretary of Energy, the head of the Atomic Energy Commission, and the CEOs of several large utility companies.

7. The signs on every wall had the same message "No Smoking Allowed."

8. The bag was full of many knickknacks, including gum balls, pennies, small plastic soldiers, and rubber bands.

9. The worst part of being overweight was: the shame.

10. Megan had a fairly well balanced lunch, a ham and cheese sandwich on whole wheat bread, some raw carrots, a small box of raisins, and a tall glass of non-fat milk.

Semicolons

In Chapter Two, you learned that two independent clauses can be joined together with a semicolon. In this usage, a semicolon functions to suggest a link between the two clauses. Sometimes that link is expressed by using conjunctive adverbs after the semicolon. Another use of the semicolon is to separate items in a list in which the items themselves contain commas.

Joining two independent clauses

The goal was obvious; the difficulty lay in reaching it.

The princess wanted to escape; however, the dragon was far too dangerous for her to attempt to flee on her own.

The illness began to overtake the patient; finally, nothing could save him from death.

Separating items in a list

The finalists for the scholarship included Christie Nguyen, a biology major; Mark Jackson, a physical therapy major; and Daemon Trundle, a physical education major.

In attendance at the speech were the following ambassadors: Lord Lightly, Great Britain; Kamala Ramaya, India; Leela Orona, Costa Rica; and Herman Stoecker, Germany.

The hardest hit cities included Montgomery, Selma, and Birmingham in Alabama; Memphis, Nashville, and Knoxville in Tennessee; and Tupelo and Jackson in Mississippi.

EXERCISE 7.3

Add or remove semicolons in the following sentences as needed. If a sentence is already correct, mark the sentence with a "C."

One sister tried to lose weight with a fad diet; the other sister changed her eating habits and started to exercise regularly.

1. The scale indicated that Bruce had gained five pounds in the last month, however, he still refused to change his eating habits.

2. The process was difficult, the payoff was going to be huge.

3. The settlement did not appear to be reasonable, still, the injured party decided to accept the deal to avoid a long trial.

4. Having an annual physical exam is an important part of maintaining one's health; indeed, such exams can often help patients take important preventive measures to avoid potential problems.

5. Several members of the committee were absent: Donald Edmundson, due to illness, Myra Corbin, due to a death in the family, and Eugene Kumar, unexcused.

6. When I saw that famous circus attraction, the bearded woman; I was reminded of my Great Aunt Gertie.

7. I think some of the greatest American plays are <u>Death of a Salesman</u> and <u>The Crucible</u> by Arthur Miller, <u>The Zoo Story</u>, <u>Who's Afraid of Virginia Woolf</u>, and <u>Seascape</u> by Edward Albee, and <u>Mourning Becomes Electra</u> by Eugene O'Neill.

8. Ezra worked hard to be a success; but he never actually was one.

9. The bricklayers came early to Charles's home; they left late in the evening, task finished.

10. In the end, nothing could stop her, no one even tried.

Dashes

A dash forces a break of greater strength and emphasis in the thought of a sentence than any other internal punctuation mark and should be used with caution. The dash can replace a comma or a colon for more emphasis. A dash can be used by itself or in pairs.

Interrupting the logic within a sentence

I'd like to buy the orange—no, forget that. I want to buy a doughnut instead.

The diet begins today—oh, let's make it tomorrow.

Setting off a series of items at the start of a sentence

Paris, Venice, Vienna—these were the cities on our honeymoon itinerary.

Quarters, nickels, dimes—all these silver coins lack the charm of a shiny, new penny.

Setting off a single word to show emphasis

Nicole never managed to get the one thing she wanted—respect.

Only one American president—Thomas Jefferson—can lay claim to having achieved excellence in so many different areas.

Making a comment or explanation within a sentence more emphatic.

All of his dreams—the big house, the fast cars, the beautiful women—came to an abrupt end when he was arrested for embezzlement.

Mark Twain—a giant of American letters—is still one of the most often quoted writers.

Parentheses

Parentheses are always used in pairs. They enclose relatively unimportant information—comments that are not essential to the meaning of a sentence. Sometimes parentheses can be used in the place of a pair of commas. Remember, using parentheses will draw more attention to the comment than a pair of commas will.

Enclosing dates

Robert F. Kennedy (1925–1968) served as his brother's Attorney General.

President Bill Clinton's impeachment trial (1999) was only the second such trial held in the history of the United States.

Enclosing information

A modern symposium (formed from two ancient Greek words that mean "drinking party") is often an informative yet dull convention.

James Joyce's *Ulysses* (first published in the U.S. in 1934) was the subject of an important obscenity trial.

EXERCISE 7.4

Add or remove dashes and/or parentheses in the following sentences as needed. If a sentence is already correct, mark the sentence with a "C."

1. Pepper, curry, and paprika these are spices I use quite often.

2. The three sisters, April, May, and June, certainly had parents with an odd sense of humor.

3. The Watergate scandal 1972–1974 shook the nation like no scandal ever has since.

4. A second-year college student is referred to as a sophomore meaning "wise fool."

5. Film, television, stage, the famous actress had mastered them all.

6. The report on the crisis in American health, of great concern to everyone, had very distressing conclusions.

7. The few surviving members of the platoon—Ricardo, Jerome, Terence, and Albert—made their way back to the base during the night.

8. I wanted to state clearly, no, wait, forget what I was saying.

9. Only one type of person, a dentist, scared him.

10. Alonzo, the guy seated next to Patricia, is her newest fiancé.

Quotation Marks

Quotation marks, like parentheses, are always used in pairs. Quotation marks have three main uses: to set off direct quotations, to indicate the title of a short literary or artistic work, and to emphasize a particular word or phrase.

Setting off direct quotations

The train conductor shouted, "All aboard!"

"I love you," she whispered to him.

"I'm not sure," he hedged, "if I should be helping you or not."

Note: The comma is used after the formal introduction to the quotation and the quotation itself. If the direct quotation is at the start of the sentence, a comma ends the quoted material but is placed inside of the quotation marks. End punctuation goes inside the quotation marks as well.

The mechanic asked, "Who forgot to put the oil filter on this car?"

"I can't see!" he exclaimed.

Indicating the titles of short literary works or artistic works

I was reading the essay "The American Scholar" by Ralph Waldo Emerson the other day for a class.

Heather's favorite coffee mug has a reproduction of Van Gogh's "Starry Night" on the sides.

Emphasizing a particular word or phrase

Annette often refers to Peter as a "technocrat" because he has a lot of practical knowledge of how to get things done.

The jury's verdict seemed to rest on the definition of the words "with malice aforethought."

Italics.   Italics can sometimes be used indicate the titles of long literary works, such as books, plays, and epic poems. Italics can also be used to indicate the names of magazines, journals, newspapers, movies, music CD's, and even the names of ships, airplanes, and trains.

We knew that riding on the *Orient Express* would be a once in a lifetime experience.

Robert enjoys reading the *New York Times* each morning on the Internet.

My goal this summer is to read all of *The Iliad.*

Note: If the words in italics are not visibly distinct from a regular print or typewritten words, underlining these titles and names is another option. Check with your instructor to see if he or she has a preference.

EXERCISE 7.5

Add or remove quotation marks in the following sentences as needed. If a word should appear in italics, indicate so by underlining the word. If a sentence is already correct, mark the sentence with a "C."

"I loved the movie American Beauty so much I saw it three times!" exclaimed Beverly.

1. Apparently, she cried, you have lost your faith in me.

2. I decided to improve myself this summer by reading War and Peace by Tolstoy.

3. Professor Rother maintains that the Rolling Stones' album Exile on Main Street is one of the last true rock albums made.

4. Ron asked if he could borrow a cup of mayonnaise for a tuna salad he was making.

5. Did you just ask me to run a marathon? questioned Susan.

6. The photograph of the Maine, whose sinking under mysterious circumstances was used to justify a war against Spain, shows a magnificent ship.

7. I hate Nashville, insisted Les, and I want to move back to Lubbock tomorrow.

8. The new book called Painless Ways to Lose Weight While Eating Everything You Want is a best seller.

9. The quest for universal health care has been derailed, claimed the senator, by special interest groups protecting their selfish interests at the expense of the poor.

10. The critic said, The number of people who see a movie is not necessarily an indicator of the quality of that movie. Look at Titanic, for example. Popular, yes, but not that great of a story.

Apostrophes

The apostrophe is a frequently misused or neglected punctuation mark. Good writers should have a solid understanding of when to use, and not use, apostrophes.

Forming the possessive

Use 's to indicate possession with a singular noun or with plural nouns which do not end with an s.

Rod's business

the cat's meow

the trial's conclusion

the women's claims

the media's obsession

her teeth's appearance

Use an apostrophe only to show possession if the noun is plural and ends with an s. In some cases, to avoid difficulties in pronunciation when a singular noun ends with an s, you may choose to use an apostrophe only.

the attorneys' bills

the airline passengers' complaints

the states' governors

Carlos Fuentes's newest novel

Jess's baked cookies

the moss' color

Use an *'s* to show possession with compound words according to the logic of the sentence.

Ben and Jerry's ice cream (ice cream made by Ben and Jerry)

Elvis Presley's and Chuck Berry's musical styles (two different styles by two different performers)

Use an *'s* to show possession with most indefinite pronouns.

anybody's game

no one's car

everyone's goal

Forming contractions

Use an apostrophe to indicate contractions (words formed by combining two different words together).

it's (it is)

I'm (I am)

can't (can not)

Shortening dates and indicating unusual plural forms

Use an apostrophe with shortened dates or to indicate the plural of letters, numbers, and words.

the summer of '69

the class of '80

the '49ers

There were many more A's and B's than D's and F's.

How do you write your 8's?

The large number of um's and uh's in his speech was annoying.

Hyphens

Hyphens have four common uses.

Setting off prefixes such as "ex," "self," and "all"

the ex-quarterback

the path to self-awareness

the all-powerful wizard

Setting off prefixes that are used before proper nouns or adjectives

the anti-American sentiment

the pro-Africa lobby

a pre-Columbian ruin

Creating compound adjectives that form a single idea

the hard-won victory

the follow-up appointment

the blue-green tint

Creating fractions and compound numbers between 21 and 99 when written out

two-thirds   twenty-one

seven-sixteenths   ninety-nine

EXERCISE 7.6

Add or remove apostrophes and/or hyphens in the following sentences as needed. If a sentence is already correct, mark the sentence with a "C."

I'll find out if it's possible to get a self-starting engine.

1. The city has decided to use it's tax surplus to repair some streets.

2. Three quarters of the club members have voted in favor of the proposed changes.

3. Since I graduated in the Class of 99, my twenty year reunion will be held in the year 2019.

4. Martin cant tell which pair of sunglasses are James.

5. It was sad to see the exfootball player endorsing a gambling outfit.

6. She was always proud of being a self taught woman.

7. Please do not cross your 7s like some Europeans do.

8. The bone fragments state of decay made them difficult to analyze.

9. Although its clear to the trainer what Tony needs to do, he himself wont do it.

10. Nolans' children want to attend camp this summer.

GRAMMAR REVIEW

Make whatever changes to each sentence are necessary by adding the correct punctuation marks. If a sentence is already correct, mark it with a "C."

1. Jed left his home in Florida last week, he plans to start a workout studio in northern Michigan.

2. Sex, drugs, betrayal, and violence the movie script had it all.

3. There was one thing the friends all had in common ambition.

4. According to the Washington Post, smoking tobacco is one of the worst things anyone can do to their health.

5. The new self help book didnt sell well, the trouble was the title Im Not Sure Im Ok, But I Know For Sure Youre Not Ok.

6. The hard driving reporter was setting herself up for an early heart attack.

7. I cant help thinking, said Clint, that somehow this could have been avoided.

8. How much do you think Picasso's Guernica would fetch at an auction? asked Bert.

9. The famous response of the American officer was just one word Nuts.

10. Catherine still maintains that Chinatown was the best movies ever, Andrews taste tends more toward Dumb & Dumber.

Applying the Grammar Lesson

Examine your first draft, and underline the internal punctuation marks (other than commas). Then check to make sure that the marks are used correctly. Make any corrections necessary. Here is an example of Makena's first draft, with the internal punctuation underlined:

Sometimes friends and family can get in the way of people who are trying to improve their health. I have a friend (Shara) who has a weight problem. She tried to cut back on eating, but her mother wasn't supportive at all. She says to Shara, Why <u>arent</u> you eating everything I give you? <u>Dont</u> let that food go to waste. Shara said <u>"</u>she didn't want to eat so much.<u>"</u> and her mother actually got angry with her. Shara is having a hard time because<u>:</u> she wants to lose weight but she doesn't want to make her mother angry either. Sometimes it happens in other ways. When she and her boyfriend go to the movies, he always wants butter on the popcorn. Do you know how unhealthy that stuff is? Well, Shara wants her own popcorn without butter, and he told her she's <u>"</u>stuck up<u>"</u> now. Shara just wants two things<u>;</u> to lose weight and keep her friends. But it's like as if they're making her choose<u>:</u> that isn't right. I try to be supportive because I want her to be healthy, and I've always been pretty healthy myself. I eat lots of salads, fish, and chicken, and I try to stay away from fried foods, butter, and desserts. It seems to me that friends should help each other—that's what it's all about, right?

Check the underlined passages to see how Makena corrected her punctuation errors.

Sometimes friends and family can get in the way of people who are trying to improve their health. I have a friend<u>,</u> Shara<u>,</u> who has a weight problem. She tried to cut back on eating, but her mother wasn't supportive at all. She says to Shara, Why <u>aren't</u> you eating everything I give you? <u>Don't</u> let that food go to waste. Shara said_she didn't want to eat so much<u>,</u> and her mother actually got angry with her. Shara is having a hard time because she wants to lose weight but she doesn't want to make her mother angry either. Sometimes it happens in other ways. When she and her boyfriend go to the movies, he always wants butter on the popcorn. Do you know how unhealthy that stuff is? Well, Shara wants her own popcorn without butter, and he told her she's_stuck up_now. Shara just wants two things: to lose weight and keep her friends. But it's like as if they're making her choose. That isn't right. I try to be supportive because I want her to be healthy, and I've always been pretty healthy myself. I eat lots of salads, fish, and chicken, and I try to stay away from fried foods, butter, and desserts. It seems to me that friends should help each other—that's what it's all about, right?

Writing the Second Draft

Now that you have completed the Grammar Lesson, you are ready to write the second draft of your Chapter Writing Assignment. Complete this draft before beginning the Sentence Lesson. Respond to the revision questions as you work on your rewrite.

Revision questions

- Does your topic sentence respond directly to the question you have chosen?
- Examine your paragraph. Have you chosen your words carefully, keeping in mind your subject, purpose, and audience?
- Have you been careful to avoid slang, contractions, and overly formal language?
- Does your paragraph have at least one semicolon, one colon, and one other type of internal punctuation? If not, make sure that you include at least one of each of these in your second draft.

After examining her paragraph, Makena realized that a number of her punctuation marks were incorrect, and that a few others needed to be added. In addition, she decided to work on making her paragraph more formal, choosing words that would help convey a more academic tone to her writing. This is her second draft:

Sometimes friends and family can get in the way of people who are trying to improve their health. I have a friend, Shara, who tried to loose weight, but her mother wasn't very supportive. She says to Shara, "Why aren't you eating everything I give you? Don't let that food go to waste."

When Shara said she didn't want to eat so much, her mother couldn't except it. Shara is having a hard time because she wants to loose weight, but she doesn't want to upset her mother to. Her mother's anger really effects her, but that isn't her only problem. When Shara and her boyfriend go to the movies, he always wants butter on the popcorn. Now Shara wants popcorn without butter, and he told her she's stuck up. Shara just wants two things: to loose weight and keep her friends. But its as if their making her choose. That isn't right. I try to be supportive because I want her to be healthy, and I've always been pretty healthy myself. I eat lots of salads, fish, and chicken; I try to stay away from fried foods, butter, and desserts. Friends should help each other, specially to be healthy.

SENTENCE LESSON

Usage

The word **usage** refers to how words are used in a sentence. Usage errors can occur in several forms, some of which you have already learned. For instance, one common usage error occurs with the incorrect use of adjectives and adverbs, as discussed in Chapter Five, or the errors in using the proper pronoun case, as discussed in Chapter Six. However, some usage errors occur when writers chose the wrong word. This can happen with words that have identical or similar pronunciation, but are spelled differently.

Learning which word to use in a given sentence requires a good knowledge of vocabulary; nevertheless, you can be aware ahead of time of words which are *likely* to be misused. The following list of items includes many of the more commonly misused words. The words are listed, and their proper usage described, with examples.

accept, except

"accept" is a verb that means "to receive"
"except" is a preposition which means "but"

Examples: No one **accepted** responsibility for the accident.
             All of the students **except** Camille understood.

advice, advise

"advice" is a noun that means "an opinion which is offered as a means of assistance"

"advise" is a verb that means "to offer advice or recommendations"

Examples: The counselor offered sound **advice** to her client.

The senator **advised** the president to veto the bill.

affect, effect

"affect" is a verb that means "to influence or change"

"effect" used as a verb means "to bring about or cause something to occur"

"effect" used as a noun means "a result"

Examples: The alcohol **affected** her judgment.

The owner **effected** drastic changes in the management structure of his company.

The **effects** of this drug are not yet clear.

all ready, already

"all ready" shows a state of readiness

"already" is an adverb that means "before or earlier"

Examples: The apartment was **all ready** for the landlord's check out inspection.

Your date is **already** here and waiting in the driveway.

all right, alright

"all right" is the correct form. Do not use "alright."

Examples: I think the injury will be **all right** for now, but we must get you to a doctor soon.

allusion, illusion

"allusion" is a noun that means "a reference to something else"

"illusion" is a noun that means "a false image or perception"

Examples: Luanne made an **allusion** to Shakespeare, but it went right over Jean's head.

The magician's tricks relied on **illusions.**

alot, a lot

"alot" is incorrect. "A lot" is the correct spelling.

Examples: Sean wants to make **a lot** of money this summer for college.

amount, number

"amount" should be used with things that cannot be individually counted

"number" should be used with things that can be individually counted

Examples: The large **amount** of admiration and love people had for Betty Lou was evident at her funeral service.

The **number** of refugees continued to grow.

complement, compliment

"complement" used as a verb means "to complete or balance"

"compliment" used as a verb means "to show appreciation for"

Examples: The white baby's breath **complemented** the other flowers in Christina's wedding bouquet.

The bride was **complimented** on her beautiful gown.

conscience, conscious

"conscience" is a noun that means "a moral sense or guide"

"conscious" used as a verb means "to be aware"

Examples: The businessman's complete lack of a **conscience** was a key aspect of his financial success.

Penny was **conscious** of a problem in the quality control department.

could of, should of, would of

All are incorrect usage. The correct forms are "could have," "should have," and "would have."

Examples: Sylvester **could have** been a contender.

The applicant **should have** been given greater consideration.

The police **would have** arrested the murderer if they had realized that he was already in their custody on an unrelated charge.

farther, further

"farther" refers to physical distance

"further" refers to distance in degree or time or space

Examples: Phoenix was **farther** from the Grand Canyon than he had realized.

The Jurassic period is **further** back in history than the Cretaceous period.

fewer, less

"fewer" should be used to describe things that can be counted individually

"less" should be used to describe things that cannot be counted individually

Examples: There are **fewer** people on unemployment than there were ten years ago.

Less hatred and prejudice is only possible if people are willing to set aside old stereotypes.

hanged, hung

"hanged" refers to a method of execution

"hung" refers to the suspension of something above the ground, such as a picture.

Examples: In the old west, horse thieves were **hanged** because their crime was a direct threat to the life and livelihood of the horse owner.

Jackie **hung** the tapestry above the mantel.

it's, its

"it's" is a contraction meaning "it is" or "it has"

"its" is the possessive case of "it"

Examples: **It's** clear now that you will not help me.

The dog is heading out to find **its** master.

Note: Avoid the spelling **"its'"** as there is no such word.

lay, laid

"lay" means "to set something down." Lay requires a direct object.

"lay" also is the past tense of "lie"

"laid" is the past tense of "lay"

"lie" means "to be reclining." Lie does not take an object.

Examples: Parker **lays** his journal on his bedside table before going to sleep each night.

Parker **laid** his journal on his bedside table last night.

My grandmother **lies** on the couch to take her daily nap.

My grandmother **lay** on the couch to take her nap yesterday afternoon.

loose, lose

"loose" as a verb means "to untie or unbind"

"loose" as an adjective means "untied or unbound"

"lose" means "to misplace" or "to be defeated"

Examples: The knot on the package **loosened** as it was handled.

Your shoelaces are **loose.**

I don't want to **lose** my train of thought.

many, much

"many" should be used to describe things that can be counted individually

"much" should be used to describe things that cannot be counted individually

Examples: This soda pop has too **many** calories.

This soda pop has too **much** sugar.

principal, principle

"principal" means either "main or most important" or "a head administrator of a school"; "principal" can also refer to money used as a fund to gain interest or pay off debt.

"principle" means a "concept or idea"

Examples: The **principal** problem with enforcing the law has been a lack of cooperation between federal agencies.

After we receive our inheritance, we plan to invest the **principal** and live off the interest.

The ancient Greeks formulated some of the basic **principles** of geometry.

set, sit

"set" means "to place." "Set" requires a direct object.

"sit" means "to occupy a seat" or "to rest." "Sit" does not require a direct object.

Examples: Go ahead and **set** that box over there by the door.

The box is **sitting** by the door.

than, then

"than" is used to show comparison

"then" is used to indicate a sequence in time

Examples: Deb would rather work for a little and feel good about her job **than** get paid a lot and hate her work.

First, I'll finish repainting the wagon, and **then** I'll start refinishing the wooden table.

their, there, they're

"their" is the possessive case of "they"

"there" is an adjective that means "a specified or indicated place"

"they're" is a contraction for "they are"

Examples: The new owners were appalled to find the shape **their** house was left in by the previous owners.

Over **there** is where the grave site will be.

I talked to three doctors and **they're** in agreement about their diagnosis.

To, too, two

"to" is a preposition used to show the direction or a condition of something; may also be used to form the infinitive of a verb

"too" is an adverb meaning either "also," "excessively," or "very"

"two" is a number, used as either a noun or an adjective

Examples: Marisa and Sandra rode the bus **to** the mall.

Deborah was **too** embarrassed for words by her boyfriend's boorish behavior.

You have only **two** options: quit right now or stay until the end of season.

who's, whose

"who's" is a contraction for "who is" or "who has"

"whose" is the possessive case of "who"

Examples: **Who's** going to walk the dog tonight?

Whose coffee mug is this on the counter?

woman, women

"woman" is the singular

"women" is the plural. Avoid the incorrect use of "women" for "woman"

Examples: Now, there is a **woman** I would like to see elected President.

The issue of **women's** rights will continue to be of great importance in the twenty-first century.

your, you're

"your" is the possessive of "you"

"you're" is the contraction of "you are"

Examples: This Barry Manilow CD must be from **your** collection.

Everyone says that **you're** going to be a great success in whatever you do.

Sentence Review

Examine each of the following sentences. Circle the correct word to use in each sentence.

1. The new environmental laws will (affect, effect) air pollution levels.

2. My grandpa always gave me good (advice, advise).

3. It's important that (their, there, they're) ready to go when the train arrives.

4. Make sure that the broadcast has (all ready, already) started before trying to record it on the VCR.

5. The pictures should be (hanged, hung) along that wall over there.

6. There would be (fewer, less) problems in the world if people in rich countries did not eat so much.

7. The (principal, principle) factor in our success will be our marketing and sales effort.

8. Laurie exclaimed, "(You're, Your) lying to me about the Cadillac!"

9. The only trouble with fame is (it's, its) hard to get rid of when you want to.

10. The new exercise class is led by a (woman, women) with a master's degree in physical education.

11. Alex wanted to see if any of his teeth were (loose, lose).

12. To stop a fleeing car, the police officer (laid, lay) a barrier across the freeway.

13. Sam has traveled (farther, further) than anyone else to be with us here today.

14. The political couple's public display of a happy marriage was actually an (allusion, illusion).

15. We (could have, could of) starved waiting to be served in that restaurant!

16. I know I have made (alot, a lot) of mistakes in how I've tried to lose weight.

17. The vase is (setting, sitting) on the stand near the door.

18. Be careful that you do not (lay, lie) down on any snakes when you're outdoors.

19. The large (amount, number) of food you consume is not healthy.

20. If you skip your exercises, it will be on your (conscience, conscious), not mine.

Applying the Sentence Lesson

Examine your second draft for errors in usage. Correct any errors that you find. If you are uncertain about a word's meaning, look it up in a dictionary to double-check.

Here is Makena's second draft, with her usage errors corrected:

Sometimes friends and family can get in the way of people who are

trying to improve their health. I have a friend, Shara, who tried to ~~loose~~ **lose**

weight, but her mother wasn't very supportive. She says to Shara, "Why aren't you eating everything I give you? Don't let that food go to waste."

When Shara said she didn't want to eat so much, her mother couldn't
accept
~~except~~ it. Shara is having a hard time because she wants to **lose** ~~loose~~

weight, but she doesn't want to upset her mother **too** ~~to~~. Her mother's
affects
anger really ~~effects~~ her, but that isn't her only problem. When Shara and

her boyfriend go to the movies, he always wants butter on the popcorn.

Now Shara wants popcorn without butter, and he told her she's stuck
lose
up. Shara just wants two things: to ~~loose~~ weight and keep her friends.
it's   **they're**
But ~~its~~ as if ~~their~~ making her choose. That isn't right. I try to be

supportive because I want her to be healthy, and I've always been pretty

healthy myself. I eat lots of salads, fish, and chicken; I try to stay away

from fried foods, butter, and desserts. Friends should help each other,
especially
~~specially~~ to be healthy.

Writing the Final Draft

Rewrite your second draft, making sure that you check all the words to avoid any errors in usage. This will be your final draft. Respond to the revision questions as you work on your rewrite.

Revision questions

- Does your paragraph have a strong sense of structure, with a beginning, middle, and end?

- Have you provided effective transitions as you move from one idea to the next?

- Have you provided sufficient examples and illustrations to support the main idea in your topic sentence?

- Have you checked your paragraph for careful use of language throughout? Rewrite any language that is inappropriate for an academic audience.

- Have you checked your paragraph for usage errors?

Hand in the final draft, with the materials from your prewriting, first draft, second draft, and any other materials you created in the process of writing this assignment.

After Makena corrected her usage errors, she decided that she could improve her paragraph by emphasizing why Shara's mother and boyfriend were not supportive. She also worked to remove any unnecessary words. Here is her final draft:

Sometimes friends and family can stop people from improving their health. My friend Shara is trying to lose weight, but her mother hasn't been very supportive. She says to Shara, "Why aren't you eating everything I give you? Don't let that food go to waste." When Shara said she didn't want to eat so much, her mother couldn't accept it. Shara wants to lose weight, but she doesn't want to upset her mother, too. Her mother is angry because she cooks all the time, and when Shara doesn't eat, she seems to think Shara is rejecting her. Shara's mother isn't her only problem. When Shara and her boyfriend go to the movies, he always wants butter on the popcorn. Now Shara wants popcorn without butter, and he told her she's stuck up. That's unfair: she's not stuck up, she just wants two things: to lose weight and keep her friends. Her boyfriend is making things difficult because he's a bit heavy himself. It's like they're trying to force her back into bad habits. I try to be supportive because I want her to be healthy, and I'm healthy myself. I eat lots of salads, fish, and chicken; I stay away from fried foods, butter, and desserts. No one should have to choose between friends and health. Friends should help each other, especially to be healthy.

PORTFOLIO CHECKLIST

In your portfolio, you should now have the following:

1. your Asking Questions prewriting.
2. a First Draft. The first draft should have internal punctuation marks underlined and corrected where needed.
3. a Second Draft. The second draft with any usage errors underlined and corrected.
4. a Final Draft.

PARTING SHOT

1. Why are fad diets attractive to people?
2. How have advertisers exploited our interest in being healthy?
3. How have we confused health with vanity?

GOALS IN REVIEW

In this chapter, you learned about

- asking questions as a prewriting strategy
- choosing your words carefully
- end punctuation and internal punctuation
- word usage

PRACTICE CHAPTER TEST

Part I

Correct each of the following sentences for punctuation errors. If a sentence is already correct, mark it with a "C."

1. I just can't wait, said Leo, for the sequel.

2. Abraham Lincoln, Woodrow Wilson, Franklin Roosevelt, these great American presidents never served in the U.S. military.

3. I like many ethnic foods, such as: egg rolls, tamales, and gnocchi.

4. The traffic seemed to be at a standstill, however, those on motorcycles were moving freely between the lanes of cars.

5. Malcolm's favorite television show of all time was Home Improvement.

6. The class was required to read Stephen Crane's short story, The Open Boat.

7. Its clear that the apostrophe is slowly disappearing from our language.

8. "I just wish to say, no, forget I even said that."

9. "Ouch that frying pan is still hot," exclaimed Freida.

10. The four year old child thought the joke was so funny she told it again and again and again.

11. The factory gates lock down at 1 am whether anyone is still inside or not.

12. World War II 1939-1945 devastated the world like no other war before or since.

13. The news was joyous the baby had been born healthy.

14. We went to see John and Dianes first home as a married couple.

15. He contracted a rare disease on his visit to Southeast Asia, therefore, he had to be quarantined immediately.

Part II

Choose the correct word in the parentheses.

1. I'm not sure that I would rather be a hammer (than, then) a nail.

2. Victoria was looking to see which candidate would stand firmly by his (principles, principals).

3. There are a lot (less, fewer) young fans going to baseball games than in the past.

4. The (complements, compliments) the actress paid to her fellow cast members were shallow and insincere.

5. Don't bother me because I have (a lot, alot) on my mind.

6. Sheldon (could of, could have) gone to medical school if he had had better grades.

7. The hotel appears to be (farther, further) from the tourist attractions than we would like.

8. Calvin (hanged, hung) his diploma on his office wall.

9. The water had too (much, many) chlorine to be safe.

10. The criminal (lay, laid) his gun on the floor after the police had wounded him.

8

The Environment

CHAPTER GOALS

In this chapter, you will learn about

- creating an outline as a prewriting strategy,
- tone,
- capitalization and spelling, and
- parallel structure.

The theme of this final chapter is the Environment. The environment is not simply a beautiful forest miles away to be enjoyed in pictures and visited on the occasional vacation—the environment is the natural world in which everybody lives. However, there is little agreement on how to treat the environment: some take the attitude that environmental concerns are exaggerated; others believe not nearly enough is being done to save the environment. The issues related to the environment are important because they truly affect everyone.

OPENING SHOT

QUESTIONS ABOUT THE PICTURE

1. What are the effects of the automobile—and the culture it has created—on the environment?

2. How can we balance our needs, such as for automobiles, with concern about the environment?

3. What kinds of physical environments do you find most stressful? What kinds reduce your stress?

READING

Questions to Consider

1. How are environmental issues related to lifestyles?

2. Do you do anything to help preserve the environment, such as participating in recycling programs or boycotting firms that abuse the environment?

3. Have advancing technologies been good or bad for the environment?

Words to Watch

aerie	an elevated, secluded dwelling; a bird's nest high on a cliff
resonance	able to evoke a response
greenhouse gas	an air-borne chemical compound that contributes to the greenhouse effect—raising the temperature of the Earth
ecofreaks	environmental extremists
ethos	the distinguishing character or beliefs of a person
exhort	to urge strongly
greenwashing	the practice by companies to proclaim themselves environmentally friendly when they are not
think tank	a group or institution organized for the purpose of conducting research into a social or technology problem, or for examining issues from a particular political or social viewpoint
black ink	showing a profit

The Battle for Planet Earth
Sharon Begley

1   During her two years in the redwood tree dubbed "Luna," Julia (Butterfly) Hill became a much-admired symbol as she sacrificed personal comfort to a higher cause. To protest the clear-cutting of ancient forests, she endured 90-mile-an-hour winds, El Niño downpours, almost constant damp and cold, and deprivation (she lived mostly on raw fruits and vegetables, and used a plastic-lined bucket for a toilet). But during her time in the 6-foot-by-8-foot plywood aerie in California's Humboldt County, which left her barely able to walk when she finally came to the ground last December, the whine of the buzz saws never ceased. Pacific Lumber Corp. left the 180-foot-tall Luna standing, as well as 2.9 acres around it. But the rest of the company's redwoods, scattered across 10,000 acres, were fair game.

2   And so Hill has become a symbol of a different sort, one that has special resonance as the country approaches the thirtieth anniversary of Earth Day this weekend. Saving a tree only to lose a forest, her protest against logging forced activists to confront a disturbing possibility: that individual actions on behalf of the environment pale beside the actions of big business and big government.

3   "Well-meaning people frequently focus on personal responsibility, partly because they see it as a way of doing something, without looking at how effective it's going to be," says long-time environmentalist Barry Commoner of New York's Queens College. "It's an escape on their [environmental groups'] part." No matter how many of us switched from aerosols to roll-ons, the CFCs that powered spray cans continued destroying the ozone layer—until the manufacture and use of these chemicals began to be phased out worldwide by the 1987 international agreement known as the Montreal Protocol. Millions of us might walk to the mailbox rather than drive, but the effect on emissions of the greenhouse-gas carbon dioxide (which comes from burning coal, oil and natural gas) is minuscule compared with the effect of more than 68 million SUVs on American roads. A single decision by the chairman of Royal Dutch/Shell has greater impact on the health of the planet than all the coffee-ground-composting, organic-cotton-wearing ecofreaks gathering in Washington, D.C., for Earth Day festivities this weekend. Obviously, if 1 billion people in the developed world stop driving, switch to solar energy and replace old appliances with superefficient new ones, greenhouse emissions would plummet. The question is whether that mass action, or comparable steps by a few businesses and governments, is easier to bring about.

4   The message of the first Earth Day—April 22, 1970—had a certain innocence, imbued with a certain can-do-ism; individual actions would roll back the damage done to the planet. In that spirit, some 20 million people participated in Earth Day events, such as dumping five tons of roadside trash on the steps of a West Virginia courthouse to protest litter, or burying a car in San Jose, Calif., to protest the air pollution produced

by a nation of drivers. The emphasis on the individual was picked up in best sellers like (notice the pronoun) "50 Things You Can Do to Save the Planet," as well as in public-service campaigns that hectored us to carpool, bicycle to work, recycle, boycott rain-forest wood, buy only "dolphin-safe" tuna.

5   Earth Day 2000—April 22—reflects the new ethos. The theme of events that will be staged by more than 5,000 groups in the 185 participating countries is climate change and the threats—rising seas, shifting agricultural zones, more extreme weather—that a warmer world poses. The Earth Day 2000 slogan, "Clean Energy Now!," calls for replacing energy sources that produce heat-trapping greenhouse gases with energy sources (solar electricity, wind power) that do not. Although some of the most ecorighteous have unplugged their homes from the electricity-utility grid in favor of solar panels on their roofs and fuel cells in their basements, at the rate that is happening there will be orange groves in Anchorage, Alaska, before the greenhouse effect is wrestled into submission.

6   If there was a single case that opened activists' eyes, it was one with a hamburger inside. Environmentalists had been protesting the use of McDonald's "clamshell" boxes because of the ozone-destroying CFCs used in their manufacture. Customers were exhorted to boycott the Golden Arches. But—surprise!—burger lust beat save-the-planet fervor hands down. The Environmental Defense Fund saw a better way, and began working with McDonald's to design a box that would keep the burger hot but not harm the ozone layer. In 1989 McD's phased out the Styrofoam clamshell in favor of paperboard.

7   That success began to redirect some green activism. Environmental Defense (it recently dropped the "Fund") has worked with UPS to use more recycled paper and plastic in its packaging. (Recycling was a nonstarter as long as there was no market for the newspapers we all dutifully bundled and the plastic bottles we put outside.) Conservation International has advised Starbucks on growing organic coffee plants in Mexico, and the Gap uses organic cotton. Environmental Defense is back with McDonald's, finding ways to cut energy consumption by at least 10 percent at every Mickey D's.

8   Whether such moves are driven by a company's desire to be a good corporate citizen or to gain economic advantage by draping itself in green bunting is hard to say. There is no question that some "greenwashing" is going on. Bayernwerk, a Bavarian utility, began selling "Aqua Power" last year when Germany began to let customers choose their electricity supplier. Bayernwerk markets Aqua Power as 100 percent green, renewable, hydroelectric energy. But any consumer who signs up gets power from the same mix of sources as before: hydro, gas, coal, and nuclear. Nothing changes except some accounting, and there's no net benefit to the environment. There is a benefit, though, to Bayernwerk, which charges more for Aqua Power and has been swamped with orders for it.

9   Greenwashing takes many forms. "Companies often advertise themselves as environmentally friendly even though they might have some

pretty hideous environmental records," says Jill Johnson of the group Earth Day 2000. California's PG&E, the utility that settled out of court after the real Erin Brockovich accused it of polluting groundwater, runs pro-environment ads. But PG&E is due in court in November on charges of polluting wells in a second California town. "PG&E has a very good environmental track record," says spokesman Greg Pruett, citing recycling and waste reduction. Weyerhauser, the timber company, cuts old-growth trees in Canada but trumpets the 100 million tree seedlings it will plant this year.

10   Overall, the greening of corporate America is real and hasn't been as hard to achieve as some activists imagined. That is especially true for greenhouse gases and climate change, the focus of Earth Day 2000. "Now there's more recognition by companies that there may be an economic advantage to reducing emissions of greenhouse gases," says Paul Portney, president of the think tank Resources for the Future. More and more companies are changing the way they heat and light their buildings and design their factories to reduce greenhouse-gas emissions as well as their energy bills. (Energy-efficiency upgrades can save a company roughly $1 per square foot of office or factory space every year.) The reductions often exceed those called for in the 1997 international agreement on greenhouse warming called the Kyoto Treaty, whose goal of reducing greenhouse emissions 7 percent from their 2000 levels is deemed so threatening to the economy of many oil, coal, and chemical companies that the White House does not dare submit it to the Senate for ratification.

11   Corporations from Xerox and Compaq to Du Pont, 3M and Toyota have realized that green behavior can mean black ink, says Joseph Romm, director of the nonprofit Center for Energy and Climate Solutions. Royal Dutch/Shell is reducing emissions of greenhouse gases at its plants by 2002 to a projected 25 percent below levels of 1990, to 100 million tons. For an equivalent annual cut, every car in New England would have to be taken off the road for five years. Du Pont is cutting its greenhouse emissions 40 percent from their 1991 levels by this year, to 58 million tons. Anyone who dutifully unscrewed the old incandescent light bulbs and subbed in compact fluorescents, scowling every time the &%# things dim, can ponder this: Boeing's lighting upgrade reduced its use of electricity for lighting 90 percent and saves 100,000 tons of carbon dioxide every year. Some 500,000 people would have had to change a light bulb to achieve that. Companies that can't squeeze out another single kilowatt hour of energy savings in their own facilities can bankroll someone else's. Shaklee, the consumer-products company, and Interface, Inc., a $1.3 billion floor-covering manufacturer, are paying to upgrade school boilers from coal to natural gas, which produces fewer greenhouse emissions. "There has been tremendous change in the corporate world," says Gaylord Nelson, who as a senator from Wisconsin conceived the first Earth Day.

12   None of this is to say that individual decisions do not matter. They do: the lemming-like movement from cars to SUVs has resulted in some 200 million more tons of carbon-dioxide emissions every year than if everyone had stayed with his nice little Taurus. But individuals can exert

greater force for environmental good by pressuring companies and governments than by lecturing their Navigator-driving friends. Or by spending two years in a tree.

PREPARING TO WRITE

Creating an Outline

Making an **outline** is a way to organize your thoughts or materials before you begin writing. An outline is a plan of what you are going to write. When you write an outline, you have a better sense of how different details of your topic relate to each other, and to the topic sentence of your paragraph.

There is more than one way to create an outline. You might think that an outline needs to have a strict format, using Roman numbers (I, II, III,) followed by capital letters (A, B, C,) and then Arabic numbers (1, 2, 3,). Indeed, such an outline, called a **formal outline,** can be very useful when you are planning an extended work. However, in many writing situations, a formal outline is unnecessary or impractical because of the multiple levels of detail it requires.

For shorter works, such as a single paragraph, an **informal** or **scratch outline** might be all you need. In a scratch outline, you begin with a general statement (which could eventually become your topic sentence) and specific details that support that statement. Here is an example of a scratch outline on the topic of dams:

Building dams on rivers causes enormous environmental damage.

> animals must find new homes
> plant life is killed
> areas downstream are destroyed by the change in water supply
> the creation of an artificial lake wreaks havoc on the local ecosystem

Preparing Yourself to Write

In order to create an outline, you must already have some knowledge of your topic. The point of an outline is to organize ideas and special details that you already have. Because of this, the creation of an outline could follow the use of other prewriting techniques that you used to generate ideas. You might also need to go to the library to do some research on your topic.

Once you have assembled your ideas, formulate a general statement. This statement essentially serves as the first version of your topic sentence, so make sure that it states the point or argument that you want to make. If you are responding to a writing question, such as a Chapter Writing Assignment question, the sentence should directly respond to the question.

After you have written your general statement, you list specific details underneath. Make certain that you supply enough details for the length of the writing assignment. An outline with too few details will not be of much use.

Another benefit of your scratch outline is that you can easily see if certain details don't actually belong with the others. Each detail should be directly related to the general statement. Look at the following scratch outline. The unrelated items have been struck through:

Cell phones are a great invention for parents of teenagers.

parents keep track of their teens

teens can contact parents in a moment if there is trouble

cell phones are becoming more affordable so everyone in the family can have one

~~beeping cell phones can be very annoying~~

parents can contact friends of their teenagers in case of emergency

~~cell phone technology is quite amazing~~

cell phones provide an additional sense of security for everyone

A final benefit of creating an outline is that you can check the *order* of your details. You want to have your details arranged in some logical fashion. One logical order is *spatial order,* in which details are arranged according to their physical relationship to each other, such as left to right, or nearer to farther away. Another logical order is *chronological order,* in which details are arranged according to their time sequence.

Often, though, your topics lead to creating an order based on *importance.* You can lead with your strongest point and end with your weakest, or begin with your weakest and end with your strongest. There are advantages and disadvantages to each. However, since you're already starting your paragraph with a topic sentence, the next most important position in your paragraph is at the end. For this reason, many people prefer the weakest-to-strongest order.

To prepare for her Chapter Writing Assignment, Tien decided to do an outline based on Question #3. The following is her result.

Rich countries like the US do have a big effect on the environment

we use up so many natural resources

global warming is getting worse because of our pollution

sea levels will rise

weather will get worse

wealthy nations are wasteful of resources

we need to start recycling

Prewriting

Now that you know how to create an outline, do a scratch outline for a topic within the subject of the environment, or choose a question from the Chapter Writing Assignment. After you complete your outline, examine what issues have been raised in the outline and whether or not you want to pursue any of those.

CHAPTER WRITING ASSIGNMENT

Write a 100- to 200-word paragraph in response to one of the following writing assignments. Instructions in the chapter will guide you through the writing process. At different points in the chapter, you will be asked to produce more work on this assignment. By the end of the chapter, you will have completed your final draft.

1. How is the size of the human population related to the state of the environment? Explain, being specific.

2. Can human beings survive while destroying substantial parts of the earth's ecosystem, such as rare species, habitats, and vegetation? Explain your answer, being specific.

3. Many people argue that people living in wealthy nations are going to have to scale back their consumption of material goods, or enormous environmental devastation will occur. Do you agree or disagree? Explain, being specific.

4. In "The Battle for Planet Earth," Sharon Begley argues that individual actions to help the environment are not as important or effective as actions taken by large corporations or governments. How important do you think individual efforts to preserve the environment are, and why?

WRITING LESSON

Tone

In your personal life, you are probably conscious of the importance of tone in conversation. Statements such as "It wasn't so much what he said, it was how he said it" reflect an awareness of the importance of tone in conveying a message. If, for example, your roommate comes home one day, slams the door, drops her books on a table in a huff, and in response to your polite "How was your day?" answers growling, "Fine. Just perfect," you know that her day was actually not fine. The tone conveyed anger, not satisfaction.

Your writing can carry tone in the same way that your voice can. Indeed, correct use of tone is an effective tool for a writer. The following are some of the ways that tone can be described:

serious	more formal, unemotional, and also more public. More likely to use vocabulary that includes abstract words
ironic	saying one thing while meaning another
humorous	funny. Often casual, perhaps even employing slang.
solemn	like the serious tone, but more grave, somber. Often used for public or religious ceremonies.
joyful	a positive, upbeat feeling
mournful	deeply sad from a feeling of loss. Might be personal or public in its expressions and use of vocabulary.
sarcastic	harshly ironic; a critical, insulting form of humor

As a student, you will usually be expected to write in a **serious** tone when confronting academic subjects. In order to fulfill this expectation, you should keep in mind several characteristics of a serious tone:

- word choice is key. As discussed in Chapter Seven, when your audience is a general academic audience, you need to avoid using many personal pronoun references, avoid the use of contractions or abbreviations, and avoid the use of slang.
- The individual words are important, but how you use them is also important. When you are writing in a serious tone, you are attempting to communicate to a reader through the force of your ideas. What you are not trying to do is emotionally manipulate the reader. For example, you must avoid **slanted language.** Slanted language conveys emotional approval or disapproval towards its subjects.

Slanted

The jocks in the back of the classroom are whining about flunking the test.

Words such as "jocks," "whining," and "flunking" are emotionally-laden with disapproval. No sensible reader could examine that sentence and not know that the writer is showing disapproval unfairly.

Not slanted

The student-athletes in the back of the classroom are complaining because they failed the test.

- The content of the writing conveys tone, as well. Writing is serious if it addresses its subject in a serious fashion, by using facts, statistics, and expert opinions to bolster whatever is being said. Asking a reader to consider statements without specific details to support those points merely invites the reader to criticize the writer as superficial.

Non-specific

No one in business really cares about the environment at all.

Specific

Utility companies that dispose of hazardous wastes directly into rivers, lakes, and oceans are showing a lack of concern for the effects of the waste on the environment.

- A serious tone cannot be conveyed if the writing is littered with frequent errors in grammar, spelling, and punctuation. Technical matters are important; they help the reader to understand the writer. Technical errors undercut the value of whatever the writer is saying, and ultimately, the reader might even question the writer's credibility. Therefore, check your work carefully, work with a tutor if you find it helpful in preparing your work, and always proofread materials before turning them in.

ZOOM-IN PRACTICE

Spend five minutes writing a slanted passage on any subject. Then, rewrite the slanted passage using a serious tone that could be used for a general academic audience.

Writing the First Draft

After Tien had completed her outline, she was ready to write the first draft of her Chapter Writing Assignment. She chose to answer Question #4. The following is her paragraph:

Here in the united states, were people have everything it seems, we

don't realize that what we're doing can have such a big affect on the

environment. But that's the problem because we DO cause so much damage, like with the ozone and also we cause air polution. We're useing up so many natural resources. In my biology 130 class, the instructor told us that Global Warming is making the earth hotter every year, and if it goes on long enough, the poler ice caps will melt, causing the sea level to rise. There could be tons of storms, hericanes, and there will be drouts to in other parts of the world. dirty air, missing ozone, and there is water polution—these are all problems that are mostly caused by wealthy nations like america. It really makes me mad, especially when I see jerks all around me being so wasteful, like everything is going to be their forever, like magic or something. We have to start conversation efforts, like recycling, reusing products, and also we can make things out of more environmentaly safe materials. Because this is the only world we have—and don't you forget it!

Now that you have completed your prewriting assignments, you are ready to write your first draft in response to one of the questions in the Chapter Writing Assignment. Complete this draft before beginning the Grammar Lesson.

GRAMMAR LESSON

Capitalization and Spelling

Capitalization and spelling are important in English because they are part of the keys to communicating well. Inconsistent capitalization and poor spelling mark writing as amateurish or even incompetent. The result is that the reader of such writing is less likely to take the writer seriously, no matter how valid or important the message.

Capitalization

Most fluent writers of English have a knowledge of the basic rules of capitalization, but there are some situations in which confusion can occur. A review of the rules of capitalization can help clarify misunderstandings you might have.

1. **Begin a sentence by capitalizing the first word of a sentence. If the first word is a number, spell out the number unless it is a year.**

   The table had uneven legs.

   Thirty-six years ago, a miraculous event occurred.

   1984 did not turn out to be that bad of a year after all.

   Note: Some instructors prefer that sentences not begin with a year as a number.

   The year 1984 did not turn out that badly after all.

2. **Capitalize people's names, place names, professional or personal titles, and other proper nouns.**

   My Uncle Michael graduated from the University of Notre Dame.

   The New York Yankees may be the most famous team in all of sports.

   Professor Sullivan was visiting from Portland, Oregon.

3. **Capitalize directions only when they refer to a specific place or region.**

   Turn south when you get to Newbury Highway.

   The representatives from North Dakota were given special treatment.

   The problems in the Middle East seldom seem to go away.

4. **Capitalize the days of the week, months, and holidays.**

   Tuesday marks the last day of Mardi Gras in New Orleans.

   This December, my family plans to have its first Kwanzaa celebration.

   The Fourth of July is the most important national holiday of the year.

5. **Capitalize the names of academic subjects only if they are referred to as proper nouns, such as a language, or as a specific course followed by a number.**

   I heard that Math 101 was the hardest class on campus.

   Jane is a political science major, but Harriet is going to major in Spanish.

   The faculty decided to cut Music 213 from its offerings this semester, but there will still be several courses offered in piano and music appreciation.

6. **Capitalize all references to a supreme being, including pronouns.**

   References to God appear frequently in his poetry.

   The sinner asked Him for forgiveness.

   Americans are starting to learn more about Islam and its worship of Allah.

EXERCISE 8.1

Change the sentences to reflect proper capitalization. If the sentence is correct, mark it with a "C."

my favorite Vacation Spot is lake louise in alberta, canada.

My favorite vacation spot is Lake Louise in Alberta, Canada.

1. nineteen children had the flu last winter at my son's daycare, parker's playground.

2. i read a book called <u>inventing mark twain</u> last march.

3. douglas wanted to go to ucla for graduate school, but he had to accept an offer from usc instead.

4. the student claimed that she was dropping her french class because her math 22 class was taking up too much of her time.

5. a.d. 1066 was an important year in english history.

6. the declaration of independence uses the word "providence" as a means of referring to god.

7. marion found ancient greek mythology, with its gods and goddesses, to be fascinating.

8. the distinction between optometrists and ophthalmologists eludes me.

9. presidential candidates consider labor day the official start of the election season even though they begin campaigning long before that.

10. the opera *aida* is known for its dramatic staging as well as its music.

Spelling

Learning to spell correctly can be one of the more frustrating experiences for writers. Keep in mind that very few people are perfect spellers—that's one of the reasons why there are spelling bees, after all. There might be certain words that give you trouble, but with vigilance and caution, you can be on guard for them. Keeping lists of troublesome words is one way to combat this problem. Proofreading a work carefully before it is handed in is another way to catch spelling errors before others see them.

Ultimately, spelling in English can be difficult because it is not standardized. Learning the basic rules is important, but most rules have exceptions, and there are sometimes exceptions to the exceptions. The best advice is to work on your spelling by keeping spelling lists, looking words up in a dictionary frequently, and remembering that no one can spell every word correctly!

1. **Use "i" before "e," except after "c," unless sounded like "a" as in "neighbor" or "weigh."** This old rhyme works for many words, such as the following:

I before E	Except after C	Unless sounded like "a"
believe	deceive	vein
piece	receive	sleigh
grief	conceive	veil
thief	ceiling	freight

However, there are a number of common exceptions:

weird   foreign   leisure
neither   seize   forfeit

2. **If adding a suffix to a word which ends with a silent "e," and the suffix begins with a vowel, drop the "e." If the suffix begins with a consonant, keep the silent "e."**

mate + ed = mated   hate + ful = hateful
shake + able = shakable   extreme + ly = extremely
love + ing = loving   base + ment = basement
fate + al = fatal
immune + ity = immunity

However, there are a number of exceptions to this rule, including the following:

true + ly = truly
argue + ment = argument
canoe + ing = canoeing
peace + able = peaceable
dye + ing = dyeing

3. **If a word ends with a consonant preceded by a vowel, and you are adding a suffix that begins with a vowel, double the consonant if the word has only one syllable, or if the last syllable is accented.**

drop   dropped
fit   fitting
fat   fattest

commit	committed
prefer	preferring
expel	expelled
occur	occurred

But do not double the last consonant if the last syllable is not accented:

travel	traveled
offer	offered
label	labeled
equal	equaling
lumber	lumbering

4. **When adding a suffix to a word that ends in a "y" preceded by a consonant, change the "y" to "i" unless the suffix itself begins with an "i."**

society	societies
baby	babies
happy	happiness
vary	varied

But:

marry	marrying
vary	varying
party	partying

However, for words in which the "y" is preceded by a vowel, maintain the "y" when adding the suffix.

toy	toyed
attorney	attorneys
portray	portrayed

5. **When forming the plural of words, remember that most words form the plural by adding "s." Words that end with an "s," "ch," "sh," or "x" form plurals by adding "es." Most words that end with an "o" also form the plural by adding "es."**

oranges

cats

guns

glasses

churches

dishes

boxes

foxes

heroes

potatoes

tomatoes

However, there are exceptions, including the following:

pianos

stereos

radios

sopranos

6. **Some words form the plurals by changing their spelling in irregular fashion. If a word ends with an "f," change the "f" to a "v" and add "es." In other cases, the changes may be internal to the spelling, and in some cases, the spellings are determined by foreign languages, including Greek and Latin.**

knife	knives
leaf	leaves
wife	wives
man	men
woman	women
tooth	teeth
child	children
alumnus	alumni
syllabus	syllabi
curriculum	curricula
datum	data
medium	media
analysis	analyses
basis	bases
crisis	crises
parenthesis	parentheses
criterion	criteria

EXERCISE 8.2

Write the correct spelling for the following words:

allready   *already*   potatoe   _____

alot   _____   analysises   _____

definate	_____	swiming	_____
accross	_____	arguement	_____
thier	_____	lunchs	_____
its'	_____	beleive	_____
millenium	_____	profitted	_____
allright	_____	heros	_____

100 Commonly Misspelled Words

The following are one hundred of the most commonly misspelled words. Check the list to see which ones you misspell frequently.

absence	academic	accept
accidentally	accommodate	accuracy
achieve	acknowledge	acquaintance
admittance	advertisement	aggravate
altogether	amateur	analyze
anonymous	apparatus	apparent
argument	arithmetic	athlete
audience	awkward	beginning
behavior	benefited	breath
breathe	calendar	conscience
conscious	criticism	criticize
definitely	dependent	desirable
disastrous	development	dissatisfied
echoes	effect	eighth
eligible	embarrass	equipped
exaggerate	familiar	February
fictitious	fiery	finally
fulfill	gases	grievance
guarantee	harass	illegal
intercede	judgment	knowledge
lightning	loneliness	maintenance
mathematics	mischievous	ninety
noticeable	occasion	occurred

omitted	pastime	personnel
pneumonia	possess	precede
proceed	questionnaire	repetition
restaurant	rhyme	rhythm
secretary	separate	September
sergeant	sophomore	succeed
temperament	thorough	through
unanimous	usage	vacuum
valuable	villain	Wednesday
women	writing	written
yield		

GRAMMAR REVIEW

Correct the spelling errors in the following sentences. If a sentence is correct, mark it with a "C."

1. The restuarant near the dry cleaners just went out of busyness.

2. They told me to take this job application to the Personal Department.

3. Its' clear that noone has the right to that sort of a money.

4. Weather you agree with me or not, there is know doubt the industry has been two lacks in the inforcement of environmental laws.

5. we cited the balled eagel high in the mountains.

6. the minister was known as a firey speaker.

7. The test results where disasterous, so everyone blamed everyone else.

8. Societies expectations were to much for him to bare.

9. The cold air made his breathe steam.

10. English teachers exagerrate the need for correct spelling, don't they?

Applying the Grammar Lesson

Examine your first draft and check it for correct capitalization and spelling. Use a dictionary to double-check your spelling. Do not rely strictly on a computer to check your spelling since computers often do not find usage errors or spelling errors that inadvertently create a different, unintended word. The following is Tien's paragraph with the misspelled words underlined. Letters that need to be capitalized are circled. Letters that should not be capitalized are struck through with a line.

Here in the United States, were people have everything it seems, we don't realize that what we're doing can have such a big affect on the environment. But that's the problem because we DO cause so much damage, like with the ozone and also we cause air polution. We're useing up so many natural resources. In my Biology 130 class, the instructor told us that Global Warming is making the earth hotter every year, and if it goes on long enough, the poler ice caps will melt, causing the sea level to rise. There could be tons of storms, hericanes, and there will be drouts to in other parts of the world. Dirty air, missing ozone, and there is water polution—these are all problems that are mostly caused by wealthy nations like America. It really makes me mad, especially when I see jerks all around me being so wasteful, like everything is going to be their forever, like magic or something. We have to start conversation efforts, like recycling, reusing products, and also we can make things out of more environmentaly safe materials. Because this is the only world we have—and don't you forget it!

Writing the Second Draft

Now that you have completed the Grammar Lesson, you are ready to write the second draft of your Chapter Writing Assignment. Complete this draft before beginning the Sentence Lesson. Respond to the revision questions as you work on your rewrite.

Revision questions

- Does your topic sentence respond directly to the question you have chosen?
- What kind of tone do you want your paragraph to have? Do the words in the paragraph convey that tone?
- Examine your paragraph. Have you used capitalization and spelling correctly? Correct any errors that you find.

Here is the second draft of Tien's paragraph. She corrected her paragraph for capitalization and spelling, but she also tried to improve her use of tone so that her writing would be taken more seriously.

We need to scale back on how much of the world's resources we use. Here in the United States, where people seem to have everything, we don't realize that we can have such a big effect on the environment. But that's the problem: we do cause so much damage. Our cars, factories, and the way that we live hurts things like the ozone layer and also we cause air pollution. We're using up too many natural resources. In my Biology 130 class, the instructor told us that global warming is making the earth hotter every year, and if it goes on long enough, the polar ice caps will melt, causing the sea level to rise. There could be many storms, hurricanes, and there will be droughts too in other parts of the world. Dirty air, missing ozone, and there is water pollution—these are problems that are mostly caused by wealthy nations like America. I feel anger when I see people being so wasteful, like everything is going to magically be there forever. We have to start conservation efforts, like recycling, reusing products, and also we can make things out of more environmentally-safe materials. Because this is the only world we have, and we shouldn't forget it!

SENTENCE LESSON

Parallelism

Whenever you present a sequence of things or ideas, you need to make sure that the sequence is parallel. This means that the words in the sequence are presented in the same form and same order. Here is a simple example of a sentence that is not parallel:

Ernest liked fishing, hunting, and to sail.

The items "fishing" and "hunting" are both gerunds (a noun that uses the -ing form of a verb), but the third item "to sail" is an infinitive. In order to make this sentence parallel, either the first two items should be changed to infinitives, or the third item should be changed to a gerund.

Ernest liked to fish, to hunt, and to sail. (all infinitives)

or

Ernest liked fishing, hunting, and sailing. (all gerunds)

In both sentences, the items in the sequence are now parallel. Either sentence can be used—they're both technically correct—but it's likely that most readers will find the second sentence preferable since it uses fewer words to say the same thing.

Of course, at other times, sequences are not so simple. When sentences are more complicated, the principle remains the same: use the same word-forms in the same order.

William stepped up to the counter, grabbed a tray, ordered his meal, watched the server place the food on a plate, and paid for his lunch at the cashier.

In this sentence, there are five actions in the sequence. Each action begins with a verb, followed by any needed objects or phrases. As a test to see how these items are in parallel, you could actually divide this sentence into a "trunk" (the unchanging part of the sentence) and its branches (the changing parts).

Trunk	Branches
William	stepped up to the counter
	grabbed a tray
	ordered his meal
	watched the server place the food on the plate
	paid for his lunch at the cashier

You can see that if you place any of the branches in front of the trunk ("William"), the resulting sentence is grammatically correct. Furthermore, each of the branches begins with a verb in the simple past tense.

Now, examine this sentence:

The candidate claimed he would lower taxes, increase spending, and balancing the budget.

Trunk	Branches
The candidate claimed he would	lower taxes
	increase spending
	balancing the budget

In this sentence, the last item in the sequence, "balancing the budget," is not parallel with the other branches. The form must be changed from "balancing" to "balance." Read the sentence, rewritten for parallel structure:

The candidate claimed he would <u>lower</u> taxes, <u>increase</u> spending, and <u>balance</u> the budget.

Sometimes writers create sentences that use parallel structure at the start but prematurely break off the sequence, often by creating a new clause.

The kitchen was clean, well-equipped, and it was easy to use.

The first two items in the sequence are adjectives: "clean" and "well-equipped." Instead of continuing to use adjectives, however, the writer suddenly creates a second independent clause "it was easy to use." The resulting sentence is awkward because it is out of parallel. Rather than introduce the second clause, the writer should use another adjective.

The kitchen was <u>clean</u>, <u>well-equipped</u>, and <u>easy</u> to use.

This sentence can be broken down as follows:

Trunk	**Branches**
The kitchen was	clean
	well-equipped
	easy to use

EXERCISE 8.3

Complete the trunk and the three branches outlined below. Then, rewrite the completed sentence, demonstrating the parallel structure.

Trunk	Branches
Weaker environmental laws led to	*more pollution*
	more environmental devastation
	more health problems

Weaker environmental laws led to more pollution, more environmental devastation, and more health problems.

1. The new car was   expensive

                                 luxurious

                                 _____

Complete sentence: _____

_____.

2. The princess felt

obligated to obey her mother-in-law

frustrated in her marriage

_____

Complete sentence: _____

_____.

3. Their baby was already

walking

jabbering

_____

Complete sentence: _____

_____.

4. Our new family dishwasher is

quieter than the last one

more spacious

_____

Complete sentence: _____

_____.

5. The speaker told his audience that the future would be

hopeful

exciting

_____

Complete sentence: _____

_____.

6. The damage to the forest was due to

careless campers

littering hikers

_____

Complete sentence: _____

_____.

7. Raymond's goals in life were   to own a house on a golf course

to drive a black Porsche

Complete sentence: _____

_____.

8. The general addressed his troops by telling them that they would   have to make great sacrifices

_____

_____

Complete sentence: _____

_____.

9. Joyce played her violin with   skill

_____

_____

Complete sentence: _____

_____.

10. Irving decided to quit his job because   the pay was too low

_____

_____

Complete sentence: _____

_____.

Of course, you may also find parallel structure at the start of a sentence as well.

To act, to sing, to dance—these were skills Jennifer hoped to develop in order to become a great stage actress.

Laughing, giggling, screaming—all the typical sounds of a young children could be heard in the back yard on April's birthday.

Softly, smoothly, but insistently, Joanne tugged at Richard's arm.

Sentence Review

Rewrite any of the sentences below that contain errors in parallel structure. If a sentence is correct, mark it with a "C."

1. Before he died, the explorer wanted to find the source of the Nile, climb Mount Everest, and he also wanted to travel to the North Pole.

   _____

   _____

2. The computers of tomorrow will be less expensive, more powerful, and having more special features.

   _____

   _____

3. The farm had to be sold because the crops were no longer profitable, the loans were overdue, and the younger family members were moving into the city.

   _____

   _____

4. Tom Cruise is a major movie star because of his charm, his good looks, and he can play a wide range of sympathetic characters.

   _____

   _____

5. The Declaration of Independence was written for King George III, the people of England, and also it was written ultimately for all people.

   _____

   _____

6. Before he left the fantasy baseball camp, Emil wanted to bunt for a base hit, steal second base, and scoring on a head-first slide into home plate.

_____

_____

7. To learn everything he could learn, to apply what he had learned in his job, and getting a promotion eventually were all reasons that Burl decided to return to college.

_____

_____

8. The train left its tracks, plunged down a hill, and settling at the bottom of a creek.

_____

_____

9. Abraham Lincoln said that the government was "of the people, by the people, and for the people."

_____

_____

10. The pollution could have been caused by a factory upstream, by automobiles traveling along the nearby interstate, or another likely source of the pollution was the town's waste disposal site.

_____

_____

Applying the Sentence Lesson

Examine your second draft for errors in parallel structure. Correct any errors that you find. Make certain that you have at least two sentences that use parallel structure.

The following is Tien's second draft. The sentences that lack parallel structure are underlined:

We need to scale back on how much of the world's resources we use. Here in the United States, where people seem to have everything, we don't realize that we can have such a big effect on the environment. But that's the problem: we do cause so much damage. <u>Our cars, factories, and the way that we live hurt things like the ozone layer and also we cause air pollution.</u> We're using up too many natural resources. In my Biology 130 class, the instructor told us that global warming is making the earth hotter every year, and if it goes on long enough, the polar ice caps will melt, causing the sea level to rise. <u>There could be many storms, hurricanes, and there will be droughts too in other parts of the world. Dirty air, missing ozone, and there is water pollution</u>—these are problems that are mostly caused by wealthy nations like America. I feel anger when I see people being so wasteful, like everything is going to magically be there forever. <u>We have to start conservation efforts, like recycling, reusing products, and also we can make things out of more environmentally-safe materials.</u> Because this is the only world we have, and we shouldn't forget it!

To correct her errors in parallel structure, Tien rewrote her sentences as follows:

Original

Our cars, factories, and the way that we live hurt things like the ozone layer and also we cause air pollution.

Rewritten

Our cars, factories, and lifestyle hurt the environment, such as poking holes in the ozone layer or causing air pollution.

Original

There could be many storms, hurricanes, and there will be droughts too in other parts of the world.

Rewritten

The result could be many storms, hurricanes, and droughts around the world.

Original

Dirty air, missing ozone, and there is water pollution—these are problems that are mostly caused by wealthy nations like America.

Rewritten

Dirty air, missing ozone, and water pollution—these problems are mostly caused by wealthy nations like America who use up so many natural resources.

Original

We have to start conservation efforts, like recycling, reusing products, and also we can make things out of more environmentally-safe materials.

Rewritten

We have to start conservation efforts, like recycling raw materials, reusing products, and buying only environmentally-safe materials and products.

Writing the Final Draft

Rewrite your second draft, making sure that you have at least two sentences that demonstrate your use of parallel structure. This will be your final draft. Respond to the revision questions as you work on your rewrite.

Revision questions

- Does your paragraph have a strong sense of structure, with a beginning, middle, and end?
- Have you provided effective transitions as you move from one idea to the next?
- Do you have enough specific details to illustrate the points you are trying to make?
- Does the paragraph convey the proper tone?
- Does the paragraph properly use capitalization and spelling?
- Do you have at least two sentences that demonstrate your use of parallel structure?

Hand in the final draft, with the materials from your prewriting, first draft, second draft, and any other materials you created in the process of writing this assignment.

Tien corrected her errors in parallel structure. Then, she rewrote her paragraph, trying to be more specific. Here is her final draft:

We need to scale back on how much of the world's resources we use. Here in the United States, where people seem to have everything, we don't realize that we can have such a big effect on the environment. But that's the problem: we do cause so much damage. Our cars, factories, and lifestyle hurt the environment, such as poking holes in the ozone layer or causing air pollution. In my Biology 130 class, the instructor told us that global warming is making the Earth hotter every year, and if it continues, the polar ice caps will melt, causing the sea level to rise. The result could be many storms, hurricanes, and droughts around the world. Dirty air, missing ozone, and water pollution—these problems are mostly caused by wealthy nations like America who use up so many natural resources. On a personal level, I get angry when I see people being so wasteful by driving very short distances, letting water taps run when they're not being used, or leaving lights on in rooms where no one is. We have to start conservation efforts, like recycling raw materials, reusing products, and buying only environmentally-safe materials and products. This is the only world we have, and we can't forget it!

PORTFOLIO CHECKLIST

In your portfolio, you should now have the following:

1. your outline.
2. a First Draft. The first draft should have misspelled words underlined, letters that need to be capitalized circled, and letters that need to be lower case with a line struck through them.
3. a Second Draft. The second draft should have any errors in parallelism underlined and corrected.
4. a Final Draft. Make sure you have at least two sentences that use parallel structure.

PARTING SHOT

1. Have you ever lived through a natural disaster, and how did it affect your life?
2. Are some areas of the United States environmentally safer than others? (For example, fewer natural disasters, less traffic, less pollution.)
3. Do you think it is possible to control the environment?

GOALS IN REVIEW

In this chapter, you learned about

- creating an outline
- tone
- capitalization and spelling
- parallelism

PRACTICE CHAPTER TEST

Part I

Correct the following sentences for errors in capitalization and spelling.

1. Societies love of the Automobile has created many Environmental Problems.

2. She claims to be from northern texas, but from her accent I'd say she's from south carolina.

3. If you turn South at the intersection, you'll find an highway that runs East and West.

4. The judge decided that the timber company was guilty of harrassing protestors outside it's work sight.

5. My vaccuum cleaner is made by hoover, a famous manufacterer of vaccuums equipment.

6. The embarassed secretery submited her resignation, cleaned her desk, and left without filing a greavance.

7. If you see the movie <u>pyscho</u> by alfred hitchcock, you might have trouble taking a shower afterwards.

8. I originally enrolled in japanese 101 just to satisfy a general requirement, but I've decided now I want to spend a Summer in japan.

9. That politician sure talks about god a lot.

10. 34 people were injured when a bus hit a stalled car.

11. The theifs decieved all of us, accept Marion, that is.

12. She's a loving wive and a devouted mother, but she's also a payed assasin.

13. My uncle has had trouble with his back after he fell from a tree, but my aunt gertrude is doing everything she can to help him.

14. One of the easiest majors on campus is economics, and one of the hardest is russian.

15. The city decided that this labor day a big Parade would be held Downtown near the Convention Center.

Part II

Examine the following sentences. If a sentence contains errors in parallel structure, mark it with a check. If a sentence is correct, mark it with a "C."

_____ **1.** To soar higher, to breathe freely, and seeing all that could be seen were the reasons why Margaret decided to take up hang-gliding.

_____ **2.** The work required a lot of heavy lifting, some paper shuffling, and little else.

_____ **3.** Conn wanted to move to Ireland because of the beautiful scenery, the friendly people, and he also likes their stout.

_____ **4.** Movies today seem to lack the depth of character, subtlety of situation, and mature vision of human nature that movies made twenty years ago had.

_____ **5.** Madonna, Michael Jackson, and a rocker named Bruce Springsteen were enormously popular in the 1980's.

_____ **6.** My grandfather enjoyed fishing, boating, and he liked to cook.

_____ **7.** The children left their toys under the chairs, behind the sofa, and a few were also thrown on top of the dresser.

_____ **8.** By examining the evidence, questioning witnesses, and interviewing the suspects, the detective arrived at his conclusion.

_____ **9.** The artist's works were considered masterpieces because of his brilliant use of color, his excellent technique, and the fact that they displayed a new approach to traditional subjects.

_____ **10.** In her purse, the woman carried her keys, a compact, a packet of tissue papers, and a wallet along with carrying a checkbook.

CREDITS

INDEX

315